All About
COMMODITIES

TOM TAULLI

New York Chicago San Francisco Lisbon London
Madrid Mexico City Milan New Delhi San Juan
Seoul Singapore Sydney Toronto

ISBN   978-0-07-176998-3
MHID   0-07-176998-6

e-ISBN   978-0-07-176999-0
e-MHID   0-07-176999-4

This publication is designed to provide accurate and authoritative information in regard to the subject matter covered. It is sold with the understanding that neither the author nor the publisher is engaged in rendering legal, accounting, securities trading, or other professional services. If legal advice or other expert assistance is required, the services of a competent professional person should be sought.

—*From a Declaration of Principles Jointly Adopted by*
a Committee of the American Bar Association and a
Committee of Publishers and Associations

McGraw-Hill books are available at special quantity discounts to use as premiums and sales promotions or for use in corporate training programs. To contact a representative, please e-mail us at bulksales@mcgraw-hill.com.

This book is printed on acid-free paper.

CONTENTS

Chapter 11

Chapter 12

Chapter 13

Chapter 14

Chapter 15

Chapter 16

CHAPTER 1

Introduction to Commodities Investing

Key Concepts

- Look at the main drivers of commodities prices
- Understand the benefits of investing in commodities
- Discuss the risks

Commodities are pervasive throughout the world economy. Every day we buy food and energy. We drive our cars, which are made out of an assortment of metals and other materials. We live in homes and apartments, which are also made out of various commodities. Without these valuable materials, civilization would vanish. It's that simple.

On a global basis, commodities markets are massive and trade in trillions of dollars on a daily basis. There is also much diversity. For example, investors can invest in the following categories:

- **Agriculture:** Includes corn, wheat, soybeans, cotton, sugar, cocoa, orange juice, coffee, and oats.
- **Livestock:** Includes live cattle, feeder cattle, pork bellies, and lean hogs.
- **Precious metals:** Includes gold, silver, and platinum.

- **Industrial metals:** Includes copper, palladium, aluminum, tin, nickel, zinc, lead, and cobalt.
- **Energy:** Includes crude oil, unleaded gasoline, natural gas, coal, heating oil, uranium, ethanol, and electric power.

There are also a variety of ways for investors to participate in these markets. For example, these include buying and selling futures and options. There are also exchange-traded funds (ETFs), mutual funds, hedge funds, and managed futures. And yes, you can even buy the physical commodity, such as gold or silver, and put the metals in a vault.

COMMODITY MANIA?

Over the past decade, there has been a major bull market in commodities. In fact, it has become a popular topic on cable business channels like CNBC and even mainstream websites. Perhaps one of the most interesting signs of the fervor is that even criminals are focusing on stealing commodities. For example, copper has seen a spike in thefts. After all, the high prices could mean substantial profits. It also helps that you cannot trace copper back to the source.

Criminals are stealing power lines and cooling pipes. Unfortunately, this poses serious problems to communities. Because of this, law enforcement agencies have been putting more resources into combating this new crime wave. Consider that a criminal was able to extract the copper from an irrigation system in Pinal County, Arizona. There was about $10 million in damages. The theft even ruined a harvest. In 2008, a report from Electrical Safety Foundation International (ESFI) listed over 50,000 incidents of copper theft in the United States. The total damages were $60 million.[1]

But for investors, is this a classic sign that the commodities market is in a bubble and will peak soon? Perhaps, but the fact is that bull markets can easily last 15 to 20 years, and some commodities experts believe that the commodities markets are in a bullish "super cycle" that could last for several decades. If you don't believe this is possible just take a look at Table 1-1. It details the bull markets in commodities that have taken place since the beginning of the twentieth century.

---

[1] http://www.businessweek.com/magazine/content/10_49/b4206066273601.htm.

TABLE 1-1

Commodities Bull Markets for the Past Century

1906–1923
1933–1953
1968–1982
2000–?

During the first three periods, the biggest commodities bull market was actually during the Great Depression. Even during bad times, people still buy commodities. Also, because of the difficulties in raising capital, there were continued difficulties with entrepreneurs to find new sources of commodities (this also happened during the 2008–2009 global recession). In other words, a drop in supply could have a huge impact on prices.

Why consider the long trends? A key reason is the difficulty of extracting commodities. To understand this, let's take a look at an example. Suppose that copper prices have surged and are likely to increase for some time. To capitalize on this, you decide to start up a copper mine. To do so you will first need to explore for a large deposit. This requires sophisticated scientific equipment. It also probably means you will need to focus on areas of the world that are treacherous, in terms of the geography and politics. The exploration process can easily take several years. Assuming you find a rich deposit, you will then need to negotiate the copper rights and get the necessary governmental permits. To do this, you will likely need to raise a substantial amount of capital from investors. This process can take several years. After you lock up everything, you will then need to hire miners and purchase expensive equipment to extract the copper. It can take a year or two to get any substantial amount of the commodity.

As you can see, it takes a great deal of time to find new sources of commodities. Thus, price increases can last a long time because the supply will lag. But, when the supply hits the market, there can quickly be an overabundance. The excess could also last 10 to 20 years. But over this time, there will eventually be an underinvestment in the commodity and the supply will slowly contract, which will set the stage for the next bull market.

In the case of the current bull market, there are some major demand forces that are likely to keep prices robust. The main one includes the growth in emerging markets.

COMMODITIES IN BRIC COUNTRIES

The main players in emerging markets—Brazil, Russia, India, and China—are known collectively as the BRIC countries. Combined, these countries have 42 percent of the world's population and are responsible for about 23 percent of the world's output.

Brazil

Brazil is a country that has had its share of turmoil. Until the mid-1980s, the government had military dictatorships and populist leaders. The country also experienced severe bouts of inflation and economic slumps. But over the past decade, Brazil has made great strides. Then again, the country has rich natural resources and a large workforce.

Because of its tropical climate, it is possible to grow crops year-round in Brazil. Some of the key crops include coffee and sugarcane.

Oil is another big commodity. Over the years, there have been major discoveries off its shores. Brazil also has the second-largest mining company in the world, which is Vale. It produces nickel, coal, aluminum, and other commodities.

The gross domestic product (GDP) of Brazil is roughly $2.2 trillion and the economy grew by about 7.5 percent in 2010. Because of the strength of its economy, the country has been a popular destination for foreign investment.

Russia

Since communism was abolished in the early 1990s, Russia has undergone extreme changes. During 1998, the country defaulted on its foreign debt. The result was an economic plunge. Despite all this, Russia remains a major power. Besides being a big producer of oil and natural gas, the country also has large deposits of iron ore, bauxite, and gold.

The GDP is \$2.2 trillion and the economy grew by 3.8 percent in 2010. However, there are still big challenges. Corruption is a big problem in Russia. Moreover, Russia has had difficulty in attracting foreign capital because of the uncertainty regarding property rights.

India

Because it was originally under British rule, India has a Western legal system and other institutions. This certainly makes international trade easier. But since gaining independence in 1947, India has seen lots of problems. The Gandhi and Nehru governments focused on a pro-socialist agenda, which had a dampening impact on the economy. Yet since the early 1990s, there has been a move toward free-market economics. As a result, growth has been particularly strong and India has become a leader in industries like information technology.

With a population of 1.2 billion, India has a GDP of about \$4 trillion. In 2010, the economy grew by about 8.3 percent.

China

When it comes to investing in commodities, perhaps the most important driving factor is China. The country has shown an insatiable appetite for many commodities and the demand is likely to continue for many years.

China is no stranger to global power. The country has had the largest economy for 18 of the past 20 centuries. China has a long history of innovation and international trade. But during the twentieth century, there was mostly turmoil. During the first half of the century, Japan invaded China several times. Then in 1949, Mao Zedong came to power and created a communist state, called the People's Republic of China. There were purges, famines, and massive takeovers of private businesses. The upshot was a substantial decline in the national economy.

But in the late 1970s, there was a major shift. Deng Xiaoping, who was a key player in the communist revolution, began the process of economic reforms. Interestingly enough, he said that "being rich is glorious."[2]

---

[2] http://www.businessweek.com/magazine/content/06_06/b3970072.htm.

The reforms certainly paid off. Over the past 26 years, China has had the fastest growing economy in the world, with its GDP increasing by roughly ten times. The economy is now ranked second in the world and is expected to surpass the economy of the United States by 2027. Even with the global financial crisis of 2008, China was able to recover quickly. Consider that within two years, the economy was already 20 percent higher.

With the economic growth, China has undergone significant urbanization, as rural populations moved into the cities. From 2004 to 2008, the urban population increased from 542.8 million to 606.7 million, representing 45.7 percent of the total population. The result has been a surge in demand for housing and consumer goods. And of course, this will mean tremendous demand for commodities like oil, coal, copper, nickel, and zinc. Keep in mind that by 2035, China is expected to account for one-fifth of all global energy, according to the International Energy Agency (IEA). With its rising wealth and dependence on the importation of commodities, China has been aggressive in buying mines, energy properties, and commodities. These investments came to $2.4 billion in 2010 and will probably increase over the years.

Looking back at economic history, China is no aberration. There are certainly other examples of the impact of emerging economies on commodities prices. Just look at what happened after World War II. Countries like Japan and South Korea had to rebuild their economies. This meant a substantial long-term demand for commodities. A key indicator of this was the staggering rise in oil consumption. Back in the 1960s, it was roughly 2 barrels of oil per person in Japan. Now the ratio is 15 barrels per person. As for China, it is about 2 barrels per person. So despite the strong growth since the early 1980s, the country appears to still have much room to catch up with developed countries.

OTHER MEGATRENDS

While the growth in emerging economies should have a lasting impact on commodities prices, there are yet other megatrends. Because of industrialization, there will be changes in climate. This could result in more constraints placed on the supplies of commodities, especially in agriculture. At the same time, global pools of money are coming into commodities markets. This should result in even more pressure on prices.

Global Warming

Global warming refers to the general increase in the average temperature on the earth. In the twentieth century, the average global temperature increased by 1.33 degrees Fahrenheit (°F). Of course, many scientists believe that this was the result of the emissions of carbon in the atmosphere, which creates the Greenhouse Effect. The primary sources of carbon emissions are from fossil fuels and deforestation. Since the Industrial Revolution, there has been a 40 percent increase in carbon levels. While temperatures are expected to increase, it is far from certain what the temperatures will be during the twenty-first century. Keep in mind that scientists rely on sophisticated computer models, which are based on new data and changing assumptions.

There is still much political controversy about the causes of global warming. Some people believe that the science is far from exact. Yet investors are not concerned about politics. Instead, investors are interested in the *impact* of climate change. Already, there is a growing number of examples of the impact. Just look at 2010. The price of cotton spiked 92 percent, reaching an all-time high, and corn was up 52 percent. Some of the driving factors included snowstorms in the United States and Europe, a drought in Russia, and floods in Pakistan and Australia.

Based on reports from the National Aeronautics and Space Administration (NASA) and the National Oceanic and Atmospheric Administration (NOAA), 2010 saw temperatures that tied the record set five years earlier—1.12 degrees Fahrenheit higher than average, which was 57 degrees Fahrenheit in the twentieth century. It was the thirty-four straight year that temperatures were higher than the century average. In fact, nine of the ten warmest years recorded were from 2001 to 2010.

Institutional Interest

Institutions—including insurance companies, endowments, and pension funds—represent some of the largest buyers and sellers of investments. These organizations are typically large and have long-term perspectives. Traditionally, institutions have focused mostly on equities and fixed income. No doubt, these will continue to represent a major part of their portfolios. These investments provide long-term growth potential and offer much liquidity, making it easier to sell the investments.

However, institutions are focusing more attention on alternative investments. These typically include private equity, hedge funds, and venture capital. For a typical institution, the percentage of a portfolio's stake in alternative investments is usually 5 percent to 10 percent. But of this segment, little is invested in commodities. There are several reasons for this. First, some institutions are not legally able to own physical commodities. Next, commodities are usually not a part of investment theory. Thus, a portfolio manager may not have much experience in this asset class.

Yet as commodities continue to increase in value, it is inevitable that institutions will invest more in them. Actually, with the emergence of ETFs and commodities hedge funds, it is getting easier for institutions to put money into this asset class. Because of this, there has been growing investment demand for commodities, which should remain a key driver for rising prices.

Rise of Sovereign Wealth Funds

As a country accumulates wealth—such as through its exports—it may decide to create a fund to manage and grow it. This is known as a sovereign wealth fund (SWF). This sector is expected to experience substantial growth, going from $3 trillion in 2007 to $12 trillion in 2012. Part of this growth has actually come about from the commodity boom. For example, the oil-rich Middle Eastern countries have major SWFs. Singapore is also a large player. And of course, China is also bolstering its SWF, called the China Investment Corporation (CIC). Started in 2007 with $200 billion, CIC has grown to over $332 billion in assets.

A sovereign wealth fund often has a wide investment mandate, such as putting its money into mines, companies, and hedge funds. When it comes to investments in companies, they usually have minority positions, such as 5 percent to 10 percent stakes. The reason is that there will be little political concerns about control of key assets. Despite this, the demand from SWFs is likely to be a significant factor in the commodities industry. These funds will want to diversify into other commodities that their country does not have much supply. In the case of the CIC, the fund has been making key investments to get access to strategic metals.

Going Beyond Equities and Fixed Income

Investing in equities will remain a key part of any individual investor's portfolio. If a portfolio is diversified—and there is exposure to foreign markets—there should be long-term growth from capital gains and dividends. Fixed income investments are also critical to a portfolio. While the capital gains may not necessarily be as strong as with equities, these investments tend to provide higher income and are often less volatile. Despite all this, equities and fixed income asset classes can undergo grueling bear markets. From 2000 to 2010, the U.S. stock market underwent a brutal period. Known as the Lost Decade, the Standard & Poor's 500 Index (S&P 500) averaged a loss of 0.5 percent per year. This was even worse than what happened during the Great Depression.

In the case of fixed income, this asset class suffered tremendous losses during the 1970s because interest rates had increased to high levels; they reached 20 percent by 1980. This caused the value of fixed income investments to plunge in value. A big problem was the spike in inflation. Because of this, investors began looking at alternatives. For example, some investors began looking for companies to short sell. This means making money when the value of a stock falls (for more on this, you can check out my other book, *All About Short Selling*).

Investors also began looking at alternative asset classes. One of the most interesting is commodities. Interestingly enough, some investors think that the commodities asset class is not an asset class. One reason is perception. The fact is that there have been many colorful promoters in the industry. For example, there are the gold bugs. They believe that the world is on the verge of collapse and that purchasing gold is their only salvation for survival. Thus, commodities have historically had a credibility problem.

All asset classes have their fringe elements. There are penny stock schemers and real estate scammers. So, like any asset class, it is important to be vigilant and to do the necessary research. The upshot is that there should be better investment results for any asset class.

THE BENEFITS OF COMMODITIES

Despite all the controversy, the fact is that the commodities asset class is an effective way to diversify your portfolio. It is often the case that when commodities prices are in a bull market, the stock market is in the bear phase. Why? A key reason is that companies get squeezed by higher materials prices. If sugar prices surge, then it will be more expensive for Hershey's and Mars to manufacture their treats. While these companies will be able to pass on some of the higher prices, there are limits to this. In the end, the candy manufacturers are likely to have lower profits as well as stock prices.

Other key benefits to investing in commodities include: the lack of obsolescence and the inflation hedge.

Obsolescence

When investing in stocks, there is always the risk of obsolescence. There are many famous examples. Consider the travel agency business, which quickly evaporated because of the emergence of the Internet, where people can book their own airline flights and vacations. Other examples of obsolescence include the destruction of classified ads because of Craigslist, the fall of the *Encyclopedia Britannica* because of Wikipedia, and the disappearance of pay phones because of cell phones.

When there is obsolescence, the outcome is destruction of shareholder value. Just look at former highfliers like Tower Records and Blockbuster Video. But with commodities, the threat of obsolescence is fairly minimal.

There are cases when a commodity will be impacted by an advancement in technology. An example of this was the growth of digital photography. When this happened, there was less demand for silver, which is a critical element for developing photos from film. Despite this, the overall demand for silver has still been particularly strong since there are many other uses for the commodity.

Think about it: What's the likelihood of the world not wanting cotton, wheat, pork bellies, and sugar? Indeed, commodities are not subject to complete obsolescence, so there is little chance of them becoming worthless (this is certainly in contrast to stocks). There have been some rare exceptions—but these only lasted for a short period of time. During the depths of the Great Depression, sugar actually traded at a negative price. The reason was that there was an overabundance of the commodity.

Inflation Hedge

Inflation refers to a general increase in the prices in an economy. This is not necessarily bad. Actually, a moderate amount of inflation is normal, say 1 percent to 2 percent. But when the rate starts to accelerate, there are often problems. This is especially the case for investors.

One reason is that the purchasing value of the currency falls. In other words, it takes more and more money to buy the same amount of goods and services. To understand this, let's look at an example. Suppose you buy a bond that pays a 3 percent annual interest payment. However, inflation is at 5 percent. This means that the purchasing value of your interest is *negative* 2 percent. This is known as the real interest rate, which is the current interest rate minus the inflation rate. If the real interest rate is below zero, then investors are losing value.

It is the role of the Federal Reserve (often referred to as the Fed) to restrain inflationary pressures. This is through changes in interest rates and the money supply. But, if inflation has too much momentum, the Fed often must take tough measures and substantially increase interest rates. This risks an economic downturn, which can mean lower profits and stock prices. This is what happened during the early 1980s.

Interestingly enough, commodities can act as a hedge against inflation. How? Basically, investors want to put their money into hard assets. Regardless of the economic environment, hard assets will have some minimum value. So commodities represent a safer place for investors. Perhaps the best hedge against inflation is gold. Since it has historically been an alternative to a currency, gold is a normal place for investors to find a way to deal with inflation.

The fear in the United States is that there may ultimately be much higher inflation. True, after the 2008 financial crisis, this seems remote. If anything, the United States has been in jeopardy of deflation. This refers to a general fall in prices in an economy and can be terrible for economic growth. Back in the 1930s, the U.S. economy suffered from a bout of deflation, which did not end until the country entered World War II. But as for the current environment, the Fed has taken major steps to pump money into the economy. The hope is to stimulate economic growth. Yet, if there is too much in the system, it could mean higher inflation. And if history is any indication, it can take much time to get this under control.

There is an even worse form of inflation, that is, hyperinflation. This is when prices increase by a minimum of 50 percent per month. Famous examples of hyperinflation include Germany in the 1920s, Hungary in the mid-1940s, and Zimbabwe in 2008. When hyperinflation hit these economies, there was a quick meltdown. Unemployment soared and there was political instability. In the case of Germany, there was the rise of Adolf Hitler and the Nazi party. As should be no surprise, gold was an alternative monetary unit in these countries.

A big believer in the higher inflation scenario for the United States is John Paulson, a hedge fund manager, who has about $35 billion in assets. From 2007 to 2008, he made billions from shorting the subprime market. Now, Paulson has been using structured inflation hedges. He is a strong believer in the concept that successful investing is about the right timing, which often means getting into the market early so you can get bargains. Paulson's strategy has two main phases.

1. **Implementation phase:** During this phase, which can take several years, he researches a market and takes his positions.
2. **Monetization phase:** During this phase, he begins to sell off his holdings.

In the case of his inflation hedges—which involves a major focus on gold—he began this process in 2009. He thinks the monetization phase will be around 2013 to 2014.[3]

THE RISKS OF COMMODITIES

While this chapter has looked at many of the positive factors for commodities, there are certainly risk factors. Every investment has them.

---

[3] http://dealbook.nytimes.com/2011/01/24/paulson-recaps-big-bets-in-year-end-letter/.

A key risk factor is political instability. In the case of the BRIC countries—Brazil, Russia, India, and China—they are vulnerable to disruption, such as strikes and even social problems. What if there is an uprising in China or India? What would that do to the global demand for commodities? An uprising is certainly a possibility, since the income gaps are still so extreme in the BRIC countries. Besides, the authoritarian government in China will likely come under more pressure. The revolutions in places like Egypt have shown how change can be quick.

Another key risk is that it will not be easy for the BRIC countries to continue to grow at fast rates. As the economies get large, it becomes more difficult to eke out more production. In fact, shortages of key commodities can reduce the rate.

Geopolitical problems present yet another source of risk. India and Pakistan remain enemies. Yet both of these neighboring countries have nuclear weapons. What would happen if they go to war with each other? Keep in mind that over the past 60 years these countries have fought three wars.

THE FUTURE

Even with the risks, the bullish thesis still looks particularly strong. There are definitely major long-term forces that are likely to continue to propel commodities prices. If the super cycle theory is valid, the trends may last a decade or more.

In this book, we will look at the main commodities and understand their main drivers. We will also look at the ways to invest in them, as well as how to minimize risks and allow for sustained profits for your portfolio. In the next chapter, we will take a look at futures, discuss the main futures exchanges, and explain how electronic trading works. We'll also discuss how to set up a commodities trading account and how to effectively manage margin requirements.

CHAPTER 2

The Futures Markets

Key Concepts

- Understand how futures exchanges work
- Look at the main exchanges
- Discuss electronic trading

There are a myriad of ways to invest in commodities, such as with mutual funds, exchange-traded funds (ETFs), options, and hedge funds. Of course, you can also purchase miners and other commodity-related companies. But another common way to invest in commodities is through derivatives. These are financial instruments that reflect the underlying value of a commodity. The two main types include futures and options. In this chapter, we'll take a look at futures.

MANAGING THE RISKS OF COMMODITIES

While many of the world's commodities exchanges are electronic networks, the United States still has physical trading floors. While physical trading floors are likely to be phased out over the next few years, for now they are certainly energy-filled environments. Traders wear colorful jackets and run around the trading pits, the main locations where each commodity is traded. Because of the loud noise, traders use hand signals to make their transactions. This is known as the open outcry system. It may look like chaos but it is actually quite organized. The open outcry system has also been a part of a variety of famous television shows and movies. Perhaps, the most well-known is the movie *Trading Places*.

Each member of an exchange will have a seat. To get one, a person must meet rigorous financial requirements and have a background with no blemishes. A seat may also have lots of value. For example, it can easily cost $500,000 to get a seat on the CME Group. A seat allows a person to trade in a pit. A pit is in the form of an octagon and has steps that go downward. A pit is shaped this way to enable traders an easy way to see everyone else. Each octagon represents a commodity and each ring is the month for the contract. If a trader wants to buy a futures contract for March delivery, he or she will go to that ring in the pit. Then the runners will go to the pits and place the incoming orders to the brokers.

When a trade is placed, a broker actually does not know the identity of the purchaser or seller. This is to provide some protection. After all, if a well-known trader is making a transaction, this may alert other traders. Keep in mind that brokers are not trading the *actual* commodity. This is instead done in the spot market.

To understand this, let's look at an example. Suppose Hershey's wants to buy more sugar. To do this, the company will locate various owners of the commodity and then try to find the right price. Hershey's will then arrange for the shipment of the sugar to its facilities so it can produce its candy bars. The sum of these types of transactions will result in the spot price. This is the current price of the commodity.

In the case of commodities exchanges, the traders will instead trade futures. These are contracts that allow for the purchase of a fixed quantity of a commodity for delivery in the future. Why do this? A key reason is for hedging. This allows a company to reduce its risk levels for price changes in commodities.

To understand this, let's take a look at some examples. Suppose that ABC Airlines Corp. believes that fuel prices will surge in the next few months. Since this is a big part of an airline's costs, the company will use the futures markets to help reduce the impact of this move.

Suppose that fuel prices are $2 per gallon but ABC Airlines Corp. thinks it will go to $2.50 in the next six months. The company will execute futures contracts that allow it to buy fuel at $2.00 per barrel. Assuming that the price does rise to $2.50, the airline will save $0.50 per barrel. The reason is that the value of the futures contract will have increased by this amount, which will compensate ABC Airlines Corp. for the additional fuel costs. In light of its huge fuel needs, this could be a big savings and help maintain the company's profits. Again, since this hedging is a form of insurance, ABC Airlines Corp. will be giving up the advantage of a lower spot price. If fuel drops to $1.50, the company will still need to pay $2.00 per barrel.

With hedging, companies can also use futures to sell a commodity. For example: XYZ Corp. operates a wheat farm. The company plants the wheat in the spring and will harvest it in the summer. Suppose that the spot price is $8 per bushel. What if over the next few months, the spot price drops to $6 a bushel? In this case, XYZ Corp. will suffer a significant loss. To avoid this, the company will sell futures contracts for wheat—with the purchase price of $8 per bushel. So even if the spot price eventually plunges, XYZ Corp. will still get $8 per bushel for its crop.

How is it possible for these hedging transactions to occur? The fact is that there are many investors—often referred to as speculators—who are willing to take the opposite side. These include individual traders, investment firms, and hedge funds. Simply put, they are looking to make a quick profit. But by doing this speculators play an important function in futures exchanges, that is, they provide liquidity. Interestingly enough, the futures markets are considered a zero-sum game. This means that there is always one buyer for each seller. Ultimately, one will win versus the other, in identical amounts.

THE CHICAGO BOARD OF EXCHANGE

Before the emergence of commodities exchanges, the market was highly inefficient. Farmers typically had to go to central areas, like Chicago, to find buyers for their crops. The shipments were often extremely expensive, which could easily mean big losses or bankruptcy. Even if a farmer could find a buyer for his crops, there could still be risk. What if the buyer reneged on the contract?

To deal with these problems, there was the emergence of commodities exchanges. The first one to open in the United States was the Chicago Board of Trade (CBOT) in 1848. At first, the traders would use a forward contract, which is a variation of a futures contract.

To understand how a forward contract works, let's take a look at an example. Suppose a corn farmer has planted his crop but wants to guarantee a price per bushel. He can find a commodity trader, known as the counterparty, to negotiate a contract. The contract specifies that the farmer will deliver 5,000 bushels of corn for May. The counterparty will then agree to pay $6.50 per bushel.

But there may be some problems. First of all, will the counterparty honor the contract? Maybe there will be a dispute or the counterparty may experience financial problems. Next, it takes much time to find a quality counterparty and to negotiate the contract. Finally, it can be difficult to arrive at the right price for the forward contract. Again, this is subject to much give-and-take. To cure these problems, the CBOT introduced the futures contract. With this, the exchange would be the counterparty. This is done through system called a clearinghouse.

So, the farmer would not know who the trader on the other side of the transaction is. Basically, the CBOT agrees to take the other side of the transaction with the farmer and then sell the futures contract to a trader. The commodities exchange acts as an intermediary. The upshot is that the farmer or the trader does not have to worry about whether the futures contract will be honored. Because of the lower risk, there is much liquidity in commodities markets. It also helps that the major U.S. commodities markets have never defaulted on trades.

An exchange has the additional safeguard of regulations. The Commodity Futures Trading Commission (CFTC) is the federal agency that enforces the laws on futures trading. There is also the National Futures Association (NFA), which is an industry association that promotes its own standards and rules.

Another key advantage of futures contracts is that they are standardized. In other words, there is no need for the farmer and the trader to negotiate a contract. Instead, the futures contract will have *predetermined* delivery dates, locations, quantity, and grade.

Again, this streamlines the process, lowers trading costs, and increases liquidity.

As you can see, commodities exchanges provide a valuable service and they have grown tremendously over the years. And while they can certainly facilitate the delivery of commodities, this is a low percentage of the futures transactions. For the most part, commodities exchanges allow for a way to provide hedging, investment returns, and price discovery.

So why have forward contracts? There are several reasons. One is that there are some types of commodities that are not traded on exchanges. Also a company or investor may have unique requirements and may need to customize a transaction.

The trading that is directly between parties is known as the over-the-counter (OTC) market. It involves trillions of dollars in volume but has remained unregulated. Because of this, the belief is that this marketplace helped to contribute to the 2008–2009 financial crisis. This was primarily in the OTC trading of credit derivatives. So, the federal government has been taking steps to regulate their trading. Interestingly enough, this is likely to benefit the futures exchanges, since they have the infrastructure to bring uniformity and governance to the marketplace.

Over the years, there has been much consolidation with the futures exchanges. Keep in mind that during the nineteenth century, there were over 1,600 futures exchanges. But with the emergence of communications technologies—including the telephone and the computer—there was little need for regional exchanges. As a result, now there are less than ten exchanges in the United States. The main ones include the CME Group, which purchased the CBOT in 2007. Another major exchange is the Intercontinental Exchange (ICE). It acquired the New York Board of Trade (NYBOT) in 2006.

In fact, futures exchanges have become highly profitable organizations. They make money from charging transaction fees, as well as membership costs for traders' seats. They also charge licensing fees for data and indexes.

Take a look at the CME Group. In 2010, the company posted revenues of $3 billion and had a market value of roughly $21 billion. The company operates the CBOT, NYMEX (originally known as the New York Mercantile Exchange), and COMEX (originally known as the Commodity Exchange, Inc.). Thus, if you plan to invest in futures, you will likely be placing a transaction on the CME.

THE CME GROUP

After the horrible fire that destroyed a large part of Chicago in 1874, the Chicago Mercantile Exchange (CME) got its start. The exchange had the nickname of the Merc. In 1898, there was a major dispute and some of the members of the CME broke off and formed the Chicago Butter and Egg Board. That would not be the end of the infighting. And yes, there was also a good amount of market manipulations, which nearly destroyed the CME.

Sam Siegel and Vincent Kosuga were avid traders in the CME during the 1950s. Wanting to make a fortune, they hatched a corner on the onion market when they bought up nearly all the supply in Chicago. The price quickly spiked and then the duo went to 13 onion growers and proposed an interesting deal: If they did not buy futures on onions, Siegel and Kosuga would dump their massive holdings. So the growers started to buy. But Siegel and Kosuga instead sold futures contracts and then dumped the onions anyway. They made a tidy profit whereas the growers sustained enormous losses. In under a year, the price of onions went from $2.75 per bag to a mere $0.10 per bag. No doubt, there was much outrage and media attention. It was enough to get the attention of President Eisenhower and the Congress. As a result, they passed legislation that outlawed futures trading in onions.

After this, the future for the CME was dim. Much of the trading was in egg futures, but it was not enough to pay for the overhead. So the CME needed to find a new market. By 1961, the exchange did just that—they introduced futures on pork bellies. While it took several years to get traction, the market eventually became a nice profit generator. But it was only the foundation of more and more innovation. Over the decades, the CME has introduced many new products. The following represents a partial list:

- **Agriculture:** Corn, wheat, soybeans, oats
- **Energy:** Crude oil, heating oil, unleaded gasoline
- **Metals:** Gold, silver, copper, platinum
- **Animals:** Livestock, feeder cattle, live cattle, frozen pork bellies, lean hogs

ELECTRONIC TRADING

Over the next decade, due to ever-better technologies, it's likely that futures exchanges will be completely electronic. It's simply a matter of improving efficiencies. After all, many top commodities traders use sophisticated software systems to make their trades. So, it is important that they get quick execution on their trades.

The pioneer in electronic futures trading is the CME Group, which launched Globex in 1992. This system matches orders for futures as well as for options. There is also the benefit of the clearinghouse for all transactions and anonymity for the parties that are placing trades. Globex has 1,100 direct connections from over 86 countries. To speed up transactions, there are telecommunications hubs in places like London, Milan, Amsterdam, and Singapore. Because of its sophistication and capabilities, many other exchanges use CME Globex. At the same time, it is available from any futures and options brokerage firm.

In 2006, CME Globex began allowing side-by-side trading. This means that—during certain periods—there could be trading in the *same* futures contracts for the open outcry system and Globex. No doubt, this has resulted in even more growth in electronic trading. In the case of the energy contract, volume has tripled.

Sometimes a trader can use both markets to execute different parts of a trade. For example, a trader can buy a futures contract on the electronic market and then sell it on the open outcry system. Why? Well, in some cases, there may be more types of orders allowed on the open outcry system. Also, a trader may have a good relationship with a floor broker and believe that he or she will get better service from that person.

FLASH CRASH FOR COMMODITIES?

At 2:42 p.m. on May 6, 2010, the Dow Jones Industrial Average (DJIA) suddenly plunged by almost 1,000 points within about 20 minutes. It sliced $1 trillion in investor wealth. As a result, it became known as the Flash Crash. How did this happen? There are many possibilities, but it appears that there was a breakdown in electronic trading. Essentially, computers went haywire and started to sell en masse. In some cases, the prices were ridiculous. For example, Accenture fell to $0.01 per share.

But as commodities markets become more digitized, might there also be a type of flash crash? It certainly is a possibility. In fact, these markets are increasingly being connected to trading with other types of markets, including currencies, bonds, and stocks. For example, a trader may pull off a sophisticated trade that involves a futures contract on crude oil and the U.S. dollar (since oil is dominated in the currency) as well as the purchase of the shares of major oil companies, like ExxonMobil. If there is a malfunction, it could spread quickly. This is being called a Splash Crash. In addition, commodities hedge funds have increasingly been using strategies that are based on algorithms. These are extremely sophisticated computer-based trading techniques that involve huge amounts of volume for short periods of time.[1]

MARKET MANIPULATION

Any financial market is subject to manipulation, as investors work extremely hard to get outsized profits. The futures markets are no exception. Over the past 160 years, they have seen many colorful manipulations. Many of these occurred prior to the 1930s, when there was minimal regulation. For example, there were cases where a trader would bribe an organization to lie about a crop report.

The most common market manipulation was the corner. Essentially, this was a clever way to create the perception of a shortage, which would lead to a spike in the futures price of a commodity. A trader would buy up a significant amount of a commodity and store it. When it came time for the expiration of the futures contracts, the holders would be unable to find enough supply to meet delivery. As a result, there would be a scramble to buy the commodity. In some cases, a trader would go bust. However, the person who pulled off the corner would then unload the commodity. This would cause the price of the commodity to collapse. In many cases, a corner would last only a couple of weeks. It was a way to make a quick killing.

In the 1930s, new market regulations were helpful when dealing with corners. At the same time, the antitrust laws were another

---

[1] http://www.thestreet.com/story/10996095/1/splash-crash-the-ultimate-market-meltdown.html.

way to guard against these market manipulations. Despite all of this, there continued to be corners. One of the most notorious was from the Hunt brothers, Bunker and Herbert. The Hunt brothers were the heirs to a multibillion-dollar oil fortune, and they also happened to have quite a pessimistic outlook of the world. In fact, they thought there would be an inevitable collapse of the capitalist system. To protect their wealth, the Hunt brothers believed it was imperative to invest aggressively in commodities. Their most sought-after commodity was silver. They were avid followers of a market guru, Jerome A. Smith, who wrote *Silver Profits in the Seventies*. He urged the purchase of silver as well as gold, and he advised that the physical commodity should be stored in vaults in Switzerland. Why Switzerland? Smith believed it was the only way to avoid capture when the Soviet Union invaded Western Europe.

It was definitely fringe thinking, but the Hunt brothers put these theories into action. By using futures contracts, they amassed 9 percent of the world's supply of silver in 1974 and hired armed Texans to transport the silver in 707 jet airliners to Switzerland. From the mid- to late 1970s, the Hunt brothers continued their buying spree, and although silver prices were increasing, it was not enough for them. They wanted a grand slam. To this end, the Hunt brothers encouraged a variety of Saudi sheiks to also buy up large amounts of silver. By 1979, the commodities exchanges were running out of the metal and there was extreme concern. During the year, silver went from $20 an ounce to $34.45. A month later, it peaked at $50, giving the Hunt brothers a profit of $3.5 billion.

To deal with this, the COMEX and the CBOT adopted onerous restrictions on the purchase of silver on margin. As expected, the price started to plunge. The problem was that the Hunt brothers had borrowed huge amounts of money—backed by its silver holdings. Every day, they would receive large margin calls until they were unable to satisfy the demands. However, with a default, several major Wall Street firms would have failed. Because of this the Federal Reserve quickly arranged a bailout, with a consortium of banks, for the Hunt brothers. It amounted to roughly $1.1 billion. In 1988, a court found the Hunt brothers guilty of civil conspiracy to corner the silver market and they had to pay a fine of $134 million. Because of this, they both had to file for personal bankruptcy.

MARGIN

Beginner futures traders often confuse the concept of margin. They think it is similar to the way it works when buying stock. But there are some key differences. In the case of stocks, margin is the amount of money you borrow against your portfolio, which can be no more than 50 percent of the overall value. There are also ongoing interest charges. With futures, though, margin is really a good faith deposit or a performance bond. The idea is that both the buyer and seller of the futures contract have an obligation to perform. This means that the buyer will take delivery of the commodity and the seller will provide the commodity. The futures exchange will set the margin percentages, which vary from commodity to commodity. It will look at volatility, risks, and other factors. But for the most part, the margin percentages are quite low, say 5 percent. A futures brokerage firm might charge a higher amount—such as a couple of percentage points more.

Each day, the exchange will mark-to-market the margin for all traders. This means there will be automatic increases and decreases to all the accounts based on the closing price on each contract. Because of this, a trader will have to pay taxes at the end of each year on the gains or losses in the account. It is not possible to defer a gain into the following year. This can be a surprise to new traders. With low margin requirements, futures trading is subject to high leverage. This means a small change in the futures price will have a big impact on a trader's portfolio.

To understand this, let's take a look at an example. Suppose you buy one soybeans futures contract. The price is $5 per contract, which comes to $25,000 (the $5 price per contract multiplied by 5,000 bushels). But to trade the contract, your initial margin requirement is 10 percent of this value, or $2,500. Suppose the price increases to $5.20. This is a 4 percent increase from your $5 purchase price. But since you control 5,000 bushels, your account has increased by $1,000 (5,000 multiplied by $0.20). This is 40 percent return on your $2,500 deposit. If you close out your trade—by selling an equivalent soybeans futures contract—you will have made a tidy profit. However, leverage can also magnify losses. If the soybeans futures contract falls by 20 cents, your account will fall to $1,000 or 40 percent.

As you can see, futures trading can be fairly risky, with traders even losing all of their money. As a result, traders need to be cautious with their use of capital and monitor their trades. Traders also need to be aware of the maintenance margin requirement. This is the minimum amount of margin that must be in the account. If it goes below this level, the broker will initiate a margin call. This means the trader needs to increase the margin amount to the maintenance requirement. If not, the broker will start liquidating positions in the account.

The maintenance requirement is also used as the basis to measure equity in the account. To understand this, let's take a look at an example. Suppose you purchase one soybeans futures contract and have a minimum maintenance requirement of $2,000. Then suppose the value of the contract increases and the value in your account is $5,000. In this case, you have $3,000 in equity. This means you can take this cash out of the account or use it to make more purchases of futures contracts. But if a trader has a winning trade, he or she may have to unwind it because of the expiration of the contract. But a trader can continue with the position by rolling over a position. This means purchasing the same commodity with a futures contract.

Table 2-1 lists margin requirements for some of the most common commodities.

TABLE 2-1

Margin Maintenance Requirements for Common Commodities

Contract	Initial	Maintenance
Feeder Cattle	$1,688.00	$1,250.00
Lean Hogs	$1,485.00	$1,100.00
Live Cattle	$1,350.00	$1,000.00
Corn	$2,025.00	$1,500.00
Wheat	$3,375.00	$2,500.00
Silver	$11,138.00	$8,250.00
Copper	$5,738.00	$4,250.00
Gold	$6,751.00	$5,001.00
Light Sweet Crude	$5,063.00	$3,750.00

DEALING WITH MARGIN CALLS

A margin call is dreadful, especially for beginner investors. But like anything, there are ways to deal with a margin call, lessen the stress, and help maintain your portfolio. Keep in mind that if you are an active trader, you will get an occasional margin call. After all, the commodities markets can experience bouts of volatility.

You will typically get a margin call via e-mail. Again, it is nothing to be alarmed about. It is just the first step in a process. To deal with it, you have several options.

- **Reduce your risk exposure:** For example, suppose you have a long futures contract on corn that has gone under your maintenance requirement. You can actually purchase a put option against this, which will limit your downside.
- **Wire more money into your account:** However, if you do this, you probably should put in an amount that is 20 percent or higher than the maintenance margin requirement. The reason is that markets can move quickly. That is, you may wire money and still have an account that gets another margin call.
- **Liquidate part or all of your positions in your account to meet the margin requirement:** In some instances this may be a good approach. Some traders believe that if you get a margin call, it's an indication that you made a bad judgment on your investment reasoning and it is probably better to unwind the position.

How long do you have to cure a margin call? It varies from firm to firm, but it is usually between one to three days. Keep in mind, however, that it is best to take swift action. The longer you take, the higher the chances that a brokerage firm will automatically liquidate positions in your account. This should be avoided since the brokerage firm will show no consideration about the impact on your portfolio or strategy.

SETTING UP AN ACCOUNT

Any large brokerage firm will have a futures department. However, there will likely be gaps between the service offerings. So it is important to shop around. This also includes evaluating the fee structures, which can vary greatly. A good place to start compiling information is on the Internet, with a search in Google or various investment forums. There are two main types of futures operators.

Futures Commission Merchants

First, there are futures commission merchants (FCMs). They will handle the full cycle of services, such as taking possession of your funds, confirming trades, and making sure your account is in compliance with the exchanges. A FCM will also be a registered member of the various commodities exchanges. Some of the top FCMs include:

- E*TRADE (www.etrade.com)
- Infinity Futures (www.infinityfutures.com)
- Interactive Brokers (www.interactivebrokers.com)
- Lind-Waldock (www.lind-waldock.com)
- OptionsXpress (www.optionsxpress.com)
- PFGBEST.com (www.pfgbest.com)
- Thinkorswim (www.thinkorswim.com)
- TradeStation (www.tradestation.com)
- Vision Financial Markets (www.visionfinancialmarkets.com)

Introducing Firms

Next, there are introducing firms (IBs). They may look like regular brokerages, but they actually work on behalf of futures commission merchants (FCMs). Thus, when a trade is placed with an IB, the execution will be through the FCM. What's more, the FCM will handle the money and margin amounts. Because of this, the trader will write a check to the FCM, not to the IB. This is actually a safeguard for the client, but this can also get confusing, especially when it comes to reading confirmation statements. Will the commissions be higher since an IB will be working through an FCM? This is not necessarily the case. There is much discretion when charging commissions. To remain competitive, an IB may offer lower rates.

Discount and Full-Service Firms

Just as with stocks, futures brokers—whether introducing firms or futures commission merchants—will have discount and full-service firms. With a discount firm, the rates are much lower but it will provide less service. This type of firm will mostly try to get the most efficient execution on your trade—usually through the Internet.

A full-service firm, on the other hand, will have a dedicated broker assigned to you. He or she can help you devise investment strategies as well as minimize risks. For beginner futures traders, a full-service firm is often a good option.

Managed Account

Sometimes, however, clients require even more service. To this end, they will instead set up a managed account. With this, a professional futures trader will make investment decisions on your behalf. To do this, the managed account will require that you set up a discretionary individual account. As with any professional investment manager, you need to be selective. Make sure you spend much time evaluating various managers and analyzing their track records. Compare how managers have done during market downturns. Consider the managers' long-term average returns. Are there any complaints about the investment managers?

Even when you select an investment manager, you still need to do ongoing monitoring. Is the performance competitive? Or are returns lagging? Keep in mind that many successful commodities brokers are good at sales. After all, his or her compensation is primarily based on producing commissions. There is nothing necessarily wrong with this. If anything, salesmanship is key to many industries. However, there are instances where commodities brokers engage in high-pressure tactics. This is definitely a red flag. Most likely, this is a person who routinely grinds through many accounts and is mostly concerned about generating trading activity and not good investment results.

BACKGROUND CHECKS

Once you have narrowed down your choices for a futures commission merchant, an introducing firm, or a managed account operator, it is a good idea to perform even more due diligence. All brokers must take an exam and become a part of the National Futures Association (NFA). On the NFA's website (www.nfafutures.org), there is a database called BASIC (Background Affiliation Status Information Center). With this, you can find the career history of every broker. You can also see if he or she has committed any infractions or has been subject to arbitrations.

True, if a broker has been in the industry for a long time, there is a good chance there will be some bad marks in BASIC. This is inevitable in the high-risk futures market. But are there recurring charges year after year? Is there a pattern? It is also advisable to ask the broker about these violations. Yes, there could be a reasonable explanation.

ACCOUNT SIZE

When setting up a futures account, there will be a minimum amount requirement. In some cases, it could be as low as $2,000. While such a small amount seems like a good way to start, it is often not enough for effective trading. It may actually lead to more margin calls and limit the trading strategies. Unfortunately, a few bad trades could actually lead to major losses—even wiping out the whole account. Instead, a more reasonable account size would be $10,000. You will have more flexibility and not be under pressure to produce results. However, it is still a good idea to focus on those markets with less volatility. In fact, this usually means the margin requirements will be lower.

In this chapter, we have looked at the importance of commodities exchanges, which are efficient and safe platforms to participate in the commodities. But investors also need to do due diligence in finding a broker and understand the risks of margin accountants.

In the next chapter, we will take a look at how futures contracts are quoted and the impacts of different pricing dynamics on commodities. We will also cover important concepts like contango and backwardation.

CHAPTER 3

Understanding Futures Prices

Key Concepts

- Learn how to read futures quotes
- Look at the differences between commodities
- Understand contango and backwardation

When trading in stocks, the quotes are fairly straightforward. But this is not the case with commodities futures, as well as options on futures. The reason is that throughout U.S. history, there have been many futures exchanges. Because of this, each organization had its own standards. Even with the CME Group's merger of the Chicago Board of Exchange (CBOT) and the New York Mercantile Exchange (NYMEX), the differences still exist—and they will likely continue for some time. So to be an effective investor, you need a good understanding of how the main types of futures contracts are quoted. It is also important to understand some of the pricing dynamics, including seasonality, contango, and backwardation. These can have major impacts on commodities.

THE FUTURES QUOTE

To find trading information on a futures contract, a good place to go is an exchange's website. You will get access to timely quotes,

contract specifications, and trading history. But the quotes will usually have a delay, such as ten minutes. To get real-time quotes, you
will need to pay a fee.

Table 3-1 shows a sample of a quote for the gold futures
contract.

TABLE 3-1

Gold Futures Contract

Month	Last	Change	Prior Settle	Open	High	Low	Volume
Feb 2011	1338.0	+19.6	1318.4	1314.0	1346.6	1307.7	68,812
Mar 2011	1338.6	+19.5	1319.1	1314.8	1347.1	1308.8	2,419
Apr 2011	1339.1	+19.3	1319.8	1314.9	1348.0	1309.1	230,690
Jun 2011	1339.0	+17.6	1321.4	1316.8	1349.0	1310.9	7,690

The Month column shows the month and year that a contract
will expire. The gold futures contract goes as far as 2016. However,
trading for the later years has little volume. As for trading hours,
these will depend on whether a commodity still has floor trading,
and this is the case for gold. The open outcry trading is open from
Monday to Friday, with trading from 8:20 a.m. to 1:30 p.m. Then
there is trading on electronic markets. The CME Globex is open from
Sunday to Friday, with trading from 6:00 p.m. to 5:15 p.m. There is
a 45-minute break and then trading resumes, going from 6:00 p.m.
to 5:15 p.m.

The Last column shows the most recent trade. The Change
column shows the change in price between the most recent Last
price and the prior day's settlement price. The Prior Settle column
shows the final settlement price at the end of the prior day of trading. The Open column shows the price of the first trade for the day,
although, because of heavy volume, this may be an average of the
first group of trades. The High column shows the highest trade,
whether it is a bid or an ask. The Low column shows the lowest
trade, whether it is a bid or an ask. The Close column shows the
last trade for the day. The Volume column shows the total number
of contracts traded for the day. Then there is the Open Interest,
which is often confused with Volume, though the two are quite

different. Open Interest includes all futures contracts that have *not* been closed out with offsetting trades.

Futures have a shorthand for a ticker, which you can find on CNBC and various websites. The format is generally:

Ticker Symbol + Month + Year

Each month has its own character, as Table 3-2 demonstrates.

TABLE 3-2

Futures Quote Symbols for the Months

F—January	**J**—April	**N**—July	**V**—October
G—February	**K**—May	**Q**—August	**X**—November
H—March	**M**—June	**U**—September	**Z**—December

So, if you are looking at the February 2011 gold futures contract, the quote would be: GCG11 (GC is the ticker symbol for gold). But keep in mind that the quotes on the electronic markets will be different. This is to avoid confusion. For example, if you trade gold on the CME, the symbol is GC on the open outcry system but EGC on the electronic market. There are also different ticker symbols for mini contracts. As the name implies, these are for futures that have a lower amount of the underlying commodity. This is to make it easier for individual traders to participate in the markets.

THE BID-AND-ASK SPREAD

There will always be a difference between the bid and the ask of a futures quote. This is known as the bid-and-ask spread. This is essentially the profit for the commodities traders to carry out transactions and provide liquidity to the marketplace. It may be a seemingly small amount, but it is still a cost. The reason is that if you buy a futures contract, you will pay the higher ask price. When you sell a futures contract, the price will be *at* the bid.

In general, the more trading activity there is in the contract, the tighter the spread, which is why it can be costly to trade in illiquid commodities markets. While you will pay for a spread, there are ways to reduce it. One is to use special order types, like limit orders. We will look at these in more detail in Chapter 4.

OPEN INTEREST

When compared to investments like stocks and bonds, the concept of open interest is certainly unique. Yet it is often confusing to investors and may actually be ignored. This can be a big mistake. In fact, open interest can be a useful tool for making trades.

As mentioned previously, open interest shows all the outstanding contracts that have not been closed out. This increases when a trader buys a new contract from a seller who takes a new short position. There will be a decrease if the trader then sells the contract to someone who is already short.

But open interest will remain unchanged under certain types of trades. One case is when a trader buys a new contract from someone who was already long. Another case is when the seller of a contract covers his position from a new seller. Since every purchase of a contract involves a short position, the open interest will always have an equal amount of long and short contracts.

So, how can you use open interest? An effective strategy is to chart it. If the open interest is growing, then it shows that traders are getting more committed to the futures contract.

A bullish sign would be if both prices of futures and open interest are increasing. All in all, the bulls are adding to their positions and the momentum is likely to continue. Another bullish sign would be if both prices of futures and open interest are falling. In this scenario, the shorts are covering their positions as they think the trade has made enough profits. At the same time, new buyers are coming into the market.

As for bearish signs, this would be if prices of futures are decreasing but open interest is increasing. Essentially, bearish traders are taking on new positions and think the downtrend has yet to end. Another bearish sign would be if prices of futures are going up and open interest is going down. In this case, the bullish traders are taking their profits.

STANDARD TERMS

Each futures contract has standardized terms. The only differences include the expiration and the price.

- **Quantity:** This is what fits within a railcar. For example, the soybeans contract is equal to 5,000 bushels or roughly 136 metric tons.
- **Grade:** This is the quality of the commodity. For soybeans, there are three different levels—Yellow #1, Yellow #2, and Yellow #3.
- **Delivery date:** This is when the seller of a commodity futures contract is required to transport the contract amount to the buyer of the futures contract.

Contrary to popular myth, if you buy a futures contract this does not mean a pile of wheat will appear on your front lawn. Rather, the commodity will be delivered to a predetermined storage facility. The futures buyer will then be debited for the amount of the purchase, which can be substantial.

If he or she does not take possession, there will be fines and fees, which come to about $300. This is known as the retender process. Because of this, futures traders will typically close out their positions. Thus, if they *sold* a futures contract, they will *buy* a contract for the same delivery term, and vice versa. This must be done by the last trading day. In fact, traders will usually make offsetting trades in the last month in the term of the futures contract.

THE MULTIPLIER

It seems elementary, but it can actually be difficult to determine the profit and loss on a futures investment. Because of the differing pricing approaches, it is easy to make a mistake. But there is one core concept: the multiplier. This is a fixed amount that you multiply by the change in the price.

To understand this, let's take a look at an example. In the case of wheat, each penny change in the price is equal to $50.00. Why is this so? The reason is that each wheat contract has 5,000 bushels. When you multiply $0.01 by 5,000, you get $50.

However, the multipliers vary across the different futures contracts. So to understand things better, let's take a look at the main categories.

Grain Futures Prices

The grains are a diverse market and can be quite volatile. One of the key drivers is weather, which can result in higher or lower yields on the harvests. At the same time, demand is usually the result of population growth and dietary preferences. But some grains are even useful for biofuels. Also keep in mind that a large amount of grains go to feed livestock. Table 3-3 outlines the main futures contracts for the grains complex.

TABLE 3-3

Contract Specifications for the Grains Complex

Commodity	Exchange	Ticker	Multiplier	Contract Size	Minimum Tick	Terms
Corn	CME	C	$50.00	5,000 bushels	$12.50	Cents per bushel
Wheat	CME	W	$50.00	5,000 bushels	$12.50	Cents per bushel
Soybeans	CME	S	$50.00	5,000 bushels	$12.50	Cents per bushel
Oats	CME	O	$50.00	5,000 bushels	$12.50	Cents per bushel
Soybean Oil	CME	BO	$600.00	60,000 pounds	$6.00	Dollars and cents per ton
Soybean Meal	CME	SM	$100.00	100 metric tons	$10.00	Cents per pound

As you can see, four futures contracts—corn, wheat, soybeans, and oats—have the same multiplier. The main reason is that their contract sizes are all 5,000 bushels. These contracts are also quoted in cents per bushel.

To understand this, let's take a look at an example. Suppose that the March wheat contract is selling for 916'2. The price would be 916 and a quarter cents per bushel. The '2 is a fraction but the denominator, which is 8, is not shown. But it is 2/8, or 1/4. Let's say you purchase the wheat contract and it increases to 930'4. In this case, your profit would be 14'2. To calculate the dollar amount, you would multiply 14.25 by $50, which is $712.50.

$$14.25 \times \$50 = \$712.50$$

Wheat is also traded on other exchanges, such as the Kansas City Board of Trade (KCBT) and the Minneapolis Grain Exchange (MGEX). However, these contracts are specific to the region. So when traders think of wheat, they look to the contract on the CME.

As for soybean meal and soybean oil futures, there are some key differences. Let's first look at soybean oil futures. The multiplier is $600, which is $0.01 times 60,000 pounds. The price quote is also in decimals. Suppose that the price quote is 57.27. Traders convert this to $0.5727, or 57.27 cents per pound of soybean oil.

For soybean meal futures, the multiplier is $100 and is priced based on tons. Suppose that the price quote is 379.50. This means that the value is $379.50 per 100 metric tons. No doubt, this is fairly straightforward, at least when compared to the other grain contracts.

Livestock Futures

There is much trading in the livestock futures contracts, except for pork bellies. In fact, this contract may eventually be eliminated or changed. Table 3-4 outlines the main futures contracts for the livestock complex.

TABLE 3-4

Contract Specifications for the Livestock Complex

Commodity	Exchange	Ticker	Multiplier	Contract Size	Minimum Tick	Terms
Live Cattle	CME	LC	$400.00	40,000 pounds	$10.00	Cents per pound
Feeder Cattle	CME	FC	$500.00	50,000 pounds	$12.50	Cents per pound
Lean Hogs	CME	LH	$400.00	40,000 pounds	$10.00	Cents per pound
Pork Bellies	CME	PB	$400.00	40,000 pounds	$10.00	Cents per pound

For all of these livestock futures, the quotes are in decimals. If lean hogs are quoted at 83.950, the price amounts to 83 and 95/10ths of a cent. The decimal can confuse investors since it looks like cents, but it is actually 1/100th of a cent.

Now let's suppose that this contract increases to 89.00. The profit would be 5.05. To translate this into dollars, you would multiply this by the multiplier or $400, which is $2,020.00.

While feeder cattle is nearly the same as the others in the livestock complex, its contract has a higher size, which is 50,000 pounds. Because of this, the multiplier is $12.50.

Metals

For individual investors, the metals complex is quite popular, especially with gold and silver. The category is also less convoluted then the others. Table 3-5 outlines the main futures contracts for the metals complex.

TABLE 3-5

Contract Specifications for the Metals Complex

Commodity	Exchange	Ticker	Multiplier	Contract Size	Minimum Tick	Terms
Gold	CME	GC	$100.00	100 troy ounces	$10.00	Dollars and cents
Platinum	CME	PL	$50.00	50 troy ounces	$5.00	Dollars and cents
Palladium	CME	PA	$100.00	100 troy ounces	$5.00	Dollars and cents
Silver	CME	SI	$400.00	5,000 troy ounces	$10.00	Cents per pound
Copper	CME	HG	$250.00	25,000 pounds	$12.50	Dollars and cents

The quotes for gold, platinum, and palladium are in dollars and cents. So if gold is trading at 1250.50, it is $1,250.50. Each change in a dollar is equal to $100 in the futures contract.

Gold certainly generates much trading activity. This is not the case with platinum and palladium. Although over the past few years there has been increased interest in these metals, they do not generate much trading activity. The contract size for platinum is only 50 troy ounces. The main reason is that this metal is fairly rare.

Silver trades in cents per ounce. Thus, if a quote is for 2703.6, it would translate to $270.36. Copper—which is the high-grade version—is quoted in cents per pound. A quote of 433.20 would be 433.20 cents or $4.332.

The Softs

The softs are commodities that include various foods and fibers. However, unlike the other categories in this chapter, this area has a diverse group.

Many of the softs trade on the Intercontinental Exchange (ICE) and they tend to be produced overseas. This is important. With sugar, there are various forms, such as #11, #14, and #16. The #11 contract is the most common and is the one quoted in the table below. But if you accidentally trade #14 or #16, you will be in a market that has much less liquidity. Table 3-6 outlines the main futures contracts for the softs.

TABLE 3-6

Contract Specifications for the Softs Complex

Commodity	Exchange	Ticker	Multiplier	Contract Size	Minimum Tick	Terms
Coffee	ICE	KC	$375.00	37,500 pounds	$18.75	Cents and hundredth of a cent
Sugar	ICE	SB	$1,120.00	112,000 pounds	$11.20	Cents and hundredth of a cent
Cocoa	ICE	CC	$10.00	10 metric tons	$10.00	Dollars per metric ton
Orange Juice	ICE	OJ	$150.00	15,000 pounds	$7.50	Cents and hundredth of a cent
Cotton	ICE	CT	$500.00	50,000 pounds	$5.00	Cents and hundredth of a cent
Lumber	CME	LB	$110.00	110,000 board feet	$11.00	Dollars and cents

Unfortunately, the pricing for the softs is extremely complicated. Based on the chart above, you can see that there are a myriad of multipliers, contract sizes, and minimum ticks. Yet it does help that coffee, sugar, orange juice, and cotton are all traded in cents per pound. Yes, this is even the case with orange juice. While it's true that orange juice is sold by the gallon in retail stores, keep in mind that it is sold frozen as a commodity.

So let's take a look at a quote for cotton. Suppose it is 120.50. In this case, it would amount to $1.2050 per pound. Each one cent move would be equal to $500. Cocoa, on the other hand, is quoted in dollars per metric ton. There are no cents; there are only dollar movements.

Energy

While energy futures are popular—and trade in huge volume—they can be tough for individual investors. There are many sophisticated traders in the market and the exchange rules can change quickly. Because oil is such a critical commodity for the world, the price is highly sensitive to changes in the world economy.

Another area of confusion for beginner investors is with the price of unleaded gasoline. It is easy to assume that it is close to what you would pay at the gas pump. But this is not the case because of regional differences in the supply chain as well as taxes. Table 3-7 outlines the main futures contracts for the energy complex.

TABLE 3-7

Contract Specifications for the Energy Complex

Commodity	Exchange	Ticker	Multiplier	Contract Size	Minimum Tick	Terms
Crude Oil	CME	CL	$1,000.00	1,000 barrels	$10.00	Dollars and cents
Heating Oil	CME	HO	$420.00	42,000 gallons	$10.00	Cents per gallon
Unleaded Gasoline	CME	HU	$420.00	42,000 gallons	$4.20	Cents per gallon
Natural Gas	CME	NG	$10,000.00	10 million BTUs	$4.20	Cents per 10 million BTUs

Crude oil is easy to calculate. For example, if it is at 100.25, then the price is $100.25. Each point increase will mean a $100 increase in the value of the contract.

But the quotes for heating oil and unleaded gasoline are in cents per gallon. If a quote for heating oil is 3.5055, then this would be $3.5055.

Natural gas is quoted in BTUs, or British Thermal Units. These represent a quantity of heat. Each contract has 10,000 million BTUs.

If the quote is at 5.50, then this would be $5.50 and each dollar increase would amount to $10,000.

SEASONALITY

Seasonality refers to a recurring change in a commodities market. For investors, this can be a way to play changes in prices. But there should be some caution. As should be expected, many traders anticipate these changes. Besides, the seasonality can be more or less severe. Let's take a look at some of the main patterns for key commodities.

- **Wheat:** Winter wheat is planted in the fall and is harvested in the summer, which will mean a large supply. There is also pressure from the harvest from the Southern Hemisphere countries. To take advantage of this trend, traders will short the wheat futures contract in January and then offset the trade in the summer.
- **Corn:** Weather has a major impact on corn, especially during June and July. If the weather is severe, then there will likely be a spike in corn prices. However, prices will likely hit their lows in the fall because of the harvest.
- **Live cattle:** Demand for live cattle typically falls during May and June. The reason is that this is when a large amount of supply comes onto the market. There is also the influx of other meats, like poultry and pork.
- **Soybeans:** Traders will tend to buy up soybeans contracts in February. The reason is that there is usually a strong demand for feed for livestock in the winter months. Traders will then look to go short by May. At this point, the size of the soybeans crop will be fairly clear.
- **Sugar:** Going into June, sugar usually hits a low, as supply hits the market. But it is often a bottom and traders will go long.
- **Cocoa:** Traders will tend to go short on cocoa in March. There will be a large influx of supply from the Ivory Coast and Ghana, whose harvests are from January to March. At the same time, there will be lower demand going into the summer months.

- **Coffee:** There is generally weak demand for coffee going into May, as production ramps up in warm climates like Colombia and Brazil. But this is far from foolproof. As seen over the years, the weather can get volatile and destroy crops.
- **Energy:** Demand for crude oil and natural gas often reach a low in February and then will begin a climb. A big driver is the increase in heating use. If December is a particularly cold month, there may be low inventories of oil and natural gas in February.

CONTANGO AND BACKWARDATION

The spot price refers to the current value of a commodity. The futures price refers to the price at a fixed date in the future. Often, there is a difference between these two prices. Why? The reason is that the futures price accounts for various costs.

For example, suppose the spot price of gold is $1,340 but the futures prices—the March futures price—is $1,442.50. The additional $102.5 is likely to be the case because of storage, insurance, and financing costs.

In general, the longer the contract the higher the futures price. Table 3-8 shows this effect in action.

TABLE 3-8

Gold Futures

Month	Futures Price
Feb 2011	1342.3
Mar 2011	1342.4
Apr 2011	1342.3
Jun 2011	1344.6
Aug 2011	1345.4
Oct 2011	1343.9
Dec 2011	1346.3
Feb 2012	1351.4

The upward slope in the futures prices is called contango. At the same time, the closer a futures contract gets to expiration, the narrower is the difference between its price and the spot price. The reason is that an exchange facilitates the delivery of the underlying commodity. If the gap becomes too large, then a group of investors—called arbitrageurs—will come into the market and realize the profits.

To understand this, let's take a look at an example. Suppose that the gold futures contract has only two days until expiration yet the price is $1,450 and the spot price is $1,445. If the trader believes the spot price will remain the same, he or she will short the futures contract. So at the time of expiration, the trader will buy gold at $1,445 and sell it for $1,450, which is the contract term. Interestingly enough, it is this type of activity from arbitrageurs that will ultimately narrow the gap—which will reach zero at the time of expiration.

While contango is the typical price pattern, there will sometimes be a downward slope in the futures prices. This is called backwardation. This happens when there are high levels of demand for a commodity. Simply put, the buyers want to get a higher-than-normal supply of the commodity. The result will be a spike in the spot price.

PRICE MINIMUMS AND LIMITS

Futures exchanges set forth a variety of restrictions on the contract prices. These will vary from commodity to commodity.

One is the minimum price fluctuation, which is the smallest amount the price can go up or down. This is also known as a tick. Corn, for instance, has a $12.50 tick. Sugar has an $11.20 tick.

An exchange will also have daily limits. This is the maximum a price can increase or decrease for a trading session. This is to allow for a more orderly market and provide a cooling off period if markets overheat. For example, say the daily limit for live cattle is $0.03 per pound. If the price of the futures contract hits this limit, there will be no more trading allowed. Instead, trading will need to resume the next day. In fact, in rare occasions, it can take a week for a market to get through a limit. This can certainly pose liquidity problems for traders.

For all of these limits, an exchange has the discretion to change things. And this can happen unexpectedly—posing even more problems for investors. But the exchange's goal is to try to find ways to tamper speculation. There are even purchase limits. That is, a trader can only purchase a maximum number of futures contracts. This is meant to reduce the possibility of pricing pressures and even manipulation.

THE SQUEEZE

A fast market is when prices are either surging or plunging. It can be highly profitable for traders, but for commercial buyers it can be a big problem.

For example, going into 2011, the price of cotton futures spiked following record climbs during 2010. A key contract was for March. It's typical that a commercial buyer—such as a cotton mill or an apparel maker—would have already closed out a contract. But this was being delayed because the buyers were waiting for a decline in the price. Yet, this did not happen. So as it got closer to the expiration of the contract, there was fear that the price could go up even more—which would be a squeeze. In other words, traders would buy aggressively in the market to make a quick buck.

As a result, the Intercontinental Exchange (ICE) considered placing limits on the amount of buying traders could make.[1] This is usually based on the size of the firm and its current holdings. The hope is that this would lessen the possibility of a squeeze. Of course, it would make it tougher for the traders to make a profit.

VOLATILITY

Commodities can have sharp changes in prices. The factors include many unexpected events, like wars, weather, and recessions. For example, the 2008 financial crisis had a significant impact on the prices of commodities. Consider that by the end of the year, the price of copper saw 70 percent of its gains wiped out as the price

---

[1] http://online.wsj.com/article/SB10001424052748703652104576122001071740950 .html?mod=WSJ_Commodities_LeadStory.

fell to $2,770 per ton. Another prominent example of volatility took place during the Asian crisis of 1998. At this time, there was a financial panic that resulted in the plunge of equities and fixed income markets. This quickly led to painful recessions across Asia. It took several years for recovery for commodities prices to rise again.

Because of its size, the United States has historically been a major factor in commodities prices as well. The old saying goes: "If the U.S. sneezes, the rest of the world catches a cold." It's clear that the United States is still a major force. Yet its influence has been diminishing. Just look at the 2008 financial crisis. The U.S. and Western European economies plunged into a severe recession, which also hurt China, India, and Brazil. But interestingly enough, these emerging economies quickly recovered. Of course, this was not the case in the United States and Western Europe.

While commodities prices did fall, they were able to recover fairly quickly. In other words, the strong economies of China, India, and Brazil may act as a floor on commodities prices.

MAKING THE ORDER

Placing an order for a futures contract does take some thought. Because of the complexities, beginner traders sometimes make incorrect trades, which can result in losses. When putting together an order, it is important to think about the key elements.

- **Determine if you want to buy or sell a contract:** Buying a contract means that you will make money if the futures price increases. Selling a contract will be the reverse. Is this simple? Perhaps. But this is actually when traders make a common error. It's easy to pick the wrong one when quickly placing a trade.
- **Make sure you select the right commodity:** This means that you must know the right symbol. Keep in mind that some commodities trade on several exchanges. Typically, you will pick the one with the most liquidity so as to get the best price.
- **Indicate the delivery month of the contract:** As shown in Table 3-2, each month has its own character or capital letter.

In addition to the key elements given above, you can indicate how long the order is open. To do so you need to know how long the day is. For example, a day order will be open for how long the market is open. However, it may not terminate if the contract has electronic trading. A good-'til-canceled (GTC) order means that the order will remain in place until you take it off. Otherwise, the order will end when the contract expires. You can also try to get a certain price on the trade, called an order type.

As seen in this chapter, it's clear that futures trading can get complicated in terms of understanding the various tickers and quote conventions. Because of this, it is often a good idea to initially focus on just a few commodities in order to learn the nuances. It can help improve trading and avoid mistakes. In the next chapter, we will discuss how to develop a trading strategy plan, including managing risk.

CHAPTER 4

Futures Trading Strategies

Key Concepts

- Look at the various ways to trade futures
- Learn how to develop a trading plan
- Understand market orders and risk management

For some commodities traders, the only way to play the markets is with futures. These traders like the leverage, as well as the ease of making a quick profit. It can be an adrenaline rush. Isn't that what traders crave? Yet the good futures traders are not cowboys. They have a plan, which involves certain strategies and ways to limit risk. If not, it can be extremely tough to last in the business.

Look at Bruce Kovner, who is considered one of the best futures traders of all time. In the late 1970s, he made his first trade, which was a $3,000 wager on soybeans futures. He used his MasterCard for the capital and wound up losing $23,000. Because of this, Kovner realized he needed to use risk management in all of his trades. It was a process that took time, but it paid off. He eventually started his own hedge fund, Caxton Associates, and now has a personal net worth about $3.5 billion.

BASIC FUTURES TRADES

For investors, the most basic futures trades are long and short positions. These are also known as outright positions. A long position is when you purchase a futures contract and believe that the price will increase over time. You will typically close out the transaction by making an offsetting sell of the same transaction. If you think a futures contract will fall over time, you will short it or take a short position. This is the other side of the long position. In other words, for every long position, there is another short position.

As seen in Chapter 2, a long or short position can have lots of risk. This is because of the low amount of money that is required for the investment. Because of this, some investors will put up much more margin—which should lower the overall risk levels. But this is often not enough. Instead, traders will use various trading strategies to deal with the risk. The most common strategy includes spreads.

SPREADS

A spread refers to the buying of different types of futures contracts to take advantage of price discrepancies. A common one is the calendar spread, which involves the buying of a futures contract in one month and the selling of one in another month.

To understand this, let's take a look at an example. Suppose you think there is an opportunity to profit from a calendar spread with the two following wheat contracts:

1. March: 835'0
2. May: 843'0

As you can see, there is a $0.08 difference between the contracts. However, you know that the carrying costs—which include storage, insurance, and financing—for wheat is $0.02 per month. For the two contracts, this would amount to $0.06 (3 months multiplied by $0.02). You think that the price is off by $0.02 because the gap is higher than what the carrying costs would indicate. You will then set up a calendar trade. You will purchase the March contract and short the May contract. Assuming your analysis is correct, the premium to the carrying costs should shrink. If so, you will make a $0.02 profit. Since this trade involves buying the nearby futures contract and shorting the longer one, it is known as a bull spread. The reverse would be a bear spread. But this is fairly rare, since futures contract prices tend to increase the longer the length of the contract.

In light of the many types of contracts, traders have developed a wide assortment of spreads. For the most part, these will be based on an *earlier* crop time period and a *later* crop time period. Some typical examples include:

- Going long on July corn and going short on December corn
- Going long on May soybeans and going short on December soybean meal or oil

Wide swings in the futures generally have minimal impact on an investor's position in a spread, which means the risk level is lower. Because of this, a brokerage firm will usually have lower margin requirements. However, there may be higher commissions charged, but this is usually not a big consideration for traders.

Spreads require sophisticated analysis. For example, it is important to look back at the pricing history of commodities:

- How long do prices tend to be above carrying costs?
- Is there an upcoming news release that can greatly impact the market?

Often traders will study charts to get a feel for the pricing action. Carrying charges are only for those commodities that involve storage. So they do not include things like live cattle.

There is also the intermarket spread. With this, the trader buys contracts for the same month but for different commodities.

To understand this, let's take a look at an example. Suppose you think that gold has rallied too much and is overvalued. But you also think that silver looks cheap. In this case, you will short the February gold contract at $1,400 and you will buy the February silver contract at $30.50. Over the next month, gold actually increases by $5 and you sustain a loss of $500. But silver increases by $2.00 and you earn $800. As you can see, even if one side of your position is wrong, you can still make money on the trade.

No doubt, the strategies can get complicated. But over the years, there have emerged some popular approaches, including the following:

- **Cattle crush:** This is when a trader purchases corn and feeder cattle—both of these are feeds for livestock—and then sells live cattle.
- **Soybean crush:** This is when a trader purchases soybeans contracts and then sells the contracts for soybean meal and soybean oil. If you want the opposite, there is the reverse crush.
- **Crack spread:** This is when a trader purchases crude oil contracts and then sells the contracts for gasoline and heating oil. This is the most popular type of spread. The key to being successful with this type of spread is to understand the seasonality of heating oil in relation to crude oil, which is typically magnified during winter months.

It is tempting for a trader to leg off a spread. This means that he or she will close out the profitable position and then hope the losing contract will become profitable. While this seems logical, it is often a bad idea. After all, the goal of a spread is to reduce the overall volatility, which means you will likely have a loss on one of the trades.

DEVELOPING A TRADING PLAN

When starting a business, entrepreneurs will put together a business plan, which helps to define the goals and the necessary steps to achieve them. Traders do the same thing. That is, they have a trading plan. The old saying goes: "Plan your trades and trade your plan." It's great advice, because it works. It helps to reduce the emotion and fear in trades, which should make for better decision-making.

While it is possible for a trading plan to be unwritten, this will make it less impactful. By putting your plan on paper, it will help you think about your goals and the techniques you will focus on. A trading plan can be just one page and have bullet points. But, it should cover two main areas. One area is managing risk. You want to make sure you are not jeopardizing your portfolio because you are taking risky positions. The other area is setting the parameters for when to take profits or losses.

For example, you might be satisfied if you make a 10-percent return on a futures trade. When you reach this point, you may take half the position off.

Determining when to take losses is usually the most difficult decision for traders. Who likes to think about such things? If anything, there is a temptation to keep a trade open in the belief that things will improve. Well, this usually does not happen. In fact, the losses may pile up and wreak havoc on your portfolio. When should you sell? As in the case of the profits, you may set a loss limit at 10 percent. Or you may use other triggers. For example, this would be the case if you invest in a futures contract when the price hits the support level because you believe buyers will come in.

To facilitate their decisions, investors can enforce these trading rules by using various order types. These are specific instructions you provide for a trade. In volatile markets, order types can be an effective way to manage risk and to boost returns. There are dozens of order types, many of which can be confusing. Moreover, an exchange may only allow a subset of them. So it is important to understand the rules of the exchange that you want to trade on.

PORTFOLIO MANAGEMENT

All investing should involve strong portfolio and risk management. Even fixed income securities can be volatile. But with commodities, an investor needs to be even more mindful. Take a look at Table 4-1 to get an idea of the importance of risk management.

TABLE 4-1

Recovery Periods for Portfolio Losses

Portfolio Loss	Recovery Percentage
30%	42.9%
40%	66.7%
50%	100.0%
60%	150.0%
70%	300.0%

If your portfolio drops by 50 percent, you will need to get a whopping 100 percent return just to get back to your original value. This was the predicament for many investors in 2008 when the markets plunged because of the financial crisis. Unfortunately, some investors opted to sell out and avoid the markets altogether.

A striking example of the risks of commodities trading is MF Global Holdings. One of its traders in the Mississippi office was racking up losses in overnight trading in wheat contracts. In all, the losses amounted to $141 million. When MF Global announced the losses, the stock fell 65 percent. There were fears that clients would take their money out of the firm because there might be liquidity problems. Ultimately, MF Global was able to recover from the incident and the trader was actually indicted by a federal grand jury for wire fraud and violations of the Commodity Exchange Act.[1] Yet this highlights that even top firms may have lapses with risk management. And when this happens, the consequences can be severe. The same goes for individual investors.

When taking a position in a commodity, you need to understand how it impacts your overall portfolio. For those just starting out, it is a good idea to experiment with commodities trading. This may mean taking only a handful of positions, which may represent only 5 percent of the portfolio. But as time goes by—and you get more adept at commodities—the exposure could go up to 10 percent or even 20 percent.

Whatever allocation you decide, it is still important to have a risk-management approach for *each* trade. This essentially gives you an indication of the impact of *each* position.

One approach is the 2 percent rule. Often misunderstood, this actually focuses on the percent of risk in a position.

To understand this, let's take a look at an example. Suppose your investment portfolio is $100,000. You then purchase a futures contract on corn for $10, for a total of $10,000. You will put a stop order on the position for $9. This means your risk is $1,000 or 1 percent of the portfolio. You can increase the position by $20,000 so long as you have another stop loss at $9.

Another helpful risk management approach is the 6 percent rule. If a loss for the month is 6 percent or more, then you will stop

---

[1] http://www.businessweek.com/news/2010-04-29/mf-global-missed-chance-to-stop-broker-s-141-million-loss.html.

trading for at least a month. It is probably a good idea to reevaluate all of your positions in the portfolio. Are you taking on too much risk?

Investors will also look at diversification *across* the commodities. For example, if you trade heating oil and crude oil, then they will likely move in *similar* patterns. This means they have a high degree of correlation. The problem is that you are essentially concentrating your risk in one category. So if the market falls, it can have a major impact on your portfolio. To avoid this, a trader will look for those commodities that trade *independently* of each other. So, if one commodity goes down, the other may actually go up.

MARKET ORDERS

A market order is the most basic order type. It will get you the best possible price at the current time. This is for those who want to get into a commodity quickly. Perhaps the reason is that—based on technical indicators—it looks like there will be a big increase or big drop in the price. How fast do these orders get filled? If the trade is on an electronic market, it can be within seconds. But if it is on an open outcry market, it could take a couple of minutes.

In some commodities markets, there may not be much trading volume. In this case, the market order may not necessarily get you the current quoted price. There are even some cases when an order cannot be filled because of the lack of activity, although this is fairly rare. While market orders may wind up being more expensive—because of the bid-ask spread—the fact is that commodities brokers do attempt to get a good price for their clients. They realize that this is important for client loyalty and to encourage more frequent trading.

LIMIT ORDERS

A limit order is when the investor specifies a price to purchase or sell a futures contract. Sometimes when this order is issued, the price will change and be even better. Of course, the trade will be executed.

To understand this, let's take a look at an example. Suppose you want to buy the November corn contract, which is currently trading at $5.50. You think it is pricey and instead want to purchase it at $5.40. You will place a limit order for $5.40 on one corn contract. As trading continues, the price does fall to $5.40 and your order is filled. Suppose you decide you will be satisfied with a $0.20 profit. You then will place a limit order for $5.60 on the corn contract to sell it. Over the next couple of days, the price reaches $5.60 and the limit order is filled.

Even if the market price hits the limit order price, this does not necessarily mean there will be an automatic trade. In lightly traded markets, there may not be enough buyers and sellers to fill all the orders. Or the price may have reached the limit point for only a brief moment. Despite this, the use of limit orders is quite common. As you can see, it is also a disciplined way of trading, in terms of getting a good price and taking profits off the table.

Limit orders can also help with splitting the bid. Because of a lack of liquidity, some markets may have wide spreads between the bid price and the ask price. With a limit order, you can set a price roughly in the middle of the gap. In other words, it is a way to see if you can get a broker to take the bait and give you a better price on a purchase or sale.

However, there are some caveats with limit orders. For example, some investors focus too much on getting the best price possible. It may be a matter of setting the limit at only a few ticks above or below the current price. In these circumstances, the limit order is really not much help. If anything, it could mean missing out on a good trade.

STOP-LOSS ORDER

The main purpose of a stop-loss order is to reduce the loss on a trade. That is, a market order will be triggered if the futures price hits a certain point. A buy stop is set at a price that is *above* the market whereas a sell stop is set at a price that is *below* the market.

As with limit orders, there are no guarantees on what price you will get, since futures markets can be volatile and move in big gaps, and you may encounter some slippage, the amount that goes above or below the price you set on a stop. An order may also not be filled because the futures market has hit daily limits. In such cases, it can take several days for the orders to be executed. Despite this, stop-loss orders are still effective. One of the best futures traders, Paul Tudor Jones, always uses a stop-loss order on his trades.

To understand this, let's take a look at an example. Suppose you believe that the February wheat contract looks attractive and you buy one wheat contract at a price of 90 cents. While you are confident in the trade, you realize that wheat may be volatile. So you will set a stop at 88 cents. If the price hits this level, you will be taken out of the trade. A trader may also use a trailing stop. This means that you will increase the price point as the futures price increases. Continuing our example, let's say that wheat goes to 95 cents. You then will cancel your existing stop and will set a new one at 93 cents.

At what levels should you set a stop? This is different from trader to trader. But a common technique is to look at the difference between the support and resistance (this is explained in more detail in Chapter 7). This should provide a rough guide of the underlying volatility of the futures contract. So, if you establish a stop, it would be near the support level.

LENGTH OF ORDER TYPES

When you place an order, it is assumed to be a day order. As the name implies, this means it lasts for the trading day. Although, this may not necessarily be clear. Is it the trading day for open outcry trading or for electronic trading? You need to check with the exchange.

If you do not want a day order, you can select one of these options.

- **Good-'til-canceled (GTC) order:** This will keep the order open until you terminate it.
- **Filled-until-the-product-goes-off-the-board order:** This will keep the order open until the contract expires.
- **One-cancels-the-other (OCO) order:** This is often used for spread trades. If one position hits a trigger and becomes profitable, then the other position will be closed out because it has turned unprofitable.

TRADING MISTAKES

When trading, you can be your own worst enemy. It is tempting to chase the latest hot commodity. Yet this can be a bad move, as there are often corrections. These are sudden falls in the market, which are often about 10 percent. Even if you have done your research and have good trading strategies, they will never be fool-proof. It's futile to try to time the tops and bottoms of a commodity price. Even the best traders make bad trades. Keep in mind that getting profits on 40 percent of your positions is considered a good track record and should produce nice profits. With all of this in mind, let's take a look at some of the biggest mistakes traders can make.

- **Trading Systems:** No doubt, you will find various investors who claim that they have a top-notch trading system. Often you will find these on flashy advertisements on the Internet. The language is hyped with statements that you will make huge amounts in a short period of time. Well, be wary. It does not take much to start an online newsletter and it can be nearly impossible to verify the claims. Instead, a great way to learn is to start trading slowly and get a sense of the different types of techniques and futures contracts.

- **The Big Trade:** In the early 1990s, famed investor George Soros was convinced that the British pound would fall. He saw it as a once-in-a-lifetime trade and bet billions on it. According to Soros, he "went for the jugular." Of course, it paid off. But there are many more examples of these big trades that have gone sour and wiped out investors, even some of the best. So for individual investors, it is advisable to avoid these bet-the-ranch trades.

- **Overtrading:** Trading futures can be fun and addictive. But this can lead to overtrading, which can be fatal. Not only does this result in more commission and bid-ask costs, but the trades are most likely to be bad ones.

- **Research:** While a common problem for traders is to be rash, there is also the opposite problem. That is, a trader may spend too much time researching a trade. This is known as paralysis by analysis. Again, the fact is that you will never have perfect information and you will inevitably have losing trades.

- **Confidence:** If you do not feel sure about a trade, don't do it. Look for another trade.

- **Drawdowns:** A drawdown is any loss that happens between two peaks in equity. To understand this, let's take a look at an example. Suppose your account is $20,000. Through smart trades, it increases to $30,000. But then you hit a rough patch and the portfolio declines to $25,000. After this, you then make some better trades and the portfolio increases by $5,000. In this case, your total profit is $20,000. It went from $20,000 to $35,000. But the drawdown was $5,000, which was the drop between the first gain to $30,000 and the next one to $35,000. But if you traded your account later and suffered an initial loss of $5,000, your capital would have been $15,000.

  In other words, having a sense of the potential drawdown is important to understanding how much equity you should have in your account. You do not want to be in a position where some quick losses will rapidly eat into your equity. This goes to the idea that you should only trade on the money that you can afford to lose. You do not want to place yourself in a position where you are stressed out and pressured into generating big returns. In many cases, this only makes the trading worse. Instead, make sure you have enough money in your account to meet any reasonable margin calls.

FOCUS

There are dozens of types of futures contracts to choose from and strategies. No doubt, things can get quite complicated. You will also be competing against top-notch traders.

This is not to imply that you should avoid trading futures. In fact, many individual investors have made strong profits from these markets. But to be successful, you need to have a good understanding of the dynamics. To this end, it is usually a good idea to focus on only a few futures markets. There are many examples of successful traders who have spent years on only live cattle or wheat. But it's also important to look at those markets with lots of liquidity. You do not want to pay high bid-ask costs or have difficulty getting out of a position, which can be particularly tough in fast markets.

As seen in this chapter, it is important to put together a trading plan to find the opportunities as well as protect the downside, such as with limit and stop orders. In the next chapter, we will look at call and put options on commodities futures, including how to read option quotes and writing call and put options.

CHAPTER 5

Options on Futures

Key Concepts

- Use options to go long or short
- Understand the risks
- Analyze various options strategies

While futures trading has become more common for individual investors, it can still be intimidating. There are certainly complexities and risks. If the investor is not attentive, there is the possibility of getting delivery of the underlying commodity. Perhaps the biggest risk is losing more than one's initial investment. In a fast market, the losses can pile up. But there is another approach to play futures, but not take on some of these risks. That is, you can purchase options on futures, also known as commodity options. At first, the concept seems a bit strange. But like any new investment technique, it just takes some practice and understanding of the fundamental principles, which we will cover in this chapter.

THE BASICS OF OPTIONS

The options market is massive and has been growing at a rapid rate. But despite its size, there are only two types of options. One is a call option, which allows you to buy a certain amount of an asset at a fixed price for a period of time, say three months to a year. The value of this type of option will generally *increase* if the underlying asset *increases*. A put option, on the other hand, gives a person the right to sell a certain amount of an asset for a fixed price for a period of time. The value of this type of option will *increase* in value if the underlying asset actually *decreases*. Most investors use options with stocks. Each option gives the investor the right to buy or sell 100 shares.

One of the attractions of options is that they provide leverage. This means that an investor will pay only a *fraction* of the total value of the underlying asset.

To understand this, let's take a look at an example. Suppose you want to purchase an option on IBM. You can buy 100 shares, which trade at $170 each. Your total investment would be $17,000. But you can instead purchase an option at $4 per share for a total of $400. This investment amount, $400, is called the premium. Suppose the stock price increases by $2 and the premium also increases by $2. In this case, the return on your $400 investment would be 50 percent ($200 divided by $400). In contrast, if you had bought the 100 shares your profit would have only been 1.1 percent.

Interestingly enough, when you buy a commodity option, you are actually *doubling* the leverage. How? Suppose you want to buy a commodity option on a contract for corn. No doubt, the premium you pay on the option will be a fraction of the overall value of the futures contract. At the same time, the futures contract will be based on investors who are paying a small fraction of the total value (as we saw in Chapter 2). Because of this, the volatility in commodity options can be substantial.

Another key difference between options on stock and commodity options is the expiration. True, both types of options have fixed expiration dates. This is the time when the buyer of an option can exercise it and take delivery of the asset. This would be the *underlying stock* for the equity option. But with a commodity option, the buyer of the option can exercise it to get delivery of the *underlying futures contract*. In the case of a call option, he or she will receive a long futures contract. A put buyer will receive a short futures contract.

Some commodity options expire during the same month that the futures contract does. This is known as a standard option.

There is also a serial option, where the futures contract expiration is one more month ahead of the expiration of the commodities option. Why is there a difference? Keep in mind that some futures contracts only expire during certain months of the year. There may even be differences with commissions. With a commodity option, you will need to pay an exchange fee, which can vary. Some brokers may also attempt to charge a round turn. This is an additional fee on the purchase and the sale of the commodities. But you can usually find a firm that will not charge this. So it is a good idea to shop around.

OPTION QUOTES

To understand quotes on commodity options, let's take a look at Table 5-1.

TABLE 5-1

Commodity Options Quote on Gold

Symbol	Strike	Open	High	Low	Close	Change	Volume	Open Interest
GC Q 2010 C	1125	43.70	43.70	43.70	43.70	−8.70	31	101
GC Q 2010 P	1125	43.70	43.70	43.70	43.70	−8.70	31	101
GC Q 2010 C	1130	43.70	43.70	43.70	43.70	−8.70	31	101
GC Q 2010 P	1130	43.70	43.70	43.70	43.70	−8.70	31	101
GC Q 2010 C	1140	43.70	43.70	43.70	43.70	−8.70	31	101
GC Q 2010 P	1140	43.70	43.70	43.70	43.70	−8.70	31	101
GC Q 2010 C	1150	43.70	43.70	43.70	43.70	−8.70	31	101
GC Q 2010 P	1150	43.70	43.70	43.70	43.70	−8.70	31	101

The Symbol column has different parts. The ticker is GC, which represents the gold contract. As for Q 2010, this means it is for an expiration of August 2010. The C is for a call option and P is for a put option. The Strike column shows the price that the call or put buyer will get a futures contract for. An exchange will have a policy on the increments for each level of the prices of the commodity options. In the case of gold, it is in increments of 10 dollars. The

Open column shows the options' first trade of the day. The High, the Low, and the Close columns show the quotes for gold for the day. These are in dollars and cents.

From the table, you can see that the August contract for 1140 gold is selling for $43.70. The Volume, column shows the total number of contracts traded for the day. The Open Interest column shows how many of the outstanding contracts have yet to be closed.

GOING LONG WITH COMMODITY OPTIONS

Let's say, because of adverse weather, you believe that the corn futures contract will increase in value over the next couple of months. To make a profit, you will want to use a commodity option trade. The simplest approach is to purchase a call option.

To understand this, let's take a look at some examples. You see that the July corn option contract is selling for 20 cents or $1,000 (20 cents multiplied by 5,000 bushels). It has a strike price of 700 and the futures price is 700'0. Since the strike price and the futures price are the *same*, the option is at-the-money. After one month, the value of the futures contract *rises* to 710'0. Because this is *above* the strike price, the option is now in-the-money. If the reverse occurs and the futures contract is *below* the strike price, this would mean that the option is out-of-the-money. An in-the-money commodity option will have intrinsic value. This is the difference between the futures price and the exercise price. In our example, this is 10 cents or $500. For the corn contract, every penny represents $50. In other words, the commodity option will have at least this value.

However, there should be some extra value, which is called the time value. Why? There is the possibility that the commodity option will increase even more. Generally, as time goes by, the time value will decrease. It will go to zero at expiration. In our example, let's say that the time value is 2 cents or $100. As a result, the total value of your gain will be $600 ($100 time value plus the $500 in intrinsic value). So the profit on your initial investment will be 60 percent ($600 profit divided by the $1,000 investment).

But let's say that the investment did not go according to plan and the futures price of corn instead fell to 698'0. The commodity option will be out-of-the-money and have no intrinsic value. If your time value is $100, your investment has fallen by 80 percent. If the option remains out-of-the-money by expiration, the option will be worthless. Unfortunately, this is a common occurrence.

Estimates are that 80 percent or more of long options will ultimately have no value. Ironically investors consider this to be an advantage, at least compared to futures contracts. With a commodity option, you know that the maximum amount you will lose is the premium. A futures contract may result in additional losses and margin calls if the trade goes sour.

But yes, investors do try to avoid having their options go worthless! One way to deal with this problem is to purchase a LEAP (Long-Term Equity Anticipation Security). LEAPs have an expiration of several years. However, the premiums tend to be expensive and may not have much liquidity.

Investors can also use order types to help with risk, such as stop-loss orders and trailing stops (we explain this in detail in Chapter 4). But you need to be careful of the rules. Keep in mind that some commodity options do not trade in the overnight market. So you may get an order executed in the next day, when the prices have made a big move.

Interestingly enough, some investors are tempted to purchase options that are out-of-the money. Why? The reason is that they usually have small premiums and appear to be cheap. But be cautious. There is a reason why the values are low: the likelihood of the option getting any value is slim. This is why traders tend to focus on in-the-money options to help boost their odds of getting a profit.

GOING SHORT WITH COMMODITY OPTIONS

Let's say you instead believe that the corn futures contract will fall in value over the next couple of months. To make a profit from this, you will purchase a put option.

Continuing our example from above, you purchase the July corn option contract that has a strike price of 700'0. The premium, or investment amount, is 15 cents or $750. In about one month, the corn futures contract *falls* to 690'0 or 10 cents. Thus, your profit is $500. Again, as in the case of purchasing call options, a put option is highly risky. A large number will expire worthless.

WRITING CALL OPTIONS

Each option contract has two parties. As we've seen above, there is the buyer of the option. He or she will pay a premium for the put or call option. But this amount will then go to another party, who is known as the option writer. Actually, the writer of a call is essentially taking a short position.

Let's first take a look at the call writer. Suppose you believe that silver will fall over the next two months. But it will not be a big move. Instead, you think it could drop by 1 percent or 2 percent. To profit from this scenario, you will write a March call with a strike price of 30. The premium is 30 cents or $1,500 (5,000 troy ounces multiplied by 30 cents). You get to keep this amount. A few weeks go by and there is little movement in the silver futures contract, which is now trading at 29.90. You can actually take your profit now by purchasing an offsetting March 30 call option. This will lock in your gain. What is the gain? Well, because of the decline in time value, the call option is now only selling for 20 cents. So you have a 10-cent profit, which comes to $500.

As you can see, call writing can be an effective way to generate a stream of income. As a result, it is a popular strategy for commodities investors. However, there is a big risk. In fact, a trade has potentially unlimited risk. Let's take a look. You first need to understand the break-even point of the trade. For writing a call option, it is:

Strike Price + Premium = Break-Even Point

For the March call silver position, the break-even point is 30.00 (strike price) plus 30 cents (premium) or 30.30. So, after this point, the trade will start to lose money. In fact, for every penny above it, there will be a $50 loss. If the futures price surges, this can wind up being a big loss. Because of this, a broker will require a margin account. There will also be trading restrictions. For instance, you will likely only be able to take on a certain number of trades at any time.

Despite all this, the fact is that many trades that involve call writing prove to be profitable. Why is this the case? After all, long call options usually expire worthless. Well, the reason is that the premiums tend to be competitively priced because of the time value and volatility. In a way, an option writer is capitalizing on the volatility premium. That is, the higher the volatility, the higher the premium. Option writers also tend to focus on contracts that have a small amount of time until expiration, say 30 or 40 days. The reason is that the time value will generally decline very quickly, making for a nice profit.

WRITING PUT OPTIONS

Writing a put option is similar to writing a call option. But the profit results if the futures price *stays the same or rises*. To understand this, let's continue with our example from above. You think that silver has hit a support level and will have a small bounce, say 1 percent or so. You will write a March put on silver that has a strike price of 30. For this, you get a premium of 15 cents or $750. The break-even point is:

Strike Price − Premium = Break-Even Point

This means our trade will be profitable so long as the futures price does not fall below 29.85. Actually, there is no unlimited loss potential with writing a put. The reason is that the futures contract can fall no lower than $0. Besides, even if there is a plunge, it will likely get no where near $0. As seen with writing calls, the risk tends to be reduced because of the fall in time value.

OPTION STRATEGIES

It is fairly straightforward to buy puts and calls—and write them. However, there are many other types of option strategies. As it can be overwhelming considering the other approaches, it is a good idea to use an online stimulator to try out the different strategies. This will prevent you from making mistakes that could wind up costing you big losses. There are even a variety of options schools that have one-on-one instruction, videos, and other helpful tutorials. In this chapter, we will look at just a few of the main strategies. These include the long and short straddles, the bull call and bear put spreads, as well as the married calls and puts.

Straddles and Strangles

With a straddle, you can actually make money if the option rises or falls in value. However, the swings must be substantial. This is why a straddle makes sense if you believe there will be a big change in the futures price. For example, you could use this strategy before a major report is released.

A long straddle is when you buy a long put and a long call with the *same* expiration and strike price. Usually, the strike price is fairly close to the futures price.

To understand this, let's take a look at an example. Suppose you think the federal government will report that the wheat crop will be lower than expected. To profit from this, you will buy a July call and a put that has a strike price of 800'0. The premium for the call is 10 cents or $500; the put has a premium of 8 cents or $400. This means your total investment is $900. For this trade, there are two break-even points:

Strike Price + Total Investment = Upper Break-Even Point

Strike Price − Total Investment = Lower Break-Even Point

The upper break-even point is 819'0 and the lower break-even point is 781'0. To be profitable, the futures price has to move above or below these two ranges. Now, suppose that you are correct and the wheat production report is highly bullish. The wheat futures contract spikes to 830'0. The premium on the call is 25 cents and the put has a premium of 2 cents. So your profit is 9 cents or $450.

The problem with this strategy is if there is little volatility, then you will lose on the trade. So, if the news report met expectations and the futures price increases by 2 percent or so, you will have sustained a loss on your position. Because of this, some investors may use a short straddle. Continuing with our example above, this would involve selling an at-the-money put and an at-the-money call with the *same* strike price. Instead of paying $900, you will get to keep it. Actually, this strategy is really for when a market is likely to remain relatively flat. Yet, even a small move up or down will inevitably mean that one side of the transaction will lose money. The break-even point for the short straddle is the reverse of the one for the long straddle. That is, you will have a profitable trade so long as the futures prices remain within the upper and lower bands of the break-even points.

Bull Call and Bear Put Spreads

A bull call spread involves buying and selling a call. An investor will use a bull call spread if he or she thinks there will be a general increase in the futures price. If the investor believes that there will be a spike, then the better approach might be to purchase a long call.

To understand this, let's take a look at an example. Suppose the futures price for July gold is 1500. You will purchase an October 1550 call at $850.00 and sell an October 1590 call at $400, for a total of $450. With this strategy, you have actually limited your profit. This is based on the following formula:

[Higher Strike Price − Lower Strike Price] × Multiplier − Your Investment = Maximum Profit Potential

For our trade, this would be $4,000 (or 1590 minus 1550 times 100 ounces). You then subtract from this your investment of $450. So, your maximum profit potential is $3,550.

Why allow for a cap on your profits? Well, for this, you actually have some limited downside. That is, the loss will be no more than the initial investment of $450. Besides, by selling the call, you will have generated cash, which has reduced your initial investment. All in all, the risk is less than making an outright purchase of a call.

There is also a variation called the bear put spread. This is for those trades that will benefit from a gradual fall in the futures price. To do this, there will be a purchase of an at-the-money put and a sale of an out-of-the-money call. A bear put spread will have less risk exposure than an outright purchase of a put option.

Married Call and Put

A married put is a way for an investor to protect a gain in a position. This is also known as shorting against the box.

To understand this, let's take a look at an example. Suppose you purchased a futures contract on silver and over the past two weeks you have generated a gain of $2,000. You think there may be a temporary sell-off and then a resumption of the rise in the price. You will buy a put or short a call with a strike price that is the same as the futures price. You will have locked in the gain (at least for the period of the option). In a way, this serves as an insurance policy. The premium amount is your out-of-pocket purchase—but it should only account for a fraction of your gain.

Now, suppose that you have a short position in on a silver futures contract and your gain is $3,000. You think the futures price may rise and you want to protect your position. In this situation, you will structure a married call. This means you will buy a call option with a strike price that is close to the price of the futures price. If the futures price increases, your call option will increase in value and help to offset the losses on your short position.

THE GREEKS

In options trading, you will hear about the so-called Greeks. As the name implies, these are based on Greek characters and provide different metrics to help with understanding options. The main Greeks include:

- **Delta:** This is the ratio of the option price change to the futures price change. For example, if the futures price increases by 10 cents and the options price increases by 5 cents, then the delta would be 0.50 (5 cents divided by 10 cents). Actually, if an option is in-the-money, the ratio is typically about 0.50. But the more an option is out-of-the-money, the less delta there will be, and vice versa. This is the case for both put and call options (although, in the case of a put option, the value ranges from 0 to -1).
- **Theta:** This shows the rate of change in value decay of an option. If the theta is high, then the time value will hold up better than one with a lower theta. However, when an option has less than a month until expiration, there will typically be a bigger decline in the theta value.

- **Gamma:** This shows the rate of change in the delta of an option. If the gamma increases, then there could be a big jump in the delta, which means your option has become riskier. So, savvy traders will keep an eye on the gamma for any major changes.

OPTION PRICING MODELS

There are various pricing models for options. The most-well known one is the Black-Scholes model. This was first published in 1973, in an academic paper by Fischer Black and Myron Scholes. Then Robert Merton expanded on the model. Because of their efforts, Merton and Scholes received the 1997 Nobel Prize in Economics; Black did not win it because he had died, and the Nobel Prize is not given posthumously. The Black-Scholes model is a complicated formula, but it bases option prices on the following factors:

- Underlying futures price
- Strike price
- Time to expiration
- Interest rate
- Volatility

However, when it comes to trading in commodity futures, the model has limited use. Keep in mind that it does not account for the bid-ask spread. This is important because this can be a material gap for commodities. Despite this, the core of the Black-Scholes model points out some of the key factors that drive pricing, as we've shown in this chapter. Perhaps the most important include: the overall volatility, the time until expiration, and how close the strike price is to the underlying futures price.

In this chapter, we have provided a general introduction on commodities options. While the strategies can be highly effective—and lower risks—the complexities can be daunting. So beginning investors need to be patient when learning the approaches. In the next chapter, we will look at various indexes that track commodities, and how the main supply and demand forces affect the price of commodities.

CHAPTER 6

Fundamental Analysis

Key Concepts

- Understand the main supply and demand forces for commodities
- Learn how to locate commodities data
- Look at the various risks

Investors often look for themes. If they see that the global economy is starting to rebound, then the theme will likely be to buy commodities. In most cases, it does not matter which commodity. Investors will essentially buy up all the main categories. This is what happened during the first half of 2010.

But investment themes will run their course. In the case of the one in 2010, it lasted roughly about nine months. After this, each group of commodities traded based on their underlying fundamentals; that is, the supply and demand. This is what typically happens. In this chapter, we will take a look at the main forces that impact supply and demand, as well as how to find and interpret the various data sources. But before doing this, investors need to measure the trends for the main categories of commodities. This is done by analyzing indexes.

INDEXES

An index is a basket of investments, that is expressed as one value. There are thousands of indexes across the world. Some of them are widely followed, such as the Dow Jones Industrial Average (DJIA) and the Standard & Poor's 500 Index (S&P 500). As for commodities indexes, they usually follow a group of futures contracts. There are broad-based indexes that cover a wide array of commodities, such as agriculture, livestock, energy, and so on. There are also indexes that focus on one category of the commodities markets.

Indexes are affected by two important factors: weighting and rebalancing.

- **Weighting:** This is the percentage of the overall index that the commodity represents. In some indexes, the weighting of one or two commodities can easily be over 50 percent. This means that there will be little diversification.

- **Rebalancing:** This is when the index weightings are adjusted. This can happen once a year or more, depending on the index's policy.

Rebalancing can actually have a big impact on the markets. Keep in mind that funds based on the Standard & Poor's GSCI and the Dow Jones–UBS Commodity Index amount to over $150 billion. During the first couple of weeks of January 2011—when these indexes were rebalanced—there was actually much volatility in the commodities markets.[1] So even small changes in the allocations—say, to zinc or soybeans—can have a substantial impact on the prices of commodities. This is because the index funds will need to buy or sell futures. Those commodities that have had relatively lower performances will actually get more buying. The reason is to bring them back to their allocation percentage. However, these changes in valuation are likely to last a short period of time.

---

[1] http://online.wsj.com/article/SB10001424052748704739504576067890758039436 .html?mod=WSJ_hps_sections_markets.

EXAMPLES OF COMMODITIES INDEXES

While there are many commodities indexes—and more will likely launch in the future—there are certain ones that investors focus on. These include the Deutsche Bank Liquid Commodity Index, the Dow Jones–UBS Commodity Index, the Goldman Sachs Commodity Index, the Reuters/Jefferies Commodity Research Bureau Index, the Rogers International Commodities Index, and the COT Index.

Deutsche Bank Liquid Commodity Index

Launched in February 2003, the Deutsche Bank Liquid Commodity Index (DBLCI) tracks the performance of only six commodities. These include West Texas Intermediate (WTI) crude oil, heating oil, aluminum, gold, corn, and wheat. The weightings are based on market value, with energy at 55 percent and precious metals at 10 percent.

Interestingly enough, the DBLCI commodities tend to correlate with each other. Thus, there is not much diversification in the index and as a result, the volatility can be high. But there is a key benefit to having a small number of commodities—lower costs. Except for crude oil, the commodities in the index are rebalanced every year.

Dow Jones–UBS Commodity Index

The Dow Jones–UBS Commodity Index (DJ–UBSCI), which got its start in July 1998, was formerly called the Dow Jones–AIG Commodity Index. But in 2009, AIG (American International Group) sold its interest to UBS. The DJ–UBSCI tracks 19 commodities. The weightings include:

- 33.0 percent for energy
- 29.5 percent for agriculture
- 20.0 percent for industrial metals
- 10.1 percent for precious metals
- 7.4 percent for livestock

In other words, the index provides broad coverage of the categories for commodities. In fact, a weighting cannot exceed a third. Also, a commodity must account for a minimum of 2 percent.

Goldman Sachs Commodity Index

While subject to debate, the Goldman Sachs Commodity Index (GSCI) is the most widely followed commodities index. Actually, Goldman Sachs no longer owns it. The firm sold the index in 2007 to Standard & Poor's.

Started in 1992, the GSCI tracks 24 commodities and the weightings are based on global production. To avoid anomalies, the weightings are calculated on a five-year basis. Because of this, energy represents nearly 80 percent of the index. Investors can buy futures on the GSCI on the CME. There are also a variety of exchange-traded funds (ETFs), which include the GSCI Commodity Indexed Trust (GSG). There are also mutual funds like the Oppenheimer Real Asset Fund and the BlackRock Real Investment Fund.

Reuters/Jeffries Commodity Research Bureau Index

The Reuters/Jefferies Commodity Research Bureau Index has a long history, having started back in 1957. While it has undergone a variety of changes, the last major one was in 2005. During that year, the index added to its list of commodities, for a total of 19. There are now four main tiers of commodities: petroleum, highly liquid commodities (aluminum, copper, gold, etc.), liquid, and diversified. The goal is to create a broad index, which reflects the overall commodities market. Investors can trade futures on this index on the CME.

Rogers International Commodities Index

Famed investor Jim Rogers created the Rogers International Commodities Index (RICI) in 1998. At the time, he thought the existing indexes failed to reflect the best commodities for investors. RICI tracks 35 commodities, including exotics like silk and adzuki beans, which do not trade on futures exchanges. Yet the index has a 39 percent weighting in energy and a 34 percent weighting in agriculture commodities. Investors can purchase futures contracts on the RICI on the CME.

Commitment of Traders Reports

Major hedge funds, institutions, and commodity companies trade across the world every day. It is actually possible to see the trends in the activity, which can certainly be a helpful way to evaluate an investment, by reviewing the Commodity Futures Trading Commission's (CFTC's) Commitment of Traders (COT) reports. One report covers futures; another covers futures and options. The COT reports come out weekly. You can find these at www.cftc.gov.

There are several areas on the COT reports that investors focus on. One part is the open interest, which is the number of futures or options that have not been closed out. Then there are reportable positions. These are from clearing firms, futures commission merchants, and even foreign brokers. Often these will represent more than three-quarters of the open interest. Each trader is either commercial or noncommercial. The former is for those who use futures or options for hedging. These are often large commodities producers, like Cargill. A noncommercial operator is usually a fund, such as a hedge fund, exchange-traded fund, or a mutual fund.

When evaluating the COT reports, an investor will focus on the net position changes across reports. Are the large players going long or going short? Investors will also focus on the commercial operators. Keep in mind that these companies usually have strong trading operations and sophisticated investors.

A useful indicator is the COT Index. Back in 1990, investor Stephen Briese developed this and even wrote a book on the topic (*The Commitments of Traders Bible*). This index gives more weight to commercial operators. A rating of 0 would be extremely bearish; a rating of 100 would be highly bullish.

SUPPLY AND DEMAND

When it comes to commodities, it is critically important to understand the main supply and demand forces. It is really a matter of basic economics. If the demand falls while the supply remains constant, there should be a fall in the price of a commodity. If the supply falls, but the demand remains intact, the price of a commodity should rise. The good news for commodities investors is that the demand for commodities is growing and the supply is getting constrained.

Supply and Commodities

Let's first look at supply. Since the Industrial Revolution, during the 1800s, there has been substantial growth in the extraction of commodities. At first, it was much easier to find large reserves and produce the commodities at low prices. Just look at the case of crude oil. From 1900 to 1970, the price of oil traded at about $2 per barrel.

But eventually it got tougher to find new sources of oil. At the same time, the costs of extraction increased. When new fields are found, they are usually miles deep below the ocean. The result is that it can easily take ten years and billions of dollars to get the new sources of oil. Oil is just one example. It is actually getting tougher to find and extract many other important commodities, like copper, silver, uranium, rare earth metals, and so on.

Demand and Commodities

On the demand side, there is transformation in the global economy. The key emerging economies—including China, India, and Brazil—are in the midst of modernizing their economies. Because of this, there has been a surge in the demand for commodities. Yet even during a typical year, demand generally does not spike. Rather, demand tends to increase or decrease at a steady rate.

It is usually the supply of commodities that is much more volatile. This can be the result of many factors including strikes, government policies, and adverse weather.

Information Resources on Supply and Demand of Commodities

To get information on the supply and demand of commodities, there are certainly many resources. Because of the bull market, there are now many online sites that provide helpful data and analysis.

Another good source is the websites of commodity exchanges, like the CME.

Since investors want to get a broad view of the markets, they often go to the website of the trade association for an individual commodity. Here you will find things like news alerts, industry statistics, and tutorials. There may even be Facebook and Twitter pages for the trade associations, as well as iPhone apps. The top trade associations include:

- Aluminum Association (www.aluminum.org)
- Copper Development Association (www.copper.org)
- Cotton Incorporated (www.cottoninc.com)
- International Cocoa Organization (www.icco.org)
- International Coffee Organization (www.ico.org)
- National Association of Wheat Growers (www.wheatworld.org)
- National Corn Growers Association (www.ncga.com)
- National Mining Association (www.nma.org)
- Organization of Petroleum Exporting Countries (www.opec.org)
- United Soybean Board (www.unitedsoybean.org)

Another key resource of information is from the websites of government agencies. They include:

- Energy Information Administration (www.eia.doe.gov)
- International Energy Agency (www.iea.org)
- U.S. Geological Survey (www.usgs.gov)
- National Agricultural Statistics Service (www.nass.usda.gov)
- National Hurricane Center (www.nhc.noaa.gov)
- International Monetary Fund (www.imf.org)

As you do your research, you will quickly realize that there is an overwhelming amount of information. So to make things easier, we will focus on some of the key analytics when using the data. We will also look at important risk factors, like weather and government regulations.

MACROECONOMIC FORCES

Before investing in a commodity, investors will often look at macroeconomics. This involves the main drivers of economic growth. If they are positive, it will lead to higher consumption of commodities—and probably higher prices. Here's a look at some of the important macroeconomic factors.

Global Gross Domestic Product

Global Gross Domestic Product (GDP) is the total amount of goods and services produced in the world for the year. It is perhaps the most important factor driving commodities growth. You can find the global GDP figures from the website of the International Monetary Fund (IMF).

Investors will also look at certain categories of GDP to get a sense if the world economy is poised for strong growth. This would include jumps in durable goods production (such as cars and appliances), industrial utilization (the percentage of industrial capacity in use), and residential construction.

Per Capita Income

A general increase in per capita income will lead to more demand for commodities. But there are some nuances. That is, some commodities may increase while others fall off. An example is meat. If a person's income increases, he or she will probably focus on higher, more expensive cuts of meat and avoid less expensive cuts like ground beef.

Population and Demographics

An increase in the global population will inevitably lead to the increase in the consumption of commodities. However, investors also need to understand the changing demographics. If the population is younger, then there may be more spending on homes, cars, and appliances. The reason is that there will be an increase in family formations. But when a population ages, the demand for commodities will change. More money will go to things like medical products.

Interest Rates

Often overlooked, interest rates are an important factor in the commodities industry. There is often the need to finance capital assets to produce commodities. If interest rates increase, there will be an increase in the costs of these investments. If costs get too high, there will likely be a postponement of projects or even a cancellation of projects. This happened during the early 1980s when the Federal Reserve increased interest rates to over 20 percent. This action was enough to create a painful recession and was the beginning of a long bear market in commodities.

Inflation

Inflation is certainly a big problem in emerging economies. With strong economic growth in emerging economies, there has been a general increase in consumer prices. Of course, many of these countries have had a terrible history with inflation. In some cases, there were bouts of hyperinflation. To deal with higher prices, governments will increase interest rates, put limits on credit, and even impose price controls. But these actions can actually hinder economic growth, which will ultimately mean lower commodities prices.

For emerging economies, one of the biggest risks is surging food prices. Lower-wage people have a difficult time maintaining their standard of living and may fall back into poverty. The result could be political and social instability. Sometimes there are even food riots. Consider that according to the Food and Agriculture Organization of the United Nations, global food prices hit an all-time high at the end of 2010.[2]

The U.S. Dollar

On global markets, commodities are priced in the U.S. dollar. So when the dollar falls in value, there is an upward pressure on commodities. This is because it takes more dollars to buy the commodity. Of course, the reverse is true when the dollar increases in value.

---

[2] http://online.wsj.com/article/SB10001424052748704739504576068171365313408 .html?mod=WSJASIA_hps_LEFTTopStoriesWhatsNews.

Thus, commodity traders will focus on the movements of the dollar and try to gauge its trends. But there are some exceptions, especially with gold. The reason is that during times of political instability, there is a flight to the dollar as well as to gold.

MICROECONOMIC FORCES

Microeconomics focuses on the analysis of particular markets. As should be no surprise, this involves a heavy emphasis on supply and demand. Here's a look at some of the main microeconomic principles that apply to commodities investors.

Substitute

A substitute is a good that buyers will seek out when an alternative is increasing in price. For example, if the price of beef increases, consumers may start buying turkey. However, some goods have few viable substitutes or it may take a long time for buyers to make the switch. In this case, the good has an inelastic price. This would be the case for uranium. But if a switch is fairly easy, then the price is elastic. The result could be that a price spike for the good may not last long.

To understand this, let's take a look at the case of cotton. In 2010, the commodity skyrocketed by a whopping 92 percent (it was the highest-performing commodity). Because of this, fashion designers had a problem. It was getting expensive to make cotton clothing. To deal with this, fashion designers looked for alternatives. One was rayon, which is a fabric that has been around for about 80 years. It has had several cycles of being "in" with consumers, such as during the 1980s. Interestingly enough, the demand for rayon meant a boost for the producers of pulp wood. The stocks of some of these operators—like Fortress Paper, Tembec Inc., and Rayonier—reached new highs. So even though the price of pulp wood increased, the rise has only been a fraction of the increase in cotton.[3]

This highlights yet another economic principle: complementary goods. This is when the demand for one good increases the

---

[3] http://online.wsj.com/article/SB10001424052748703730704576066291209981236 .html?mod=WSJ_hp_LEFTWhatsNewsCollection.

demand for another. For investors, this is a smart strategy to find investment ideas.

Consumer Preferences

Consumer preferences can remain fairly stable over long periods of time. But there are times when there are structural changes. This is the case with diets. After all, in countries like the United States, there has been a move towards healthier foods. As a result, demand for beef has stagnated.

Consumer preferences are also impacted by changes in culture or even in advertising. Companies like Starbucks have helped to increase the demand for coffee.

Consumer preferences are also seasonal. An example is the holidays. During this time, there tends to be an increase in the consumption of turkeys.

Global versus Regional Pricing

Some commodities—such as crude oil—have global pricing, which means they are priced similarly around the world. The main reason is that these commodities are nonperishable.

There are also some commodities that have regional pricing. This means that there can be major price differences around the world. Why is there a difference in pricing? One factor is government policy, such as with tariffs.

Another key reason is shipping costs. You can see this with the value-to-weight ratio. The lower the value-to-weight ratio, the more likely that the commodity will have regional pricing. This is the case with iron ore, lumber, and coal.

SOVEREIGN RISK

The federal government's involvement in the U.S. economy has grown steadily over the years. This has been the case despite several pro-business Republican administrations. Even in developing countries, there has been an increase in regulatory oversight. As nations get wealthier, the population expects higher standards.

These regulations can have major impacts on the supply of commodities. In the case of the cattle industry, regulations for land-use and waste disposal are serious changes.

Of course, political systems in emerging economies can also be highly unstable. This is known as sovereign risk, which includes things like nationalization or civil wars. An example of sovereign risk occurred in Russia in 2003. President of the Russian Federation, Vladimir Putin, arrested Mikhail Khodorkovsky, the founder and leader of Yukos, which was the largest oil company in the country. Khodorkovsky eventually had to serve a nine-year jail sentence and Yukos had to be sold off in parts.

Another form of sovereign risk is strategic stockpiling. This is when a country buys up large amounts of a commodity because of fear that it will become scarce and jeopardize the national economy. No doubt, such activity will put upward pressure on prices.

MINE CONDITIONS AND REGULATIONS

The aging of existing mines is certainly a big problem for production. Some mines are over 100 years old. Such mines have a variety of issues. Often they will require more maintenance and expenses. There may even be more problems with safety and environmental discharges. In fact, an aging mine is often subject to temporary closures, which can be a major disruption to supply.

WEATHER

Weather is an important factor for a variety of commodities. One is natural gas. If there is a particularly cold winter, then there will be higher demand. Thus, investors will spend much time gauging the weather. Of course, this is no easy feat. While meteorology has made many advances, the study is still based on limited data, analysis, and probabilities.

Traders will try to determine the activity of hurricanes, since they can have a major disruption for the commodities of natural gas and crude oil. The forces of a hurricane can cause much damage to distribution facilities, refineries, and offshore rigs.

A stark example occurred during 2005. In the United States, the primary activity for hurricanes is in the Gulf of Mexico. The season goes from August until late October. Hurricane Katrina, which began as a Category 3 storm in August 2005, quickly turned into a Category 5 hurricane. It wrought destruction, which in turn caused spikes in prices for natural gas. Then a month later, in September 2005, came Hurricane Rita.

Every year, the National Hurricane Center (www.nhc.noaa .gov) provides a detailed forecast for hurricane activity. It is a must-read for natural gas traders.

NEW TECHNOLOGIES

With shortages of key commodities, manufacturers are looking at new innovations to find substitutes. This is likely to spur venture capital investments in early-stage companies and may eventually result in various public offerings. Of course, multinational companies have tremendous amounts of resources to create new technologies.

Toyota Motor Company's popular hybrid vehicles rely heavily on rare earth metals. The primary metal is neodymium, which has strong magnetic powers. Each Toyota Prius has about 2.2 pounds of the metal. However, supply has been constrained because China, which dominates the market, has been restrictive with its exports. While there has been an increase in the mining of neodymium in other countries, such as the United States, it will take several years for the production to hit the market.

In the meantime, Toyota is investing substantial amounts into research and development (R&D) to develop alternatives to rare earth metals. It has made great strides and may have some new breakthroughs. Basically, Toyota is using induction motor technology, which is fairly inexpensive. Toyota is also investing in the mining business. It has formed a joint venture in Vietnam for a neodymium deposit. Toyota is not the only automaker that is investing in R&D to find alternatives. General Motors, which develops the Volt electric car, is also making key investments.[4]

If proven successful, new technology can have a big impact. A classic case is the leach-solvent extraction-electro winning process or

---

[4] http://online.wsj.com/article/SB10001424052748703583404576080213245888864 .html?mod=WSJ_hp_LEFTWhatsNewsCollection.

SX/EW Process, which allows for the production of copper through oxidized ores and mine wastes. It was a breakthrough innovation in the mid-1980s. Because of this, it became easier for miners to extract more tonnes of copper. The additional supply, of course, had a dampening impact on prices.

THE LIFE INDEX

With increasing demand and the difficulties of finding new supplies, some commodities may be headed for extinction. This phenomenon is measured by comparing the production to the total proven reserves. It's called the reserves-to-production (R/P) ratio or the Reserve Life Index (RLI). Table 6-1 provides estimates of the R/P ratio for several different commodities. Keep in mind, however, that with new technologies and higher prices, it is likely the reserve levels will increase. What's more, some resources are renewable; that is, they can be recycled. This is the case with gold and silver. However, in the case of oil and coal, they are nonrenewable.

TABLE 6-1

The Reserve Life Index

Commodity	R/P Ratio
Oil	42
Natural gas	60
Coal	133
Iron	72
Copper	35
Silver	14
Platinum	157
Gold	17
Zinc	24
Nickel	21

While Table 6-1 does provide a general sense of the supply levels of key commodities, as seen with silver and gold, there may not be enough to mine in a couple of decades. This is likely to mean higher prices.

As seen in this chapter, there are many key factors that impact the supply and demand for commodities. Yet the overriding trends include substantial demand from emerging economies and the continued difficulties of finding new deposits of commodities. In the next chapter, we will take a look at technical analysis, which involves chart formations, patterns, and indicators.

CHAPTER 7

Technical Analysis

Key Concepts

- Understand the basics of charts and indicators
- Learn how to identify patterns, like the head-and-shoulders formation
- Look at some of the main theories, like the Elliott Wave Principle

With commodities investing, there are traders who focus on fundamental analysis. This means looking at supply and demand forces. An example of a fundamental analysis investor is Jim Rogers, who pours over huge amounts of data to find key investment trends.

There is another group of traders; they use technical analysis. This involves analyzing price and volume patterns for a commodity to determine the overall supply and demand. A technical analysis investor studies investor psychology and believes that it is possible to predict key moves and identify common patterns.

Technical analysis is popular with commodities investors. One reason is that they tend to be short-term traders, trying to find temporary profit opportunities. After all, futures contracts usually have short expiration periods, as do options. Despite this, there is much

controversy about technical analysis. In academic circles, the strategy is considered to be mostly guesswork and subjective. While
there are certainly some traders who have been successful with the
technique, such as Paul Tudor Jones, the academics just dismiss
them as outliers. But this has had little impact on the usage of technical analysis. Interestingly enough, many commodities investors
use a combination of fundamental analysis and technical analysis.
Smart investors simply want to use what works.

THE BASICS OF TECHNICAL ANALYSIS

Technical analysis can seem overwhelming, especially for begin-
ners. The reason is that there are hundreds of patterns and indicators. Even professionals cannot use all of them. Instead, they will
focus on several key tools that they find to be the most helpful for
their type of trading.

Technical analysis can generally be boiled down into two categories: charts and indicators. The most familiar one is using charts.
In fact, the use of charts goes back hundreds of years. Many of the
key principles come from Richard Schabacker, who is known as the
father of technical analysis. He wrote three pioneering books on
technical analysis—during the 1920s and 1930s—where he looked
at patterns including the head and shoulders, rectangles, and island
reversals. The focus of early technical analysts was primarily on
charts since there were no computers to crunch numbers and come
up with indicators. Indicators would not emerge until the 1970s.
Yet this does not diminish the importance of charts, which are definitely popular and useful for investors today.

Indicators, on the other hand, are quite diverse and involve
mathematical ratios, formulas, and algorithms. In many cases, they
will be in the form of an oscillator, which will have a value that
ranges from 0 to 100. An oscillator is a mathematical way to measure momentum.

VOLUME INDICATORS

There are two ways to gauge volume in a commodity. The first is to
look at the number of futures contracts traded. This is either for purchases or for sales, but not for both (this avoids double counting).

The other type of volume to consider is open interest, which is the number of contracts that have been created but yet to be offset by a liquidating transaction. Traders will avoid the last month for open interest because the contracts will typically be closed out. This will result in much lower volumes during this time period.

Both volume and open interest are key indicators of strength. So if they increase when there is a reversal or a breakout—which is an abrupt change in the pattern of the price of a futures contract—a trader will be more confident in the technical analysis. The saying is that "volume precedes the price." There are a variety of volume indicators to help commodities traders.

Ease of Movement Indicator

The Ease of Movement indicator (EMV) was created by Richard W. Arms, a top technical analyst. The EMV formula correlates the volume with the price movement of a commodity. The focus is on trying to gauge the strength of the trend. If the indicator goes above 0, then there is a buy signal, and vice versa.

On Balance Volume

Another helpful indicator is On Balance Volume (OBV). This indicator was developed by legendary investor Joe Granville during the early 1960s (from his book called the *New Key to Stock Market Profits*). While his focus was on stocks, the indicator is also applicable to commodities. To calculate OBV, you add the volume on the days the price is higher than the day before. Then you subtract the volume on the days the price is lower than the day before. The cumulative total is then provided on a chart and is called the OBV line.

Accumulation/Distribution Line

Another key volume indicator is the Accumulation/Distribution Line (ADL). It was created by investing expert Marc Chaikin. This is essentially a variation on the OBV indicator. Instead of comparing the changes in prices for a period, ADL uses a formula that looks at where the price ends. If the commodity ends the day at the midpoint for the price, then traders are bullish, and vice versa.

CHART BASICS

When charting, there are many useful websites and computer programs. For commodities, the top ones include BarChart.com and StockCharts.com. As for which is better, this is really a matter of individual preference. So it is a good idea to check several out. Many providers have free trial versions.

A typical chart can be for any time period, but in most cases a commodities trader will look at a shorter period of time, say one to six months. Each chart will be made up of vertical bars and will usually represent one trading day. Take a look at Figure 7-1, which is an example of a chart for corn.

FIGURE 7-1

Daily Futures

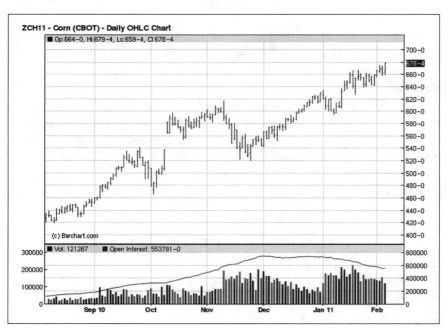

In the chart, each vertical bar will have two smaller bars, which are horizontal. These are known as tick marks. The one that goes to the right is the close and the one that goes to the left is the open. Of these, a trader will tend to focus on the close because it is the result of a full day's trading during which investors have had enough time to digest information. A trader can also get a sense of the volume for the day and see if there is growing strength on the price move. So if there is a drop in the commodities price on heavy volume, this may lead to more downward pressure for the next trading day. The top of the bar is the high for the day and the bottom of the bar is the low. If the bar is long, then this indicates much volatility in the stock. At the bottom of the chart, there will be lines that represent the volume. There may also be other technical indicators, such as the OBV line. When a commodity is volatile, a chart may actually be skewed and lead to misleading results. To deal with this, a trader can convert the chart to log-scale. This will help to smooth things out.

SUPPORT AND RESISTANCE

The two core trend lines in technical analysis are the support and resistance. A support level is the point at which a commodity will fall no further, as investors will see a bargain and start buying. The resistance level, on the other hand, is when the price gets to a high level and investors will take profits. So over time, a commodity will trade between the support and resistance levels. This is known as a consolidation, which is where the bulls and bears are equally matched. It's possible for a commodity to remain in consolidation several months to even a year.

If a commodity has been in this phase for some time, then traders will certainly take notice if the price moves above or below the range. Known as a breakout, this can be explosive on either side of the move.

To understand this, let's take a look at an example. Suppose sugar has traded in a consolidation of 50 to 55 and then the price spikes to 60. In this case, the 55 resistance becomes the support. So the new range is 55 to 60.

But a breakout may actually be a false signal, that is, a temporary move in which the price returns to its consolidation. To get a sense if there is a breakout, there are some helpful indicators. Perhaps the most important is if the consolidation has lasted for a significant period, say for a couple of months. You also want to see a major increase in volume.

UPTRENDS AND DOWNTRENDS

Another effective tool is the trend line. An uptrend line will tend to have higher lows and higher highs, whereas a downtrend line will have lower highs and lower lows. Of course, the trend lines can be jagged. But you can usually see the general trend when looking at a chart.

One of the tenets of technical analysis is: "The trend is your friend." Unless there is a breakout or some type of gap, the trend line should continue. If this holds, then it can certainly be a good way to generate returns.

What if there is a break in the trend line? A trader will be alerted and will likely start to lighten up on the position. A correction or retracement can be a large move. We will look at these in more detail later in this chapter.

When constructing trend lines, a trader can also find the channels. This is really the support and resistance lines for the uptrend or downtrend. With an uptrend, you will chart the highs. With a downtrend, you will chart the lows. This creates an interesting trading opportunity. If the commodity hits the bottom of the trend line, this is a buy signal. When it hits the top of the trend line, it is probably a good idea to lessen the position.

What if the price moves *outside* the channel? This is a breakout and is often significant since trading activity has increased. A breakout *above* the trend line is bullish. A move *beyond* the downside channel is bearish.

MOVING AVERAGES

Widely used, the moving average is a way to smooth out trends in prices. In fact, there are two types: the simple moving average and the exponential moving average.

Simple Moving Average

With the simple moving average (SMA), you will take the average for a commodity's prices over a period of time, say 50 or 200 days. Then, at the end of each trading day, you will recalculate the SMA and plot the new data point on the chart.

Exponential Moving Average

The other type of moving average is the exponential moving average (EMA). With this, the most recent prices will have more weighting. Because of this, the EMA should react to prices faster than the SMA. And since commodities traders prefer short-term trading, the EMA is usually preferred.

Comparison of Moving Average to Current Price

How do you use moving averages for trading? A popular approach is to compare the moving average with the current price. If the price is *above* the moving average, this means the commodity is in a bullish trend. If the price is *below* the moving average, this means the commodity is in a bearish trend.

Crossover

Another strategy is the crossover. This involves using two moving averages, with different time periods.

To understand this, let's take a look at an example. Suppose you are interested in the futures contract for corn. You have a 20-day moving average and a 60-day moving average. If the 20-day moving average goes *above* the 60-day moving average, then this would be a bullish signal and an entry point for a purchase. But if the 20-day moving average crosses *below* the 60-day moving average, then you would get out of your position or short the futures contract.

Moving Average Convergence/Divergence

Crossover strategies can get fairly complicated. A popular approach is the Moving Average Convergence/Divergence (MACD). This indicator was created by investor Gerald Appel in the late 1970s as a way to measure the momentum of a stock. But, it can also be effective for commodities traders. The MACD includes three steps.

1. The first is to calculate two exponential moving averages (EMAs) for the commodity. This is often for the 12-day and the 26-day moving averages.

2. Then, for each day, these two averages will be subtracted.

3. The last step is to calculate an EMA of these differences, which will be for the 9-day moving average.

You can see a chart of the MACD in Figure 7-2. The two lines in Figure 7-2 include the 12-day and 26-day moving average. There is also a histogram, which shows the positive and negative differences *between* the moving averages.

FIGURE 7-2

The Daily Chart for the MACD Technical Indicator

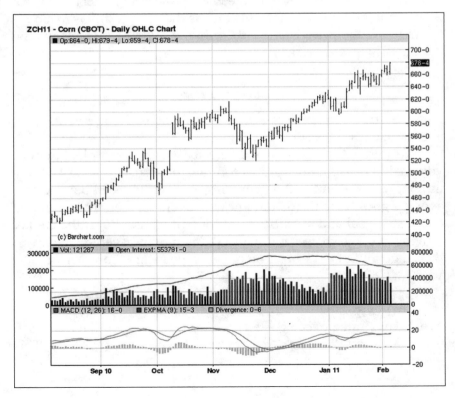

If the MACD has positive values, then the trend is bullish. If the MACD has negative values, then the trend is bearish.

But there is another level of analysis. This is done using the 9-day moving average, which is known as the signal line or the trigger line. There is a buy if the MACD line crosses *above* the signal line and there is a sell when it crosses *below* the signal line. In other words, this is an effective way to get a sense of the change in momentum and sentiment. A trader will also be alerted if there is a divergence. If the MACD is turning negative even though the commodity price is increasing, then there may be reversal.

HEAD-AND-SHOULDERS FORMATIONS

The head-and-shoulders formations, which are listed below, are the normal head and shoulders, the inverted head and shoulders, and the double top and the double bottom.

Normal Head and Shoulders

The head and shoulders is a popular chart formation. Perhaps the reason is that it has a good record of success. There are three peaks in this chart formation. The "head" represents the highest price in the move. The "shoulders"—left and right peaks—represent the lower prices.

The lows for all three should be close together and form a neckline. Yet it may also have an upward or downward slope. The neckline is critical. If it is broken when the price moves downward on the right shoulder, then this is a highly bearish signal. In fact, this move should be at least equal to the neckline and the top of the right shoulder. In other words, it can be a great opportunity to short a futures contract.

To help avoid false signals, there are some helpful techniques to gauge the success of a head-and-shoulders pattern. A key one is if the pattern has been evolving over a period of a few weeks. This shows that it is more than noise. At the same time, traders want to see growing volume on the right shoulder.

Inverted Head and Shoulders

There is also the inverted head and shoulders. This is the reverse of the normal head-and-shoulders formation, where the prices have two shoulders with similar lows and a head that has a higher low. If there is a breakout on the right shoulder, then this means there should be a bull run.

Double Top and Double Bottom

A variation of the head-and-shoulders formation is the double top and the double bottom. A double top is in the form of an M. There will be two moves that peak out. The trader will react if there is a breakout on the downside.

A double bottom is the opposite; it looks like a W. In this case, a trader looks for a breakout on the upside.

GAPS

A gap is a major move in the price of a commodity that shows up as empty space on the chart. That is, the opening price is higher or lower than the trading range of the prior day. In technical analysis, a gap has significance because the belief is that it will be filled, thus providing a trading opportunity. There are various types of gaps.

Common Gap

The common gap, as its name implies, is the gap that occurs the most. This typically happens when a commodity is in a trading range and volume is thin. So the gap should be filled quickly—often in the trading day.

Breakaway Gap

Then there is the breakaway gap. This is really a breakout, in which the price has a sharp move *outside* of its range. It is usually the first stage of a big market move. Because of this, a breakaway gap is usually *not* filled. The volume is typically strong as well.

Runaway Gap

If the price is in a big move, there can be the runaway gap. This forms in the middle of the major trend. It is an indication that the move will last for some time. Traders will often panic and aggressively take positions in the commodity so as to not miss out on the profits. Eventually, the move will end and this brings along the exhaustion gap.

Exhaustion Gap

When the exhaustion gap happens, volume spikes. Those who have made money will take their profits. This means that the trend has hit its top. The gap will likely be filled.

CONTINUATION PATTERNS

Technical analysis has many techniques that try to predict reversals. But there are cases when a trader wants to know if a trend has lasting power. To help determine this, there are several continuation patterns. Two of the most common include the flag and pennant patterns.

Flag Pattern

The flag pattern has the shape of a rectangle, which consists of two parallel lines. These are the support and the resistance. If it's a continuation pattern, there should be a slope to the rectangle, which is in the *opposite* direction of the main trend. If not, then a trader might want to move out of the position.

Pennant Pattern

The pennant pattern looks like a triangle, in which the two parallel lines are narrowing. Unlike the flag pattern, it does not matter what direction the slope has.

CONFIRMATION

Technical patterns and indicators are far from perfect. It is common for there to be false signals. So, to help things out, investors will often use several technical indicators. For example, if the Relative Strength Indicator (RSI) is overbought, you might also look to see if a head and shoulders is forming. This can get complicated, and it will certainly take time for beginner traders to learn these techniques. But over time, you will start to quickly identify market turns and know what indicators to focus on.

STOCHASTIC OSCILLATORS

The origins of the stochastic oscillator goes back to the late 1950s. The pioneer of this indicator was technician George C. Lane. He wanted to find a way to measure the momentum in an investment—that is, whether the price is in a bullish or bearish phase.

Calculating a stochastic oscillator is not easy. For the most part, it involves determining the lowest low and the highest high of a price. This is done over a 14-unit period, which could be in days, weeks, or months. On a chart, a stochastic will have two lines: the %K and the %D. Basically, when a stochastic oscillator reaches above 80, the investment is overbought.

Bollinger Band

There is an assortment of oscillators. A famous one is the Bollinger Band. The famed investor John Bollinger developed this oscillator during the 1980s. The Bollinger Band was based on Bollinger's belief that prices tend to revert to the mean. This means that if there is a big move, the prices will tend to come back to its general range. It's a pattern that can certainly be a source of trading profits.

The Bollinger Band uses a simple moving average (SMA) for 20 days. Then there is a multiplier, which is usually 2. This is multiplied by the standard deviation. This is a way to measure the volatility in the price of a commodity. With these measures, there will be an upper and lower band, both of which are charted. These will tighten when volatility falls and increase when volatility expands. If a price moves *above* the upper band, it is a bullish sign. If a price moves *below* the lower band, it is a bearish sign.

Relative Strength Indicator

Another helpful oscillator is the Relative Strength Indicator (RSI). Back in the 1970s, investor Wells Wilder developed this ocillator, which is based on the changes in prices for a certain number of days. The standard is nine days.

While the RSI has a range of 0 to 100, it will usually have numbers between 25 and 75. If the RSI moves towards 25, then the commodity is oversold. If the RSI approaches 75, then the sentiment has reached overbought levels. A reversal is likely to happen in both cases. But the RSI has its drawbacks. This is especially the case when markets are experiencing major moves. In this case, the RSI can remain overbought or oversold for an extended period of time.

POINT-AND-FIGURE CHARTS

Point-and-figure (P&F) charts are popular in commodities trading since they are helpful in providing indications for entry points and exit points. While a standard chart looks at the open-close and the high-low, the P&F approach is focused on the closing price. This was to help reduce the volatility and false signals. Figure 7-3 provides a look at a point-and-figure chart.

FIGURE 7-3

Point-and-Figure Chart

20													
19													
18					X		X						
17			X		X	O	X	O					
16			X	O	X	O	X	O					
15	O	X			X	O	X	O	X	O	X		
14	O	X	O	X	O		O	X	O	X	O	X	
13	O	X	O	X			O		O	X	O	X	O
12	O	X	O						O	X	O	X	O
11	O	X							O		O		O
10	O												

Interestingly enough, there is no axis for time. Instead, a P&F chart will help to visualize the overall levels of supply and demand in the market. A falling close will be an O. A rising close will be an X. As you can see from Figure 7-3, this produces some interesting patterns.

What triggers an X or O? This is when the price hits a certain level, called a unit of price. This is actually based on the trader's discretion and experience. But he or she will set one that will be large enough to give a sense of the overall trends.

To understand this, let's take a look at an example. Suppose you want to trade copper futures and the unit of price is $0.05. If the futures price increases by $0.15, then you will have three X's on the chart. Then, if it falls by $0.05, there will be an O. Keep in mind that each column can only have X's or O's. You will then set a reversal, which is the point when there is a new column. This may be $0.20. Thus, if the copper contract declines by this amount, there will be a new column with O's.

RETRACEMENT PATTERNS

Even when a commodity is in a bull market, there will be significant drops in the price. This is known as a retracement. A key reason is that investors are engaging in profit-taking. There are many types of retracement patterns.

Correction

A common one is a correction. This is when a commodity falls at least 10 percent. Often, this is a sudden fall, which can scare away some investors. After all, they may think that the bull run on the commodity is over.

Gann Retracement

Then there is the Gann retracement. This is a newer indicator, which came out during the early 1990s. A Gann retracement is when the price of a commodity falls by about half from its move from the low to the high. For example, suppose gold goes from $1,000 to $1,200. A Gann retracement would be a price decline that goes to about $1,100, where it will encounter resistance.

Fibonacci Retracement

There is also the Fibonacci retracement, which is based on the findings of a thirteenth century mathematician, Leonardo Pisano Fibonacci.

He realized that the Fibonacci number had many applications, such as with international trade and pricing.

So what is a Fibonacci number? It is a sequence of numbers where the new number is the sum of the past two. The series is 1, 1, 2, 3, 5, 8, 13, 21, 34, 55, and so on. As you can see, it will quickly add up. And yes, there are applications for technical analysis.

While there are many variations of the Fibonacci retracement, there are generally two main levels: 38 percent and 61 percent. In other words, these are the typical drops in the price of a commodity—especially when it is in a bull phase.

CANDLESTICK CHARTS

During the seventeenth century, the first futures markets emerged in Japan. The focus was on rice trading, which proved to be a healthy business. But traders needed some techniques to better time their investments. This led to the first use of technical analysis. Yet it is much different than modern approaches. Known as a candlestick chart, this chart has many visuals that make it easy to interpret.

Candlestick charts focus on the open and the close for a commodity. This is in the form of a box, known as the real body. There is one of these for each trading day and it provides a quick way to get a sense of the overall sentiment. A white real body is when the close was higher than the open. This is a bullish sign, especially if the real body is long, and getting bigger. A black real body is when the close is lower than the open. This is a bearish signal, and is accentuated if the real body is fairly long. Sellers are aggressively coming into the market.

For each real body, there is a stick on the top and the bottom, which are known as the shadows. There is an upper shadow and a lower shadow. These indicate the high and the low for the commodity, respectively.

Sometimes the shadow will be as large as the real body. This is a sign that investors are getting aggressive with their trading.

If there is a long upper shadow within an uptrend, then the commodity is encountering resistance. It could be a sign that there will be a fall in the price.

If there is a long upper shadow in a downturn, it means that the price is at the support level and could be poised for a rally. The same principles apply to long lower shadows. When this occurs in an uptrend, it's bullish, and vice versa.

Morning Star

There are some common candlestick patterns. One is the morning star. This starts with a large black real body and then falls to a small real body. After this, you will see a white body that is above the mid-level of the black real body. When seen on the chart, it looks like a star before the sun rises. A morning star formation essentially points to a support level and that there may be a rally.

Umbrella

Then there are umbrella candlestick patterns, which do look like umbrellas. These are a combination of several types of formations.

- **Spinning top:** This formation has a short real body. There will be minimal upper shadow. But the lower shadow will be at least twice the size of the real body.
- **Hanging man:** If you see this formation in an uptrend, it is a bearish sign.
- **Hammer:** If you see this formation in a downtrend, it is a bullish sign.

Doji Line

With the Doji line, the open and the close are the same. In other words, there is no real body. Although, there will likely be variation in the shadows. If you see two or more Doji lines after a major move in a commodity, it may be a sign that there will be a reversal. Essentially, traders are revaluating their positions.

THE ELLIOTT WAVE

Back in the late 1930s, Ralph Elliott developed a new trading system. It was based on his belief that there are clear patterns of investor sentiment, which alternate between negative to positive. Known as the Elliott Wave, it actually consists of a variety of trends.

In a bullish phase, there will be five waves on the upside, with three being corrections. In a bearish phase, there will be five waves on the downside and three waves on the upside.

The trading system is based on extensive research on prices. In fact, there are many devout followers of the Elliott Wave Principle. Yet it did not become popular until the late 1970s, when Robert Prechter wrote books on the topic and made some key predictions. But as with any system, it is far from foolproof. Nevertheless, many top traders think the Elliott Wave is useful, including billionaire Paul Tudor Jones.

There will always be skepticism of technical analysis, which can often seem like hocus-pocus. But over the years, investors have developed many solid techniques to identify patterns, as seen in this chapter. The emergence of computers and data sets has also been vitally important. In the next chapter, we will look at the gold, silver, and platinum markets, including the demand, the uses, and the suppliers of these precious metals.

CHAPTER 8

Precious Metals

Key Concepts

- Look at gold, silver, and platinum
- Analyze the impact from physically backed ETFs
- Understand the role of precious metals as a safe haven and inflation hedge

Gold has always been a controversial investment. Some investors actually think it should *not* be a part of an asset class. After all, it does not provide any dividends or earn profits. Consider that famed economist, John Maynard Keynes, called gold the "barbarous relic." Even Warren Buffett thinks gold is a bad investment. Yet from 2000 to 2010, gold has generated substantial returns for investors—far outstripping Standard & Poor's 500 (S&P 500).

Some of the world's top investors have made substantial purchases of gold. One is John Paulson. During 2007 to 2008, he made $20 billion by shorting the subprime mortgage market. After this, he started to invest heavily in gold. His belief is that there will be long-term inflation and that the precious metal will be a hedge against this. Paulson started a gold fund, which owns a variety of miners like AngloGold Ashanti Limited and Kinross Gold Corporation. Assets are about $10 billion.

Another notable gold investor is hedge fund manager, David Einhorn. He too made a fortune during the 2007–2008 financial panic. After this, he turned to gold. Besides owning futures and mining companies, he also has stocked up on gold bars. He stores them in an undisclosed warehouse in Queens, NY. However, gold is not the only precious metal. Other important ones include silver and platinum, which have also proved to be strong investments over the years.

THE BACKGROUND ON GOLD

When Christopher Columbus explored the New World, he wound up striking the biggest gold discovery in history. For Spain, it resulted in significant wealth and power. Since then, there have been other major gold discoveries. These include the California Gold Rush of 1849, the Australian Gold Rush of 1851, and the discovery of gold in South Africa in 1884.

But since the gold discoveries during the nineteenth century, there have not been any mega-deposits found. The average growth rate is roughly 1 percent to 2 percent per year. In fact, the total supply of gold produced throughout history is roughly 165,000 metric tons, which is not much when compared to many other metals. Since gold is nearly indestructible, much of the metal that has been extracted still exists today.

When it comes to the price of gold, it is actually based on the decisions of five committee members of the London Gold Market. The current ones are from major financial firms like Barclays, HSBC, Société Générale, Deutsche Bank, and the Bank of Nova Scotia. The members meet twice a day—at 10:30 a.m. and 3:00 p.m., London time—to set the price. This has been the procedure since September 1919. The process is known as the London Gold Fixing.

THE GOLD MARKET

The process of extracting gold is expensive and time-consuming. It often requires large mines and blasting rock to mine gold. The ore is then transported to a plant that crushes it to get to the gold. Keep in mind that gold is one of the most wasteful commodities. It can take crushing over 250 metric tons of rock to get enough gold to make a wedding ring. Interestingly enough, the grade of gold deposits has been declining over the years. This means that it takes crushing even more rock to extract gold.

Investors often get confused on what is an ounce of gold. There are actually two types. There is the avoirdupois ounce, which is used for jewelry. This is not the one for investors. Instead, there is the troy ounce, which is about 10 percent larger than the avoirdupois ounce.

DEMAND SOURCES FOR GOLD

There are three main demand sources for gold.

Gold for Jewelry

First, there is jewelry, which accounts for 40 percent of global consumption. This has been falling steadily over the years. No longer than a decade ago, jewelry consumption accounted for 70 percent of gold production. Yet this demand is still robust in Asian countries. While jewelry is still used as an adornment, there is another purpose. That is, it is viewed as a store of value and savings. This is certainly the case in India, where gold is a key part of a dowry. Actually, there is usually high demand during the festival seasons, such as in the summer and fall.

Gold for Investment

Investment is the next largest demand factor. It represents about 25 percent of global consumption. This includes the collection of coins and bars. But perhaps the biggest driver of gold investment has been from exchange-traded funds (ETFs). Those like SPDR Gold Shares (GLD) buy the actual metal when investors purchase shares. Keep in mind that the fund holds over 1,200 metric tons of gold.

Gold for Industrial Use

Finally, the third largest category for global gold demand is industrial use, which comes to about 12 percent. Gold is used because it is nontoxic and an effective conductor of electricity. Some of the applications include bonding wire and gold-plated contacts. Gold is also useful in dentistry, medical treatments, clean energy, and even the aerospace industry.

SUPPLIERS OF GOLD

South Africa was once the dominant global producer of gold. But since the 1980s, production has steadily declined. The country now accounts for 10 percent of the overall supply. The largest gold producer is now China, at 13 percent. The other main producers include Australia and the United States.

Roughly 17.5 percent of the world's supply of gold is not put onto the market. Why? The reason is that this is the amount of the world's gold that is held by central banks (in some cases, the gold has been in vaults for centuries). Table 8-1 outlines some of the largest holders of gold. Note that while China and India have large amounts of gold, it still represents small amounts of their currency reserves. As should be no surprise, these countries—as well as other emerging economies—have been steadily increasing their gold reserves. No doubt, this added demand could be a major factor in the price of gold.

TABLE 8-1

Central Bank Holdings of Gold

Country	Tonnes	Percentage of Reserves
United States	8,133.5	73.9%
Germany	3,401.8	70.3%
Italy	2,451.8	68.6%
France	2,435.4	67.2%
China	1,054.1	1.7%
Switzerland	1,040.1	16.4%
Russia	775.2	6.7%
Japan	765.2	3.0%
Netherlands	612.5	57.5%
India	557.7	8.1%

Source: World Gold Council (http://www.gold.org/government_affairs/gold_reserves/)

From the 1980s to the late 1990s, central banks were major net sellers of gold, which put lots of pressure on the price. The belief was that gold was losing its relevance. For example, in 1999 the British government sold 395 tonnes of the country's gold supply at $275 per ounce. It turned out to be one of the worst decisions in government finance since gold would bottom out at $252.80 on July 20, 1999. Even Switzerland's central bank was a big seller of gold during the late 1990s.

To try to provide for a more orderly process in the sale of gold—and not allow for a plunge in the gold price—the world's major central banks entered into the Washington Agreement on Gold or WAG, to limit the sales. All in all, it has been effective. But with the rise in gold prices and the growth in emerging economies, WAG may not be factor any more.

Gold Scrap

While gold mines are the largest part of the global supply, another important source is from scrap. This is the process of converting jewelry into gold bars or coins. In 2009, recycled gold accounted for 1,674 tonnes of additional supply, which was an all-time record. With high prices, this should continue to increase. Of course, a sign of this is the many television commercials from companies like Cash4Gold.

GOLD TRADING

Gold trades on many futures exchanges. The main ones include the CME and the Tokyo Commodity Exchange (TOCOM).

Actually, trading of the gold futures did not start until 1975. Why? Consider that during the Great Depression, President Roosevelt prohibited U.S. citizens from owning gold. He did this to try to increase inflation in the economy and to jumpstart economic growth. While it is unclear of the success of the policy, it certainly caused much frustration and anger. In the United States, it was not legal for individuals to own gold until 1974.

Of course, investors have a variety of gold mining stocks to invest in. Some of the major ones include Barrick Gold Corporation, Newmont Mining Corporation, Goldcorp Inc., and Kinross Gold Corporation.

GOLD AS A SAFE HAVEN

There is an avid group of investors known as the gold bugs, which is not a complimentary description. Gold bugs are perennial bears. Some believe that the world economy is on the brink of disaster. What is their solution? Of course, it is to own gold, which means having physical possession of the metal, such as in coins and bullion.

While gold bugs have traditionally been the topic of jokes, this has changed over the past few years. After all, the financial crisis of 2008 was a stark reminder that the world economy is fragile. In 2010 the Federal Reserve released the data on its programs to provide liquidity during the crisis. The loans amounted to a stunning $3.3 trillion and involved roughly 21,000 transactions. Major banks, including Bank of America and Wells Fargo, borrowed $45 billion. There were also large loans made to many foreign banks, including UBS, Société Générale, and Dresdner Bank AG. But the Fed also had to provide loans to mainstream companies, including General Electric, McDonald's, and Harley Davidson. To provide such loans, the Fed had to resort to unusual powers under the Federal Reserve Act.

The financial crisis certainly came close to bringing down the global economic system. But during the crisis, gold was one of the few investment assets that increased in value. The fact is that the precious metal is considered a safe haven. This has been the case for centuries and will likely continue in the future.

FACTORS THAT INFLUENCE THE PRICE OF GOLD

There are various factors that influence the price of gold.

Availability of Gold

One is gold's role as currency. The first gold coins were issued by King Croesus in 550 B.C. For everyday transactions, gold coins proved to be somewhat unwieldy. As a result, countries eventually adopted the gold standard. This means there would be a paper currency—or a fiat currency—that is convertible into a fixed amount of gold. Thus, if the value of the paper currency is falling, then people could start to request the metal, which should bring the system into balance again. While governments can print money—and most do—they still cannot produce more gold. Its scarcity is certainly a good trait for being the basis of a currency.

Inflation

If there is inflation, or the threat of it, the price of gold is likely to rise. This was certainly the case during the 1970s. The United States experienced bouts of double-digit inflation because of oil shocks, commodity shortages, and high government spending. From 1976 to 1980, gold surged from $100 to $850. It would not surpass the 1980's record prices until 2008.

A key event during the early 1970s was when President Nixon took the United States off the international gold standard. After this, investors could buy and sell the U.S. currency. It also made it easier for the federal government to increase the money supply. Notable economists like Milton Friedman believed that this was a key reason for the inflation during the 1970s.

The 1980s and 1990s saw relatively moderate inflation, as well as high productivity, because of new technologies like the Internet. There was also a boost in overall gold production.

From 1980 to 2000, gold underwent a grueling bear market. Commodities go through long market cycles. Since 2000, gold has been catching up after its long bear market.

In 2011, many investors believe that inflation is poised to return. The current high budget deficits and trade deficits are a big concern. In the United States, as the Baby Boomers age, this will drive up retirement and healthcare costs, which is likely to further increase budget deficits.

Other Factors

If inflation is so important, why did the price of gold rise so much from 2000 to 2010? There were various factors. One was that there was much instability during the decade, caused by the attacks on the World Trade Center and the Pentagon on September 11, the corporate scandals, the housing bust, and the financial crisis.

In the last few years, there have been uncertainties about possible sovereign debt defaults from countries like Greece and Ireland. These problems are likely to last for some time.

In light of all this, a variety of emerging economies, the BRIC countries—Brazil, Russia, India, and China—have hinted that the U.S. dollar may no longer be the reserve currency. With $4 trillion in dollars held by foreign central banks, there is lots of worry that there is too much reliance on the U.S. dollar. This does not mean the dollar will be replaced. Instead, it looks like an alternative will be a basket of currencies, which could even include gold.

China and Gold

Because of controls on currencies and investments, it has been difficult for retail Chinese investors to purchase gold. But this is starting to change. In 2010, the Chinese government allowed the creation of a mutual fund that allows Chinese investors to participate in foreign exchange-traded funds (ETFs) that focus on gold. It's certainly an indication of the rising interest in the precious metal. Also, the mutual fund could be a way for investors to deal with inflation, which has become a problem in China. It looks like this is only the beginning of these types of mutual funds. In other words, there should be growing retail demand from China for the major commodities.

THE BACKGROUND ON SILVER

Silver has the highest conductivity of any element, even copper. Silver is also strong yet malleable. Because of these qualities, silver has been a good element for coins. The first known silver coins were used by the Greeks in 700 B.C. In the late 1700s, the new U.S. government used silver for its currency. But this usage was eventually phased out in the mid-1960s. Now the only country that uses silver coins is Mexico.

There are two main grades of silver. One is pure silver, which has the highest content. Then there is sterling silver or standard silver, which is an alloy of 92.5 percent silver and 7.5 percent copper. Copper helps to increase the durability of silver.

DEMAND SOURCES FOR SILVER

Some demand sources for silver are for industrial use, for jewelry and silverware, for investment, and for photography.

Silver for Industrial Use

The largest amount of demand for silver comes from industrial applications, which accounts for 46 percent of supply. These include batteries, computer components, medical devices, and surgical instruments. In fact, silver has "green" qualities, such as being a replacement for some applications of lead.

Silver for Jewelry and Silverware

The second biggest component of demand for silver—23 percent—is for jewelry and silverware. This is a fairly steady category. However, if silver prices continue to rise, there may be a decline in demand.

Silver for Investment

Another category that has been robust is investment demand. Many investors consider silver to be a good alternative to gold. A big reason is that silver is cheaper than gold on a per-ounce basis. A big part of this has come from the popularity of ETFs, like the iShares Silver Trust (SLV).

Silver for Photography

While photography was once a substantial part of silver demand, this has declined substantially over the years. The main reason has been the growth in digital cameras.

Yet, there have been some offsetting factors. For example, in some emerging markets, there has been rising demand for traditional film. Also, there is still a large market for film for professional photographers.

SUPPLIERS OF SILVER

The largest producers of silver are as shown in Table 8-2.

TABLE 8-2

Largest Silver Producers

Country	Global Production
Peru	18 percent
China	14 percent
Mexico	12 percent
Chile	9 percent
Australia	8 percent
United States	6 percent

Source: The Silver Institute

While gold production has been declining over the years, this has not been the case with silver. It has shown a steady growth rate. Roughly 77 percent of silver production comes from mines, 20 percent comes from scrap, and 3 percent comes from government stockpiles.

However, over the next decade, there are likely to be constraints on the production of silver. The amount of scrap is declining because more silver is being used in electronics products, which are fairly difficult to recycle. Also, government stockpiles are relatively small. The fact is that much of the selling has occurred over the past 20 years.

SILVER TRADING

You can trade silver futures on the CME and the Tokyo Commodities Exchange (TOCOM). There are also a few pure play silver miners, like Hecla Mining Company and Pan American Silver Corp. The reason is that about 70 percent of silver comes as a by-product of the mining of other metals, like lead, copper, and zinc. For example, BHP Billiton is the largest silver producer in the world. Yet, the metal represents only a small portion of its revenues. Instead, the company's main profit source is from copper and iron ore.

Because silver is a by-product of mining for other metals, the supply is highly impacted by changes in the economy. That is, if there is a falloff in economic growth, miners will usually cut back on the extraction of key commodities. There will be lower silver production.

FACTORS THAT INFLUENCE THE PRICE OF SILVER

Some factors that influence the price of silver are the silver standard, the government silver holdings, and the gold-silver ratio.

The Silver Standard

Some investors consider silver to be an alternative to a currency. After all, the United Kingdom and the United States were on the silver standard until the end of the nineteenth century. But this was eventually replaced by the gold standard. Because of this, there was a long bear market in silver. In fact, by late 1932, silver reached 24.5 cents per ounce. Yet it would represent an all-time bottom in the value of the metal.

Over the next few years, silver would triple in value. A key reason was because owning gold was outlawed. So investors aggressively moved into silver as an alternative.

Since 2002, the price of silver has seen a rapid increase. Some of the driving factors include the fall in the U.S. dollar, financial instability, and the bull market in commodities. Of course, another key factor has been in the increase in industrial demand. Silver is becoming a key ingredient for high-tech products.

Government Silver Holdings

Today, few governments have silver holdings. In 2004 the U.S. government sold off its remaining supply of silver, which was roughly 2 billion ounces. This has actually had an impact on the U.S. mint, which creates American Silver Eagle coins. Traditionally, the silver would come from the federal stockpile. But now, when the United States needs to create new Silver Eagle coins, it must buy silver on the spot market. Because of this, the prices are often higher and there have been occasional delays in production.

But in light of silver's history, there has been talk that it could become part of a new currency system. There is a fair amount of production. And, it could make a good complement if the world economies adopt of basket of currencies and commodities to replace the U.S. dollar as the reserve currency.

The Gold-Silver Ratio

As with any commodity, the value of silver is largely affected by supply and demand. However, there is one interesting metric that can provide a relative valuation of the metal. This is done by using the gold-silver ratio. Throughout history, there has been a relatively stable relationship between the two metals. But, when the gold-silver ratio diverges, there may be a buying opportunity.

Basically, the gold-silver ratio shows the value of silver versus the value of gold. To understand this, let's take a look at an example. Suppose gold is trading at $1,300 per ounce and silver is trading at $30 per ounce. Then the ratio is 43.33.

Here's a look at the gold-silver ratio during important periods:

- In 1980, the gold-silver ratio was at 17.
- In 1991, when silver hit a low, the gold-silver ratio was at 100.
- In 2007, the gold-silver ratio was at 51.

Traditionally, investors would trade on the gold-silver ratio when there were extremes. Let's say that the ratio goes back to 100. In this case, an investor would essentially trade his 1 ounce of gold for 100 ounces of silver. The belief is that the ratio will eventually contract and the price of silver will increase. So what levels should an investor trade at? Like anything, there are no clear-cut rules.

BACKGROUND ON PLATINUM

When the Spanish discovered the New World, they found a new metal called *platina del Pinto*, which means "little silver of the Pinto River." It was actually considered an inferior metal. Of course, this is far from the case today. The metal, which is now called platinum, is quite versatile since it has a high resistance to corrosion.

Platinum is the main part of the so-called platinum group. This group of metals includes palladium, rhodium, ruthenium, iridium, and osmium. They are quite similar and are close together in the periodic table of elements. Because of these relationships, they tend to be found in the same mining deposits. Platinum is fairly scarce, with the annual amount at about 6 million ounces. To produce 1 ounce, it takes a mine to crush about 10 tons of ore. The process can easily take six months.

DEMAND SOURCES FOR PLATINUM

Some demand sources for platinum are for jewelry, for industrial use, and for investment.

Platinum for Jewelry

A decade ago, about 48 percent of the worldwide demand for platinum was for jewelry. But since then, this has steadily declined, reaching about 19 percent.

Platinum for Industrial Use

Platinum has proven effective for various commercial purposes, such as lab equipment, LCDs, video equipment, and electrodes. But the biggest usage of platinum—60 percent of the world's supply— is for catalytic converters. So the price of the metal is highly related to the global production of cars.

During 2008 and 2009, because of the recession, there was a plunge in the price of platinum. But in light of the growth of the auto market in China (currently the largest market) and India, the platinum market is likely to show long-term growth. Platinum is also a key part of batteries and fuel cells for hybrid and electric cars, which should be a long-term growth driver.

Palladium is also useful for catalytic converters, but it is not as efficient as platinum. Often confused, palladium and platinum are not interchangeable.

Platinum for Investment

Another key source of demand for platinum has been from investment. For some time, Europe has traded exchange-traded funds (ETFs) that are physically backed by platinum. Then in 2010, there was such an offering in the United States called ETFS Physical Platinum Shares (PPLT). In light of the small supply of the metal, these ETFs have the potential of creating pricing pressures.

SUPPLIERS OF PLATINUM

The world's largest supplier of platinum is South Africa, which provides 67 percent of the total. As a result, a disruption in this country could have a major impact. This actually happened in 2008, when South Africa had serious electricity problems. Because of this, platinum reached a record of $2,276.

The second largest producer of platinum is Russia. Yet its output has seen wide swings, from 10 percent to 20 percent of the worldwide supply.

North America is also a significant producer of platinum. The country with the world's second largest amount of platinum reserves—an amount that has not been extracted yet—is Zimbabwe. However, in 2006, the government nationalized the foreign mines, which has certainly been disruptive to production.

PLATINUM TRADING

Platinum is traded on the CME and the Tokyo Commodity Exchange. There are also several publicly traded platinum miners. Some of the largest include Stillwater Mining Co. (SWC) and Platinum Group Metals Ltd. (PLG). There are also major companies listed on the Johannesburg Stock Exchange (JSE) in South Africa.

As seen in this chapter, the precious metals have unique features in the commodities world. In the case of gold and silver, their value goes beyond supply and demand. Investors look at them as safe havens and even alternatives to currencies. Because of this, the valuations can be quite volatile, and depend on the global situation. In the next chapter, we will look at energy commodities, including crude oil, natural gas, coal, nuclear energy, and alternative energy.

CHAPTER 9

Energy

Key Concepts

- Understand the main drivers of energy commodities
- Look at crude oil, natural gas, and other energy commodities
- Learn how to invest in alternative energy

Over the decades, some of the biggest fortunes in commodities investing have come from the energy markets. Consider Marc Rich, a controversial trader who made over a billion dollars from the crude oil market. Until the 1970s, the market had little trading because the major Western oil companies—called the Seven Sisters—controlled the pricing with long-term contract arrangements. From 1948 to 1970, crude oil fluctuated from $2.50 to $3.00 per barrel. But then oil-rich third world nations realized this was against their own interests, so they nationalized the oil assets. In order to sell the oil, these countries needed the help of global financiers like Rich.

In just a few years, Rich created the spot market for oil. Yet it also meant that he traded with regimes like Cuba, Iran, South Africa, and Libya. In fact, by the early 1980s, the U.S. government pursued criminal charges against Rich and he fled to Switzerland. President Clinton eventually pardoned him in 2001.

Such controversies are normal and expected in the energy markets. After all, the money and power are enormous.

THE BACKGROUND ON CRUDE OIL

Oil is the biggest business in the world. If anything, it has been the driver of industrialization and modernization. Even with higher oil prices, oil is still a cheap source of energy—especially in terms of its power and efficiency. A barrel of oil equals the manual labor of a person for eight days.

Because of its strategic importance, oil has also been the subject of many wars. When Adolf Hitler invaded Russia, he wanted to capture the oil assets of Azerbaijan.

But it was during the 1970s when wars would be a game changer for the oil market. The first was on October 6, 1973, when Egypt and Syria attacked Israel, which nearly collapsed. Because of the United States' support of Israel, OPEC (Organization of Petroleum Exporting Countries) nations agreed to prevent oil shipments. There were also production cutbacks. The result was a spike in oil prices, which went from $3 to $11.60 per barrel. With oil shortages, the United States fell into a recession and the world experienced its first oil shock.

Then in late November 1979, there was another oil shock. A group called the Muslim Students of Imam Khomeini Line took over the U.S. embassy in Tehran. They took 63 Americans as hostages and sparked an international standoff. The following year, oil prices hit $38 per barrel and the United States fell into another recession.

After all the turmoil, the oil markets saw relative stability from 1980 to 2000. There was a spike during the run-up to the first Gulf War in 1990, but this was really an exception. In fact, the long-term low prices were likely a key reason for the strong economic growth in the United States.

But from 2000 to 2011, oil prices saw a sharp rise, reaching a peak of $147 in 2008. Even with the plunge in the price after the 2009 global recession, oil has quickly made a comeback, trading over $100 in 2011.

During the past decade, there were several major wars, such as in Iraq. There was also the continued surge in growth in China and India. At the same time, OPEC still yielded tremendous power. This cartel—whose members include Algeria, Indonesia, Iran, Iraq, Kuwait, Libya, Nigeria, Qatar, Saudi Arabia, United Arab Emirates, and Venezuela—essentially set the quotas for oil production. The result is that OPEC can have a major impact on the price of crude oil.

PEAK THEORY OF OIL

One of the biggest issues is how much oil there really is in the world. It was actually during the mid-1950s that engineers and scientists started to look at this. The most notable theory was from Dr. M. King Hubbert, who was a geophysicist at Shell Oil. In an academic paper, he set forth his peak theory of oil. Basically, he stated that there were limits to oil supplies that would eventually hit maximum output and increasingly decline from there. Based on this, he predicted that the United States would reach its oil peak in the early 1970s.

It was a shocking forecast and it was roundly criticized. However, Dr. Hubbert was eventually proven correct. Other major oil fields, such as those in the North Sea and Mexico, have also reached their oil peak. So might this happen to Saudi Arabia and other key sources of oil? If this does occur, it could mean global shortages and as a result, ever-increasing oil prices.

Keep in mind that OPEC's members do not have any independent audits on their oil reserves. As a result, it is extremely difficult to know if OPEC countries are reaching peak capacity. Yet a report from the International Energy Agency (IEA), called the World Energy Outlook 2008, says that the world would reach peak levels in 2009. It is undeniable that since the last mega-oil discovery at Cantarell Field in Mexico, it has gotten tougher to find new large sources of oil. And unfortunately, production has already peaked at Cantarell Field too.

SUPPLIERS OF CRUDE OIL

Despite all this, there are still areas that hold potentially large deposits of oil. One promising area is the northern Arctic regions. Estimates are that there could be 13 percent of the world's oil there.

Another source of crude oil energy is from tar sands, especially in Alberta, Canada. There are massive deposits of this substance, which are estimated at 175 billion barrels. If true, this would make Alberta the Number Two producer of oil in the world. However, it takes strip-mining to extract the oil and the process leads to large amounts of carbon emissions and other toxic problems. It is far from an ideal solution.

Brazil has also made various major oil discoveries. While the reserves could be as much as 80 billion barrels, the oil is in deepwater and will require expensive technologies to penetrate the ocean floor. In light of the tragic 2010 BP oil spill in the Gulf of Mexico, the regulatory requirements and systems are likely to be significant.

CRUDE OIL TRADING

Crude oil is traded on the CME, which involves two versions. One is based on light-sweet crude from Cushing, Oklahoma. The other is focused on Brent light sweet crude from the North Sea. Keep in mind that light-sweet crude has a high quality and is the most preferred by refineries. Both contracts call for delivery of 1,000 barrels or 42,000 gallons.

Predicting Crude Oil Prices

A way to predict oil prices is to estimate the spare capacity. Investors can get data from the International Energy Agency (IEA) and the Energy Information Administration (EIA). The information is primarily based on OPEC members. The rule of thumb is that if the spare capacity is 5 percent or less than the daily global oil consumption, then there would be a rise in crude prices. For example, the metric got to 1.5 million barrels or 1.7 percent during the summer of July 2008, when oil reached $145.29.

INVESTING IN OIL COMPANIES

The two main categories of oil companies are upstream, which includes exploration companies and the oil services industry, and downstream. There are also drillers and refiners.

Categories of Oil Companies

While there are many types of companies in the oil industry, they can actually be segmented into two main parts: upstream and downstream. The upstream category refers to locations where oil is extracted and refined. The downstream category refers to locations where oil is sold, such as at gas stations. Several of the largest oil companies—like ExxonMobil and Chevron—are integrated operations, which means that they have both upstream and downstream segments.

Exploration Companies

Exploration companies are upstream operators. These are often small companies that spend years trying to find lucrative deposits of oil. Oil exploration is a high-risk business, but it can have massive payoffs. However, investors need to be wary since there are many companies that have little expertise or hope of being successful.

Oil Services Industry

Another upstream participant is the oil services industry. Companies in this industry—such as Schlumberger Limited and Halliburton—provide the employees and equipment to help drill deposits. Often, this involves highly sophisticated software, 3D analysis, seismic surveys, and drill bits.

Drillers

The drillers own the rights to properties and extract the oil. Properties include land rigs or submersible rigs, if there is offshore drilling.

A key metric for the drillers is the day rates, which are published by a variety of industry organizations. These are the fees for drilling on a daily basis. If there is a steady climb, profits should begin to grow.

Another important indicator is the rig utilization rate. With a higher rate, a driller will likely generate more revenue and profits.

This is dependent on the quality of rigs, as well as their locations. Drillers will then transport their oil to refiners.

Refiners

Refiners turn oil into gasoline, fuels, and even chemicals. The industry is highly consolidated. Because of onerous government regulations, it is extremely difficult to build a new refinery.

Refiners have some problems. The main one is the day rates for drilling. If these escalate, it will mean lower profit margins.

UNLEADED GASOLINE

Unleaded gasoline is a complicated mixture, which relies primarily on crude oil. Because of environmental mandates from the federal government, some types of gasoline contain roughly 10 percent of ethanol (a combination of corn and gasoline).

Due to the close relationship between unleaded gasoline and crude oil, the prices often follow each other. But there are times when there are divergences, especially during events like hurricanes. For example, there may be a large amount of crude oil on the market yet a major storm could disrupt refineries and distribution systems. So as crude oil prices fall, unleaded gasoline prices will do the opposite.

UNLEADED GASOLINE TRADING

Unleaded gasoline futures are traded on the CME, under the symbol RB. Each contract consists of 42,000 gallons or 1,000 U.S. barrels.

HEATING OIL

Heating oil—also called oil heat—is flammable petroleum that has low viscosity. The primary uses include energy for furnaces, much of it for homes. Heating oil is stored in tanks, which are typically in basements or garages.

During the 1920s, heating oil became a popular energy source because of the introduction of the oil burner. Before this, homes were heated with coal, which was not only dirty but also a health hazard. Of course, since then there have been new technologies that have made heating oil much more efficient.

About 42 percent of the cost of heating oil is based on the price of crude oil. So if crude oil increases by $1, this should translate into a $0.025 change in the cost of heating oil. The main regions in the United States that rely on heating oil are in the Northeast (accounting for 8.1 million single-family homes). Much of the demand is from October to March.

HEATING OIL TRADING

Heating oil is traded on the CME, with the symbol HO. Each contract represents 42,000 gallons or 1,000 U.S. barrels.

NATURAL GAS

Natural gas consists mostly of methane and is found alongside fossil fuels and coal beds. As a source of energy, natural gas has many advantages. It is cheaper than crude oil and it is environmentally friendly. Consider that a natural gas plant will generate about half the amount of carbon emissions than a coal plant.

After it is drilled, natural gas is usually transported through pipelines. In fact, the distribution is to over 60 million homes in the United States. But the pipeline system is expensive.

Liquified Natural Gas

An alternative to natural gas is liquefied natural gas (LNG). It takes up six-hundredth the volume of regular natural gas, which means it is much easier to ship with tankers.

So far, liquefied natural gas is a small part of the market. But this is beginning to change. Major energy companies have started to invest large sums in LNG distribution.

INVESTING IN NATURAL GAS

Just five years ago, natural gas was in short supply as prices surged. It turned into a tremendous opportunity for investors to make huge profits. Oil tycoon T. Boone Pickens made more than a billion dollars by trading natural gas futures. He even started Clean Energy Fuels Corporation. The company manages a chain of natural gas fueling stations.

John Arnold worked as a natural gas trader at Enron. He took his $8 million bonus and created his fund, Centaurus Advisors. Because of savvy bets, Arnold is now worth $4 billion and is only in his mid-thirties.

SHALE PROCESS AND FRACKING

However, the natural gas industry underwent a disruption from new technologies during the 1990s. Keep in mind that natural gas is found in rock and shale formations. The problem was that it was too expensive to extract. But companies like EOG Resources Inc., XTO Energy Inc., and Devon Energy found solutions to the problem. Because of this, the available supply of natural gas has surged.

Extracting natural gas from shale is called an unconventional source of energy. At first, there were many skeptics but this has changed. In 2009, ExxonMobil paid $31 billion for XTO Energy Inc.

But the shale process is still controversial. It involves the use of horizontal drills and hydraulic fracturing, known as fracking. Water and sand are injected to crack the shale. The concern is that the process may contaminate water supplies. This could stunt the growth of the natural gas industry in areas like Europe, which have stringent environmental laws. Another concern is that the reserves of unconventional natural gas may be overstated. Based on results so far, it appears that a typical well peaks fairly quickly.

FACTORS THAT INFLUENCE THE PRICE OF NATURAL GAS

In the short run, the price of natural gas is heavily impacted by the weather. When Hurricane Katrina and Hurricane Rita hit New Orleans, the price of natural gas went from $3 to $15.

Natural gas tends to be higher during winter and summer months, when the usage level is higher. Yet over the past couple of years, there has been a glut of natural gas causing prices to remain depressed.

HEDGING ON NATURAL GAS

Regardless of the available supplies of natural gas, companies have continued to produce more supplies. Why? One reason is that many of the producers bought hedges at much higher prices. So it makes sense to drill for more natural gas, so as to reap the profits. What's more, the leases on many properties will expire. Thus, natural gas producers will want to get as much value from them before that happens.

FUTURE SUPPLY AND DEMAND OF NATURAL GAS

Eventually this supply will fall, especially as prices remain low. Yet, the long-term prospects for natural gas look promising. Because of environmental concerns, the United States has been aggressively building natural-gas powered electricity plants. This should be a prime source of demand for the next couple of decades. As a sign of the opportunity, ExxonMobil purchased XTO Energy Inc., a leader in natural gas, for $31 billion in 2010. Based on extensive analysis of over 100 countries, ExxonMobil has estimated that natural gas will grow three times as fast as crude oil and coal. By 2030, the company predicts that natural gas will account for 26 percent of the world's energy. This will make it the second-ranked global source of energy after oil, which is believed to be 32 percent.[1]

NATURAL GAS TRADING

You can trade natural gas futures on the CME, under the symbol NG. Each unit consists of 10,000 million British thermal units (MMBtu).

There is also a variety of natural gas ETFs. These include the United States Natural Gas Fund (UNG), which invests in futures,

---

[1] http://www.exxonmobil.com/Corporate/energy_outlook_view.aspx.

and the First Trust ISE–Revere Natural Gas Fund (FCG), which has a portfolio of natural gas companies. Investors can also purchase a variety of natural gas producers, like Chesapeake Energy Corporation and Anadarko Petroleum Corporation.

COAL

"Coal" is a combustible sedimentary rock. There are various types, which depend on the mixture of carbon, sulfur, hydrogen, oxygen, and nitrogen. The coals with the highest amounts of sulfur and ash—such as lignite and subbituminous—are considered lower quality. The higher quality coals—such as bituminous and anthracite—have better burn rates and energy levels.

The supply of coal is plentiful and the price is relatively cheap. As a result, it is the source of 42 percent of the world's power generation. This form of coal is called thermal coal.

But there are major drawbacks to using coal. Coal is dirty and toxic. It is also a major contributor to carbon emissions into the atmosphere. While there is some political pressure to place limits on coal, these seem likely to be futile.

DEMAND SOURCES FOR COAL

Countries like China and India rely heavily on coal for itself and as a key source for creating steel, known as metallurgical coal. Even the United States relies on coal for a large amount of its power generation.

SUPPLIERS OF COAL

The largest supplier of coal is the United States, with roughly a 25 percent share. Other major suppliers include Russia, India, and China. In the case of China, a large amount of its coal is in faraway northern regions. This makes it expensive to ship to the growing coastal areas. Thus, it is often more economical for China to import coal. This has certainly meant rising global coal prices. But it has also been a big boon for countries like Australia and Indonesia, which export coal to China.

COAL TRADING

Coal is traded on the CME, with the symbol QL. It is based on the price of the Central Appalachian kind of coal, which has a high quality. Traders have nicknamed the contract for this type of coal the big sandy because the coal is extracted between West Virginia and Kentucky. A contract accounts for 1,550 tons of coal.

ELECTRICITY

While Benjamin Franklin is credited with the discovery of electricity, the biggest innovation came from Michael Faraday, a British scientist. During the 1820s to 1830s, he came up with the main concepts to allow for electricity generation. It was a critical foundation for the Industrial Revolution. In fact, Faraday's principles are still in use today. Basically, electricity is created by the movement of a disc of copper that is between the poles of a magnet.

In theory, it's fairly straightforward. However, it is difficult to get electricity to homes and businesses. This involves an elaborate infrastructure of power plants, transmission lines, and equipment. The fuel can vary, such as coal, natural gas, nuclear power, or alternative energy sources. In other words, investing in these types of commodities is a way to participate from the growth in electricity power.

ELECTRICITY POWER TRADING

On the CME, there is actually a futures contract on electricity power. It has a symbol of PJM and it has large amounts of trading. Each contract is for 40 megawatt hours (MWh) per peak day.

Another way to invest in electricity power is through utilities. These tend to pay relatively high dividends and are fairly stable. But there can be problems with governmental policies. Keep in mind that utility fees are regulated. To deal with some of the problems, there has been a trend towards mergers and acquisitions with utilities. It's a way to lower costs, as well as to have enough resources to invest in new sources of energy.

NUCLEAR POWER

Nuclear power plants produce a clean form of energy; that is, there are no carbon emissions. Yet the industry has been the subject of much controversy and protests. How can someone feel comfortable about something called nuclear?

The China Syndrome refers to the possible results of a nuclear meltdown. There was a famous movie about this called *The China Syndrome*. In fact, the film came out on March 16, 1979, which was about two weeks before the accident at the nuclear power plant in Pennsylvania called Three Mile Island. There was a failure because temperatures exceeded 2,750 degrees Celsius. While the sturdy structure prevented an explosion, the event was enough to stop the growth of the nuclear industry in the United States for about twenty years. The sentiment has become more pro-nuclear over the past ten years.

Yet the industry suffered another disaster in 2011. Because of a massive earthquake and tsunami in northern Japan, the Fukushima Dai-ichi nuclear power plant sustained tremendous damage and released high levels of radiation. Thousands of people had to be evacuated. This event is likely to make it harder to build more nuclear power plants.

DEMAND SOURCES FOR NUCLEAR POWER

Despite all of the concerns about nuclear power, it is a major source of energy. It accounts for 78 percent of electricity generation in France and 40 percent in South Korea. Even in the United States, nuclear power represents 21 percent.

SUPPLIERS OF URANIUM FOR NUCLEAR POWER

The main commodity to fuel nuclear power is uranium. Most of the world's surface has some level of this. But it is usually trace amounts. The largest deposits are concentrated in Canada, Russia, Australia, and Uzbekistan.

If uranium prices increase significantly, will this put an end to the development of nuclear power? It probably will not. The fact is that uranium is still a fairly small percentage of the costs of a reactor. Besides, as prices increase, there will be more focus on bringing old plants online, as well as mining new areas. After all, the United States has large deposits of uranium. However, because of the onerous regulations, it is extremely difficult to get permits.

Interestingly enough, the current worldwide production of uranium is not enough for the reactor usage. To make up the gap, there has been the transformation of nuclear-weapon stockpiles. But over the next few years, the supplies will not be as plentiful and as a result, there may be an ever-higher price for uranium.

There are currently 445 nuclear plants across the world. According to the International Atomic Energy Agency (IAEA), the number of nuclear plants is expected to increase by another 1,000 by 2050. A big driver is China, which is already in the process of building 26 new reactors.

TRADING URANIUM

For investors, there are only a handful of options to benefit from the growth in uranium demand. Only one producer is publicly traded in the United States, which is Cameco Corporation. The company gets much of its uranium from two mines in Canada. Other producers are traded on foreign exchanges, such as in Australia and France.

There are hundreds of uranium exploration companies. They trade mostly on Canadian exchanges.

There are some exchange-traded funds (ETFs) that focus on uranium, such as the Market Vectors Nuclear Energy ETF (NLR). It focuses on the DAXglobal Nuclear Energy Index and has 38 stocks that are involved in uranium mining, enrichment, plant construction, and energy generation. The companies are located in places including Canada, Australia, and Japan.

You can also trade a futures contract on uranium on the CME. Each one is for 250 pounds of U308 and the minimum price fluctuation is $0.05. The ticker symbol is UX.

NUCLEAR WASTE

A major consideration for nuclear energy is the waste. Keep in mind that nuclear fuel rods need to be replaced about every 18 months. And yes, there are well-defined procedures to dispose of the waste. The problem, though, is where to put the waste. No community wants to be near it. Even in remote areas, there are protests against the disposal of the waste. This was the case for the proposed disposal repository in Yucca Mountain in Nevada. Because of political pressure, it was defeated.

ALTERNATIVE ENERGY

In light of the dependence on fossil fuels, there has been a major trend to invest in alternative energy. While this category represents a small portion of the market, it is growing quickly. Besides, as crude oil prices increase, it becomes more economical for alternative energy. So there are lucrative potential profits for investors.

The alternative energy segment is broad and the definition is somewhat fuzzy. For example, some would say that coal fits in the definition. Then there are others who disagree because coal produces substantial amounts of carbon emissions. Despite this controversy, there are areas that are clearly part of alternative energy. These include: solar power, wind, biomass, and geothermal.

SOLAR POWER

Solar energy is far from new. It was first introduced during the mid-1950s. There are two main approaches to generating energy from solar power.

- **Photovoltaics (PV):** This approach involves the use of solar cells called polysilicon. This element is also part of computer chips. As a result, polysilicon has seen much demand and high prices.
- **Concentrated solar power (CSP):** This approach uses mirrors and specialized lenses to create a small beam of energy. The largest installation is in the Mojave Desert in California.

The more common approach of the two is photovoltaics. In fact, based on research from Solarbuzz (Solar Market Research and Analysis), the PV market grew from 6,080 megawatts (MW) in 2008 to 7,300 MW in 2009. The market is forecasted to reach 17,400 MW by 2014.

ADVANTAGES OF SOLAR POWER

A big advantage of solar power is that the fuel is free, since it is sunlight. True, sunlight varies due to weather and time. But solar power technologies have been designed to deal with this effectively. In fact, solar energy is a good solution for peak-hours energy usage since this typically happens during sunlight.

Solar energy is the most environmentally friendly energy source, with no air or water emissions or waste generation. A solar power module is durable and requires little maintenance. A typical installation can last 25 to 30 years.

COSTS OF SOLAR ENERGY

Yet solar energy is still costly. Because of this, solar energy relies heavily on government subsidies. The governments with favorable solar energy policies include Germany, Spain, Japan, the United States, Italy, the Czech Republic, Belgium, and China.

Actually, as time goes by—and with the continued support—the costs are likely to fall. Costs are forecasted by Solarbuzz, a research firm, to drop from $2.52 per watt in 2009 to $1.52 per watt by 2014.

Interestingly enough, the natural gas supply affects the solar power industry. With lower prices, it has become a more attractive alternative than solar energy for electricity generation.

TRADING SOLAR POWER COMPANIES

As for investors, there are two types of solar power companies. There are those companies that create the photovoltaics (PV) cells. A key metric is the cost advantages. Thus, lower-wage countries, like China, have an advantage.

Then there are the raw materials providers, which make the polysilicon. This business can be volatile because there is the additional demand from semiconductor makers.

The largest publicly traded solar companies include Suntech Power Holdings Co. Ltd., Solarfun Power Holdings Co. Ltd., JA Solar Holdings Co. Ltd., and LDK Solar Company. There is also the Claymore/MAC Global Solar Energy Index ETF (TAN).

WIND POWER

For thousands of years, wind has been a key source of energy, as ancient civilizations used windmills. These helped to create foods from grains. But it was not until the late 1800s that wind was used to generate electricity. However, the problem was that the energy could not be stored. But with advances in turbine technology, this is no longer a problem. Wind is now a major source of power for Europe, Asia, and the United States.

ADVANTAGES OF WIND POWER

Wind power is cost-effective when compared to fossil fuels. The costs of wind power has fallen by 90 percent over the past 20 years.

Wind farms have little maintenance requirements and can last for decades. At the same time, the capital costs are low. Of course, there are no carbon emissions.

DISADVANTAGES OF WIND POWER

Yet there are still problems with wind power. Wind can be inconsistent. So wind power needs to be supplemented by other sources. Also, it takes up a great deal of land to be effective. A turbine that generates 2.5 megawatts (MW) can easily take up 50 yards and weigh 10 tons.

In addition, there are environmental issues with wind turbines. They produce tremendous noise and kill large numbers of birds and other animal life. And yes, wind farms can be an eyesore to look at.

THE FUTURE OF WIND POWER

Despite its disadvantages, wind power is one of the fastest growing type of alternative energy. According to a report from BTM Consult Aps (BTM-C), the capacity has grown an average of 26.2 percent per year from 2009, reaching 160,084 megawatts. Much of the growth has come from the United States and China. Wind power has had key subsidies from the massive economic stimulus of 2009. The Chinese government has also provided various strong incentives to increase wind power production.

WIND POWER TRADING

There are only a few publicly traded wind power companies, like Vestas. Conglomerates like GE and Siemens are also investing large sums in the wind power market. But as time goes by—and the growth continues—there will likely be more companies launching initial public offerings (IPOs) on U.S. exchanges.

BIOMASS

Biomass consists of organic matter. Examples include plants, wood, animal waste, and even rotting garbage. Such things absorb the sun's rays and store energy. Thus, by using equipment and specialized refiners, it is possible to turn biomass into energy.

So long as it is processed appropriately, biomass energy does not have serious environmental impact. It is carbon neutral. The reason is that the carbon emissions from biomass are reabsorbed by trees and plants.

Two key biomass fuels are ethanol—made from corn and gasoline—and biodiesel—made from soybeans and diesel fuel.

But the fact remains that biomass is far from a perfect alternative fuel. Biomass is expensive. The costs to create biodiesel are fairly high, which has stunted its adoption. The industry relies heavily on government subsidies. Also, there is not enough biomass to generate the world's energy needs, although biomass will certainly be a big help in dealing with the challenges of crude oil supplies.

ETHANOL

The major biomass fuel, ethanol, is corn-based. This has resulted in higher corn prices, which has been painful for lower-income countries.

Ethanol also requires much energy, water, and labor to create. But as crude oil prices increase, this becomes less of a problem. Even with these problems, ethanol can still be lucrative for investors. The U.S. federal government provides various tax credits to encourage production as well as tariffs to ward off cheaper imports, such as from Brazil.

ETHANOL TRADING

The largest publicly traded companies in the ethanol industry include Archer Daniels Midland Company, Valero Energy Corporation, Pacific Ethanol Inc., and Green Plains Renewable Energy Inc. The risks from investing in ethanol can be substantial. When oil prices plunged in late 2008, various ethanol producers went bust.

Investors can also purchase a futures contract on ethanol on the CME. The ticker is QE and each unit consists of 1,000 barrels. The minimum price fluctuation is $0.0001 per gallon.

GEOTHERMAL ENERGY

Geothermal energy is based on the molten magma in the earth's inner mantle. At the core, temperatures are about 8,000 degrees Fahrenheit. No doubt, this is a tremendous source of energy. To get at it, there needs to be deep drilling and sophisticated equipment. So it is important to focus on areas that do not have heavy amounts of rock, which can make the extraction quite expensive.

Finding a good source for geothermal energy is no easy task. It can be as difficult as finding a new copper or gold deposit. The most promising sources for geothermal energy are in areas with volcanic activity, like the Philippines, Indonesia, and parts of Africa.

ADVANTAGES OF GEOTHERMAL ENERGY

The geothermal industry is fairly mature and the technology risk is low. Consider that Pacific Gas and Electric Company (PG&E) has been generating this type of energy since the 1960s. Geothermal's primary uses include electricity generation, as well as heating and cooling of commercial buildings and homes.

Geothermal energy is totally renewable and has little environmental impact (mostly steam). Additionally, geothermal plants are not capital intensive—primarily because of U.S. federal government incentives and tax credits.

These plants also do not take up much room and can have lifespans of several decades, requiring little ongoing maintenance. Unlike solar or wind power, geothermal does not rely on the weather. It produces energy 24 hours per day (this is known as base-load energy).

GEOTHERMAL ENERGY TRADING

There are several publicly traded companies that have geothermal operations. One of the largest is Ormat Technologies Inc. The company has its own power plans and also sells equipment for the industry. Over the past few years, substantial demand has come from China. And it appears the growth for geothermal energy will be significant. A report from ABS Energy Research predicts a 78 percent growth in capacity from 2010 to 2015.

Even with the various types of alternative energy sources, crude oil will remain a dominant source of energy. As China, India, and other emerging economies continue to grow, the demand should continue to grow. This means that the prices for crude oil—as well as other energy sources—are likely to remain strong for the long haul. In the next chapter, we will take a look at agriculture commodities and companies.

CHAPTER 10

Agriculture

Key Concepts

- Understand the main drivers of agriculture commodities
- Look at the dynamics of agriculture companies
- Understand niche markets like lumber and rubber

Until recently, the market for corn and wheat has been mostly about surpluses. During the Great Depression of the 1930s, the situation was so bad that farmers started to destroy their crops—even though millions of people were underfed. So the federal government instituted a variety of programs to keep the price of corn and wheat at reasonable levels. Of course, this often meant that farmers were paid *not* to plant anything.

Such policies are still in effect today. Yet they look like a throwback to a bygone age. Across the globe, surpluses have changed to shortages. The fact is that agriculture has been underinvested for an extended period of time and it is getting tougher to find arable farmlands. Demand for agricultural products is also increasing—and this is likely to continue for the long term. In other words, there are strong forces that are driving the agriculture industry, which will make it a lucrative area for commodities investors.

POPULATION AND THE AGRICULTURE MARKET

For over two hundred years, there has been much worry about the population explosion. In 1798, Reverend Thomas Robert Malthus wrote the influential *Essay on the Principle of Population*. In it, he said population growth would be stopped by a variety of forces, like famine and disease. In modern times, there have been various academics that have warned about population growth. One of the most famous is Paul Ehrlich, who wrote a best-seller called *The Population Bomb* in 1968. Despite all the dire predictions, the fact is that the world has continued to grow its population—and its wealth. But at the same time, this has meant a greater demand for agriculture commodities.

It's hard to imagine but just 12,000 years ago there were only about one million people. It took until 1800 to reach one billion. From there, the growth rate accelerated. Now, the globe has a population of about 6.7 billion people. What is the projection from here? According estimates from the United Nations, the world population is expected to reach about 9.2 billion by 2050.

ANNUAL AND PERENNIAL CROPS

In agriculture, there are two main types of crops. The more common one is the annual crop. This is when a farmer plants the crop and harvests it within a year. Examples include corn, soybeans, and wheat. The other type is the perennial crop. This is a plant that lasts for at least two years. Of the two, the annual crop often has the most impact on prices.

To understand this, let's take a look at an example. Suppose that there is an oversupply of corn and the price falls. At the same time, there is a shortage of wheat and the price surges. In the next few years, farmers will replace more of its corn crop with the wheat crop. The result will likely be a correction in the prices of both commodities. However, in recent years, this impact has been muted. The main reason is that there have been rising prices in *many* annual crops, so it makes it less likely for substitution.

COCOA

The cocoa bean comes from the cacao tree, which grows in tropical areas. It takes a tree about five years to produce the beans. The tree will then be productive for about 25 years. It was not until the Spanish voyages to the New World that Europeans learned about cocoa. Ancient civilizations, like the Mayans and Aztecs, used the cocoa bean as a drink and even as a currency.

In the 1800s, British colonists started to develop cocoa crops in Africa—to Ghana in the late 1870s and to the Ivory Coast at the turn of the century. To this day, West Africa is the main production location for the cocoa crop. In the mid-1800s, a Dutch chemist, Coenraad Johannes van Houten, made a major breakthrough. He used cocoa to develop a process to mass-produce chocolate candy.

Cocoa Trading

You can purchase cocoa futures on the CME, under the symbol CJ, and the London International Financial Futures and Options Exchange (LIFFE), with the symbol LCO. Some investors will also trade consumer chocolate companies, such as Hershey's. The idea is that these stocks should increase in value if the price of cocoa falls.

Political Instability and Cocoa Futures Prices

Since cocoa is found in areas that involve political instability, like the Ivory Coast, the commodity has seen much volatility over the years. Just look at the presidential election in the Ivory Coast in 2010. There was a standoff between Alassane Ouattara and Laurent Gbagbo, the incumbent. All western governments believed that Ouattara was the winner of the election. In fact, the United Nations provided security for him. About 260 people died in the violence.

To put pressure on Gbagbo to leave, Ouattara ordered a ban on cocoa imports. No doubt, this was a major blow to the Ivory Coast economy, which accounts for about a third of the country's gross domestic product (GDP). So even though the cocoa crop was robust, it did not matter. Because of the political uncertainty—and even the possibility of a war—the futures prices surged. Keep in mind that there had been a civil war in the Ivory Coast in 2002. One big problem was the candy producers needed to get enough supply of cocoa because of the upcoming Easter season.[1]

COTTON

Cotton has been around for thousands of years. But it did not come into England until the 1600s, with the assistance of the East India Company. It quickly became a rival to the wool industry. From there, England introduced cotton to its colonies in North America. Since cotton requires much sunlight and water, the American south was an ideal place to grown cotton crops.

Eli Whitney's invention of the cotton gin, in the late 1700s, would play a crucial role with cotton. By automating the process of separating the cotton fibers from the seeds, the cotton gin would also be critical for the Industrial Revolution and the growth of the United States.

Today, cotton is still important and it is the most widely used natural fiber for clothing. China and India are the biggest importers of cotton, and the growth has been strong.

Types of Cotton

There are two types of cotton. One is long-staple cotton, which is about 1.2 inches long. It is planted mostly in the United States and in parts of Africa. It is the most common type of cotton. It is used for things like yarn and high-quality fabrics.

The other type is short-staple cotton, which is the cotton with fairly short fibers. It is useful for making tires and plastic reinforcing.

Weather and Cotton

Farmers plant cotton during April and May, when the soil and weather are generally the best. But if there is adverse weather during this time, then it can wreak havoc on the cotton crop. A stark

---

[1] http://online.wsj.com/article/SB10001424052748703555804576101492254013756.html.

example of this was during the summer of 2010. A severe drought destroyed a large portion of the cotton crop in Russia.

Cotton Trading

You can purchase futures contracts for cotton on the CME, under the symbol TT.

COFFEE

The origins of coffee go back to ninth century. The story is that in Ethiopia a goat herder saw that his herd got more energy when eating red berries from a tree. The town was called Kaffa, which became the name for coffee. During the seventeenth century, coffee then spread to Europe and India. It was during this time that coffee got the name Java, since it was popular in the Dutch East Indies.

Types of Coffee

Coffee actually comes from two types of beans: Robusta and Arabica. As the name implies, Robusta is stronger and has higher caffeine levels. Arabica, on the other hand, is more aromatic but takes more time to cultivate and is more complex.

Arabica coffee has the highest consumption (70 percent) and price. Yet both Robusta and Arabica coffee prices tend to track each other. However, when there are gaps in the valuations, there may be investment opportunities, as arbitrageurs move in.

TABLE 10-1

Global Coffee Producers

Country	Market Share
Brazil	35 percent
Vietnam	14 percent
Colombia	7 percent
Indonesia	7 percent

Weather and Coffee

A major impact on coffee pricing is from supply disruptions due to weather. An example would be a freeze in Brazil. This can happen during June, July, and August, which is the winter for Brazil. Or look at Colombia. In 2011, the country experienced torrential rains and saw a reduction in its harvest.

Coffee Trading

Investors can purchase coffee futures on the CME, with the symbol KT.

There are also a variety of coffee companies for investors to purchase shares. Besides Starbucks' shares, there are also shares of Peet's Coffee and Tea, and Green Mountain Coffee. Even when coffee prices increase, the impact may still not be as bad. After all when a cup of coffee sells for $3 to $4 a cup, there is a lot of profit margin in the product.

SUGAR

Sugar is a crystalline of carbohydrates. The main ingredients are sucrose, lactose, and fructose. Of course, the result is a sweet flavor.

Sources and Suppliers of Sugar

The two main sources for sugar come from sugarcane and sugar beets. Of these, sugarcane accounts for roughly 70 percent of global production. The main producers of sugarcane include Brazil, India, China, and Thailand. Sugar beets, on the other hand, are produced primarily in Europe, the United States, China, and Japan.

Weather and Sugar

Since sugar production is concentrated in only a few regions, it is vulnerable to weather. In 2009, a dry monsoon season in India had a significant impact on sugar prices.

Demand Sources for Sugar

A key driver for sugar demand has actually been for energy production. Brazil uses a large amount of sugarcane for ethanol. Interestingly enough, the higher oil prices go, the more attractive this fuel becomes.

Of course, sugar is used to manufacture food products. There are substitutes for sugar. One is high fructose corn syrup. If sugar prices get to extreme levels, consumers will usually move over to the sugar alternatives, which will affect the demand for sugar.

Sugar Trading

Sugar has had a volatile trading history. In the 1960s, sugar traded for below two cents per pound. But by late 1974, it reached 64 cents per pound. Since then, the range has been about 20 cents to 30 cents per pound. The demand for sugar is spread throughout the world. The highest consumer of sugar is Brazil, in terms of per-capita consumption, which is 59 kilograms of sugar per year.

There are many varieties of sugar futures. But the most common one for futures investors is Sugar No.11, which is based on the world benchmark contract for raw sugar.

You can trade the sugar futures on the CME, with the symbol YO. There is an exchange-traded fund for sugar called the iPath Dow Jones–UBS Sugar Total Return Subindex ETN (SGG).

There are also multi-commodity ETFs that have large concentrations of sugar. One ETF is iPath Dow Jones–UBS Softs Subindex Total Return ETN (JJS), which has a 29.72-percent weighting. Another ETF is PowerShares DB Agriculture Fund (DBA), which has a 12.5-percent weighting.

SOYBEANS

In the early 1920s, the A. E. Staley Manufacturing Company began to crush soybeans. It was a key innovation that led to the creation of soy oil—which is useful for cooking—and soy meal—which is used for feeding chickens and hogs. Soy meal is an excellent feed because it is high in fat. Soybeans are produced in the United States

(35 percent), Brazil (27 percent), Argentina (19 percent), China (6 percent), and India (4 percent).

Weather and Soybeans

In the United States, farmers plant soybeans from May to June. The main states include Illinois, Iowa, Indiana, Ohio, and Minnesota.

The most critical time for the soybeans crop is during pollination, or the fertilization phase, which comes in July. If there is adverse weather, it could reduce the crop. This was the case in 2011, when unusually dry weather affected the crop in Argentina.

Soybeans Trading

Seeing the importance of the soybeans industry, the CME started to trade the commodity in 1936, under the symbol S. It was called the "bean pit." The CME also realized that soybeans futures would likely have more volatility. After all, there were no federal government subsidies for it, unlike for corn or wheat (which were heavily impacted by President Roosevelt's agricultural programs).

ORANGE JUICE

About 4,000 years ago, oranges emerged in China and other Asian countries. A typical orange tree takes about four years to bear fruit and will reach its prime within eight years. An orange tree can be productive for 20 to 25 years. As Spanish ships made voyages to the New World, oranges would eventually spread to Europe. Of course, back then orange juice was fresh-squeezed.

However, by the late 1940s, there was a growth in refrigeration. The result was frozen concentrated orange juice. Because of this, the orange juice market surged.

Suppliers of Orange Juice

As of now, the orange juice industry is dominated by the United States and Brazil. Traditionally, Florida had been the dominant producer of orange juice. But this leadership position was lost to Brazil over the years. Brazil now produces about 80 percent of worldwide exports of orange juice.

Weather and Orange Juice

One of the reasons the United States have been replaced by Brazil as the top orange juice producer is the more adverse weather—frosts and hurricanes—in Florida. Bad weather can not only result in lower output but can also reduce the long-term productivity of the orange trees.

Since the commodity is primarily from two regions, the price is often volatile. A major freeze can mean a big spike in the price of orange juice. The danger times for a freeze are from December to March for Florida and from July to November for Brazil.

Disease and Orange Juice

Disease is another big problem for orange trees, which in turn can affect the production of orange juice. An example of a disease known to strike in Brazil is the infestation from citrus variegated chlorosis. In Florida, a common disease is citrus greening, which is a bacteria that kills crops.

Trading Orange Juice

You can trade orange juice on the IntercontinentalExchange (ICE), which has the symbol OJ.

CORN

The origins of corn are not clear, but it looks like it goes back at least 12,000 years. In some countries, the commodity is known as maize. The main use of corn is to make livestock feed. The key reason is that corn has a high starch content. Besides being a food for people and animals, corn is also used for the fuel known as ethanol.

Suppliers of Corn

Every year, about 525 million metric tons of corn is produced. Of this, the United States accounts for a whopping 260 million metric tons. China is also an important player, with 110 million metric tons. Brazil produces 37.5 million metric tons.

Corn Prices

From September to November, corn generally has a lower price because of the high amounts of corn on the market. Then from December to May, the prices tend to increase. In fact, this may continue throughout the summer. The reason is the potential for bad weather.

Investors will rely heavily on various reports from the Department of Agriculture. One of the most important is the Prospective Plantings report, which shows the amount of crops that farmers will plan for the new season.

Trading Corn

You can trade corn futures on the CME, which has a symbol of CC.

WHEAT

The planting of wheat goes back at least to 10,000 B.C. and has been a key source of food grain. In fact, the Roman Empire was known as the Wheat Empire. As of now, wheat is still a dominant commodity, ranked second in food production. Of the world production, about two-thirds is for food consumption, with much of the rest for livestock feed. But there are other uses including seeds.

Wheat Producers

Annual wheat production comes to about 20 billion bushels. The leading producers include China, the European Union (EU), and the United States.

It helps that wheat can be planted in many types of climates. But wheat does require a heavy amount of rainfall.

Types of Wheat

There are several types of wheat. The three main types are listed below.

- **Hard Red Winter Wheat:** This type is grown in Kansas, Oklahoma, Texas, and Nebraska. With little rain and low temperate, the climate is ideal for planting. Much of this type of wheat is found in bread.
- **Hard Red Spring Wheat:** This type is grown in the northern plains states like Minnesota. This wheat is also useful for bread.
- **Soft Red Winter Wheat:** This type is the most common. It is found in the northeastern states and is useful for snack foods, crackers, and pastries.

Trading Wheat

You can trade futures for Hard Red Winter Wheat on the Kansas City Board of Trade, under the symbol KW. You can trade futures for Hard Red Spring Wheat on the Minneapolis Board of Trade, which has a symbol of MW. You can also trade the futures on the CME, with the symbol W.

BARLEY

Barley is a grain, which is used for cereal, malt for beer, distilled beverages, and even animal fodder. It is quite popular in Africa and parts of Europe.

Barley Producers

Barley is planted once a year, usually in the spring. The main producers include the United States, Russia, Turkey, and Canada. Barley crops have low water and land requirements.

Trading Barley

There are futures on barley on the ICE Futures Canada, with a symbol of AB.

RICE

Rice is a grain that represents the main staple for billions of people in Asia, the Middle East, and Latin America. Rice is the second-most produced grain, with the biggest being corn. However, unlike rice, corn has nonhuman consumption purposes like ethanol.

The production of rice is labor-intensive. So production is most economical in low-wage countries, like Thailand and Vietnam.

Factors Influencing the Supply and the Price of Rice

Rice crops require a large amount of rainfall. But there have been pressures on the rice supply because of droughts and flooding in areas where it is grown.

Another supply constraint has been the surge in the prices of other grains, like corn and wheat. The result is that farmers have been pushing production of these commodities. This in turn has lowered the plantings of rice crops.

Rice is also subject to major governmental control, especially in Thailand and Vietnam. If there are key changes in policy, this could have a big impact on rice prices.

Trading Rice

Investors can trade futures on rough rice on the CME. Rough rice is rice that comes after a harvest. The product symbol for rough rice is RR.

OATS

The origins of oats go back to the Middle East in 3,000 BC. The oat is a cereal grain, which is grown for its seed. Nearly 90 percent of oats is used for oatmeal. But the commodity is also useful to feed horses, chicken, and other livestock. Oats are even a part of various dog foods.

Oats are usually planted in the spring, but may be planted in the summer months. In the United States, production is mostly in the Midwest, including Minnesota and Wisconsin. Countries like China, India, and Russia are also major producers. Over the years, demand has been declining. Instead, the focus has been on soybeans and corn.

Trading Oats

You can trade oats futures on the Chicago Board of Trade (CBOT) of the CME. The product symbol for oats is O (open outcry) and ZO (electronic).

WATER

A typical American accounts for 100 gallons of water each day. In fact, it takes large amounts of water to create many things. Consider that to make a pair of jeans requires roughly 3,000 gallons of water. By far, the biggest user of water is agriculture. But there are other important uses. The next biggest user of water is nuclear energy.

Unfortunately, millions of people across the world have much less access to water. It is fairly common for the poorest to have just about five gallons a day. But with the world population expected to increase by 50 percent over the next 40 years, there will be a growing demand for water. And yes, it will need to be fresh, clean water. All in all, it will not be an easy task to meet this demand.

Even though 70 percent of the world's surface is water, about 97 percent of it is salt water. Unless there is desalinization, which is the costly process of removing salt from the water, this type of water is unusable. Actually, only 1 percent of the world's water is fit for human consumption. Yet there are many threats to that water, from toxins, environmental leaks, and fertilizer runoffs.

Some analysts consider that water will be the next oil, since it will be critical for growth in emerging economies. It's even possible that some U.S. states—like California, Nevada, Colorado and Arizona—may experience stunted growth due to long-term droughts.

Trading Water

To invest in water, there are several options. One is "publicly traded water utilities." These tend to be steady companies and pay competitive dividends. But the fees are regulated by the government, so it can be tough to grow the top line. Many of the water utilities focus on local areas, but this may change. Over the years, there has been more consolidation in the water utilities industry.

Investors can also invest in bottled water companies. True, this market is mature in the United States, but there appears to be much growth in emerging markets, as they get wealthier.

An investor can also participate in those companies that are building the infrastructure for water. Examples include GE and Siemens.

Then there are exchange-traded funds (ETFs). They track indexes like the Palisades Water Index (ZWI) and the Dow Jones U.S. Water Index (DJUSWU), which track the performance of companies that manufacture pumps, irrigation equipment, and water filters.

Government and the Price of Water

Because water is so essential, governments have underpriced it. The problem is that this has made water less attractive for companies to make investments. But as time goes on, it seems likely that governments will have little choice but to increase prices.

LUMBER

There are two types of wood in the lumber industry: softwood and hardwood. Softwood comes from trees whose seeds, known as conifers, are protected by cones. Examples of softwood trees are pine, fir, larch, spruce, and hemlock. For the most part, softwood is easy to saw and nail. Because of this, it is the primary source of lumber production used in construction. The main areas for lumber production are the Baltic area in Europe and North America.

Hardwood comes from trees whose seeds, known as angiosperms, are protected by a covering. An acorn comes from a hardwood tree. The main trees are broad-leaved. Examples of hardwood trees are deciduous trees like oak. Hardwoods are primarily used in furniture manufacturing. Hardwoods are also used for wood flooring, construction, panels, and kitchen cabinets.

Lumber Production

The processing of lumber is time-consuming. A tree must be felled and the branches removed. From this, logs will be created and trucked to sawmills. Depending on the demand, the lumber will be cut into various sizes. Then the lumber is either shipped via truck or rail. Freight can constitute 20 percent to 30 percent of the overall price of lumber.

Lumber Prices

Of the construction market, housing is the biggest user of lumber. The average home has about 14,400 board feet of softwood. This is why investors closely watch the housing starts report, published by the U.S. Department of Commerce, to get a sense of the prices for lumber. In light of the depressed real estate market over the years, lumber has been an underperformer.

The U.S./Canadian exchange rate is also important for predicting the price of lumber. If the U.S. dollar increases, there will usually be more demand for Canadian lumber. The Canadian government also owns substantial lumber properties. So its policies can certainly have a major impact on prices.

Trading Lumber

Lumber trades on the CME, under the product symbol LB. Each contract is for 111,000 board feet of random length 8 to 12 foot 2 × 4s. This is the wood mostly used in construction.

There are a variety of lumber exchange-traded funds (ETFs). Examples include Guggenheim Timber ETF (CUT), which tracks 25 stocks in the lumber industry, and the S&P Global Timber & Forestry Index Fund (WOOD), which is invested in 23 companies.

There are also several lumber companies, such as Potlatch Corporation (PCH), Plum Creek Timber Company (PCL), and

Weyerhaeuser Company (WY). Many are structured as real estate investment trusts or REITs. These are special securities that shield a company's income from taxes if 90 percent or more is distributed to shareholders. This means that a REIT tends to pay relatively high dividends. This can be a way to reduce volatility because the income acts as a buffer. Although, the shareholders still have to pay taxes on their dividend distributions.

Over the long run, lumber companies may offer the possibility of a new market: cleantech or clean technology. Companies like Weyerhaeuser are investing in new technologies to turn lumber into bio fuels.

RUBBER

Rubber comes from the Para rubber tree, which is found in Central and South America. Ancient tribes used it for balls, containers, and even shoes. But it was not until the late 1700s that there were commercial applications. Joseph Priestley realized that rubber was effective for erasing pencil marks. In the late 1830s, rubber saw its major breakthrough. Charles Goodyear developed the vulcanization process. This is a chemical reaction that turns rubber into a more durable material.

Rubber Supply

Much of the supply of rubber comes from Asian countries like Thailand, Indonesia, Malaysia, and China. Interestingly enough, during World War II, the United States experienced a severe shortage of the commodity because of its war with Japan. To deal with this, there was the creation of synthetic rubber.

Demand Sources for Rubber

As of now, about half of rubber consumption is for tires. Other uses include balloons, rubber bands, adhesives, gloves, and engine parts.

Trading Rubber

You can trade rubber futures on the Tokyo Commodity Exchange. The product symbol is JN. The contract is for 5,000 kilograms.

POTASH

Potash contains a mixture of salts that have potassium. Interestingly enough, this was an innovation from Samuel Hopkins, who developed it in 1790. It became the first patent ever issued in the United States. Potash may seem generic but it has actually become quite important as a fertilizer (for roughly 95 percent of the world's farms). It has been effective in increasing yields and improving resistance to disease. Potash even helps improve the quality of crops, in terms of the taste and color. It is also helpful with producing livestock.

Potash Trading

The potash industry is large, with operators like the Potash Corporation of Saskatchewan, Agrium Inc., and The Mosaic Company. These companies have been fast growers, which has led to strong stock prices.

The barriers-to-entry for the potash industry are significant and there are no substitutes for the commodity. The result is that there is much pricing power. The supplies are also concentrated in a few countries like Canada and Russia.

In 2010, BHP Billiton made a $39 billion hostile bid for Potash. It was another sign of the long-term potential of the industry. However, because of pressure of the Canadian government, BHP Billiton eventually dropped its bid.

FARM EQUIPMENT MAKERS

Another way to participate in the agriculture boom is to invest in the farm equipment makers. There are actually only a handful in the world. They include John Deere, CNH Global N.V., and Agco. Because of their dominant positions, they are like an oligopoly. In other words, these companies have a high-degree ability to maintain prices for their equipment. The result is that profit margins tend to be fairly high.

When it comes to valuations, investors have often been cautious. The reason is that farm equipment makers have been cyclical. That is, the companies perform quite well during booms but perform poorly during recessions. But in light of the long-term growth potential in global agriculture markets, some investors think the cyclicality is diminishing and that these stocks should have higher valuations.

FOOD PROCESSORS

Another type of agriculture stock is food processors. These include companies like Kraft Foods, Sara Lee Corporation, and ConAgra Foods. They are huge buyers of commodities. So if there is a spike in prices, there may ultimately be a hit to their profit margins.

These companies will use the futures markets to hedge their supplies, but this is difficult to sustain over the long term. Other approaches include actually reducing the food amounts in their products and passing along the higher prices to consumers. But again, these have limits.

FARMLAND

With the surge in agriculture prices over the years, there has also been a growing demand for farmland. However, like any type of real estate investment, there are big risks. There is the problem of liquidity; that is, it could take a while to sell the farmland or refinance it. Another big issue is bad weather or pestilence, which could wipe out a crop. It is also difficult to find available arable land.

Farmland Trading

Despite the risks, farmland has been a consistently strong invest-ment—at least from 2000 to 2010. This has been reflected in the NCREIF Farmland Returns Index from the National Council of Real Estate Investment Fiduciaries, as well as from data from the U.S. Department of Agriculture.

But it can be difficult for investors to participate. There are some farmland stocks, but they trade on foreign exchanges, such as in Argentina and the United Kingdom. But one alternative is an exchange-traded fund (ETF) like Market Vectors–Agribusiness (MOO). Or, an investor may want to select a hedge fund.[2]

In this chapter, we have seen that the agriculture market is quite diverse. There are also strong forces that should increase prices over the long term, especially with industrialization and the increase in the world's population. In the next chapter, we will look at the main industrial metals and learn how to invest in them.

---

[2] http://www.cnbc.com/id/40784051.

CHAPTER 11

Industrial Metals

Key Concepts

- Look at the main industrial metals, including copper, aluminum, and steel
- Understand the main drivers of industrial metals
- Learn how to invest in exotic categories, such as rare earth metals

As the name implies, industrial metals are used for construction and other infrastructure development. Of course, the biggest users of these commodities are the fast-growing economies of China and India.

For investors, it is tough to find a company that focuses on only one industrial metal, due to the significant mergers and acquisitions in the mining industry. Companies like BHP Billiton, Rio Tinto, Vale, and Xstrata have diversified deposits across various commodities. For example, Vale gets 46 percent of its revenues from iron ore and 15 percent from nickel whereas Rio Tinto gets 43 percent of its revenues from aluminum and 30 percent from iron ore. As a result, investors will tend to focus on exchange-traded funds (ETFs) or futures when investing in industrial metals.

MAIN DRIVERS OF THE INDUSTRIAL METALS MARKET

In the age of the Internet and mobile technologies, the market for industrial metals seems antiquated. Interestingly enough, the Industrial Revolution of the 1800s was similar to the modern-day technology boom. Efficient production of steel and other metals were key to the rapid growth in the United States and European nations. At the core was the emergence of the railroads, which also led to the emergence of large metropolitan cities.

During the twentieth century, the metals industry was still a growth market. One of the biggest contributors was the auto industry. Then after World War II, there was the real estate boom in the United States.

Few industries can continue to grow for three centuries, but it looks like this will be the case for industrial metals. No doubt, it is the rapid economic development in China, India, and other emerging countries that is resulting in high levels of demand for industrial metals. This trend is likely to continue for decades—and make for robust investment opportunities.

Yet the fact remains that industrial metals are still highly sensitive to changes in the economy. After all, when the global economy fell into a recession in 2008 to 2009, many of these commodities collapsed. So did the companies in the industry. So investors need to understand the volatility and the risks of the industrial metals market.

For investors, the key metals include copper, aluminum, and steel. They all have unique qualities, in terms of the use and supply/demand profiles. Because of the complexities, many investors will focus on just a few of the industrial metals.

There are differences in how industrial metals are mined. Some industrial metals are mined directly, which means that the metal is the primary focus. But in the process, a miner might extract other industrial metals. These are known as by-products. While they represent only a fraction of the primary metals, they can still be quite profitable.

The mines for industrial metals are usually large and require substantial capital costs. Because of this, it can take a great deal of time for there to be increased production. But if prices of industrial metals remain high, there should eventually be more investments.

Mines for industrial metals also last for many years. In some cases, they can remain productive for over a century. This makes it easier to justify the large upfront investments for opening a mine. However, as a mine ages there can be many problems. It is not uncommon for there to be supply disruptions.

In light of the importance of industrial metals, many involve long-term contracts. Often miners and purchasers will set up these arrangements on an annual basis. The goal is to bring stability to the markets. But as seen from 2000 to 2010, there continues to be much volatility in the prices for industrial metals. In fact, some of the largest consumers of industrial metals—especially China—do not like long-term contracts. So these may eventually fade away.

COPPER

The mining of copper extends back as far as 13,000 B.C. and is actually the first-known industrial metal. As a sign of its importance, copper became the basis of the Copper Age during prehistoric times. Copper was a critical metal for civilizations like the Egyptians and the Romans. Benefits of copper include its strength, durability, and malleability. It is also an effective conductor of electricity and was essential for the Electric Revolution during the nineteenth century.

Copper miners typically use open-pit mines to process large amounts of low-grade ore. The copper is then crushed and then sent to a smelter. After this, there is a refining process that removes much of the oxygen and impurities. The end-product is cathode and wire rods, which are then sold to copper fabricators.

Copper is also alloyed with other metals. The combination of copper and tin will create bronze. The alloy of copper and zinc will result in brass.

Dr. Copper

Copper is often called Dr. Copper. The reason is that it's considered the metal with a Ph.D. in economics. All in all, copper is a key indicator in gauging the status of the economy. Consider that at the end of 2008, there was a 4 percent drop in copper demand. While this may seem insignificant, it was actually a major event. For savvy investors, the drop-off was a tell-tale sign that the global economy was falling into a recession.

Demand Sources for Copper

By 2010, the overall demand for copper spiked by 9 percent. A big part of this increase came from China, which represents 40 percent of global copper consumption (this compares to just 4 percent in 1976). The European Union is ranked second in copper consumption, at 17 percent. The United States is ranked third, with 9 percent. And yes, the recovery of demand presaged an economic rebound.

Currently, the per capita consumption of copper is roughly 4 kilograms in China. This is well below that of other advanced economies like Japan, which has a per capita consumption of about 9 kilograms. India will be another big consumer over the long haul. It currently has a per capita consumption of copper of about 0.5 kilograms.

The most common use for copper is for construction. The average U.S. home contains about 400 pounds of copper. Copper is also used in plumbing, heating systems, solar installations, and the desalination of water.

World's Supply and Reserves of Copper

Based on research from the United States Geological Service, there are large amounts of copper reserves in the world. The latest estimate is 550 million tonnes, which should be enough supply for 30 years or so.

Currently, the world produces about 15.9 million tonnes of copper a year.[1] In terms of physical volume, copper is Number Three in the metals market. The largest copper producer in the world is Chile, with 34 percent.

---

[1] http://minerals.usgs.gov/ds/2005/140/copper.pdf.

Factors that Influence the Supply of Copper

Despite the abundant supply of copper, there are major constraints on the mining of the supply. These include exploration costs, political instability, labor problems, and environmental issues.

Exploration costs
Finding new copper deposits is extremely difficult. It often means exploring remote regions and using sophisticated technologies. In light of the higher copper prices, the costs of obtaining the mineral rights have also increased.

Political Instability
Much of the new sources of copper are in Africa and Latin America, where it can be difficult to launch new mining projects. The African countries of Zambia and the Democratic Republic of the Congo account for around 85 percent of Africa's copper supply. However, both countries have a long history of political instability.

The big problem is finding deposits in politically stable areas. But it appears that there are some promising locations, such as in Mongolia, in Asia. But it can easily take a decade to bring on new production.

Labor Problems and Environmental Problems
Chile, the world's biggest producer of copper, has its own host of issues. These include labor problems, as well as power and water shortages. The 2010 Chilean earthquake had an effect on the supply of copper.

The Mines' Age
In addition, the age of the mines causes supply problems. Five of the top ten mines in Chile are over 50 years old. As a result, these mines typically have higher costs, more problems, and produce lower grades of copper. At the same time, there are no plans to open new large-scale mines.

Copper Scrap
Another major problem affecting supply is the lack of copper scrap. Over the years, this has been a major supplement for the copper

supply. But it is getting tougher to find scrap. The reason is that it is unlikely that in countries like China—where there have been large increases in the use of copper in cars, buildings, and appliances—there will be high levels of recycling.

Copper Prices

Over the past 24 years, copper has definitely seen major swings in prices. During this period, the price has ranged from $1,000 per tonne to $9,000 per tonne. Since 2003, the trading has been at persistently higher levels. But when adjusted for inflation, the prices are far from those in 1974, when copper peaked at $13,811.70.

Copper Trading

You can purchase futures contracts on copper on the CME, under the product symbol HG. Each unit represents 25,000 pounds of the metal. The minimum price fluctuation is $0.05, or $12.50 per contract. You can trade copper on the London Metal Exchange (LME), with the product symbol CA.

While there are many large copper companies, many are traded on foreign markets or owned by governments. Other miners like BHP Billiton, Rio Tinto, and Xstrata are also larger producers. But copper represents a relatively small portion of their overall revenues.

The biggest U.S. mining company that is traded is Freeport-McMoRan Copper & Gold Inc. About three-quarters of its revenues come from copper, with the remaining revenues from other metals like gold (17 percent), silver (3 percent), and molybdenum (5 percent). The company generates roughly $18 billion in revenues. However, the stock price of Freeport-McMoRan can be volatile.

One of the big problems for copper companies is that it is tough to cut back on production when there is a recession. This was the case in 2008. Inventory levels actually peaked in late 2009, when the economy was in the process of recovering from the downturn. As a result, copper companies saw large drops in revenues and profits.

There are also exchange-traded funds (ETFs) on copper. The iPath Dow Jones–UBS Copper Subindex Total Return ETN (JJC) fund tracks copper with futures contracts. There are also ETFs from JP MorganChase and Blackrock that are physically backed by copper. In other words, they store the metal and handle all the costs for insurance.

PALLADIUM

Back in 1803, William Hyde Wollaston discovered palladium. He named it after the asteroid Pallas. Palladium is part of a group of elements called the platinum group metals (PGM), which include platinum, rhodium, ruthenium, iridium, and osmium. While they have many similar properties, palladium has the lowest melting point.

Demand Sources for Palladium

Some demand sources for palladium include for industrial use and for jewelry.

Palladium for Industrial Use
There are many uses of palladium, such as in electronics and dentistry. However, the most common use is for catalytic converters, which accounts for 57 percent of demand. Thus, the global demand for cars has a significant impact on the price of palladium.

Palladium for Jewelry
Palladium has also seen strong growth from jewelry. In the past decade, the increase was 264 percent. The total worldwide demand is now 11 percent.

Suppliers of Palladium

The global supply of palladium is fairly limited. From 1999 to 2008, the production was about 8.1 million ounces per year. The biggest supplier is Russia, with 45 percent. But this has been declining over the years. In 1999, Russia produced about 65 percent of the world's supply. To make up for the decrease in supply, South Africa has become a major palladium producer. It now accounts for 29 percent of the world's supply.

Palladium Trading

You can trade palladium on the CME, under the product symbol PL. You can also trade palladium on the Tokyo Commodity Exchange, under the product symbol JMA. The CME is the largest trader of the commodity; it has been traded on the CME since 1974. The ETFS Physical Palladium Shares (PALL) is backed by a hoard of palladium, which has become a popular way to invest in the metal.

There are other exchange-traded funds (ETFs)—like the iPath Dow Jones–UBS Platinum Subindex Total Return ETN (PGM) and the UBS E-TRACS CMCI Long Platinum Total Return ETN (PTM)— which involve holding shares of palladium companies. Another UBS product, the CMCI Short Platinum (PTD), offers short exposure to platinum.

TIN

Tin has a silvery color, is malleable, and is resistant to oxidation. It is used to help prevent corrosion for other metals. It was actually in 3000 B.C. that tin and copper were first combined to create bronze. Then after 600 B.C., the commodity was critical for the development of pewter. In modern times, tin is used for food packaging because it is nontoxic.

Suppliers of Tin

The biggest producers of tin are China (37 percent), Indonesia (33 percent), and Peru (12 percent). There is no tin production in the United States.

Tin Trading

You can trade tin on the London Metal Exchange (LME), under the product symbol SN. The minimum price fluctuation is $5.00 per ton, or $25 per contract.

NICKEL

Nickel is malleable and hard and has a silvery-white color. It can also withstand high levels of heat. Nickel has been in use as far back as 3500 B.C. But it was not until 1751 that Axel Fredrik Cronstedt classified nickel as a chemical element (Ni).

Demand Sources for Nickel

The main use for nickel is for stainless steel, which accounts for about two-thirds of the global production. Other uses include coins, batteries, and plating.

By far, the biggest consumer of nickel is China. It is a key to its economic growth because of the production of stainless steel products.

Suppliers of Nickel

The top producers of nickel include Russia, Canada, Australia, Indonesia, Colombia, and China. A variety of diversified miners—like Vale, BHP Billiton, and Norilsk—extract the commodity. The mining of nickel is quite difficult because it requires sophisticated technologies and mining techniques.

Nickel Trading

You can trade nickel on the London Metal Exchange (LME), with the product symbol NI. A contract represents six metric tons of nickel with a 99.80 percent purity. The minimum price fluctuation is $5.00 per ton.

ZINC

Zinc has been around since prehistoric times. Zinc is a bluish-white color and is a brittle metal. Through metal galvanization, zinc helps to prevent rust and corrosion of other metals like steel or iron.

Demand Sources for Zinc

As stated above, zinc's primary use is to prevent rust and corrosion of other metals. Zinc is also used in rubber making, paint pigment, batteries, and agriculture fungicides. It is even used in some dietary supplements. Zinc is alloyed with copper to form brass.

Suppliers of Zinc

The main producers of zinc are China (25 percent), Australia (12 percent), and Canada (7 percent).

Unlike other industrial metals, this commodity has sufficient supplies to meet current demand. In fact, there are several mines that will come online over the next few years. But by 2015 or so, the supply profile is expected to change as there will be closures of several major mines.

Zinc Trading

You can trade zinc on the London Metal Exchange (LME), with the product symbol ZS. The minimum price fluctuation is $0.50 per ton, or $12.50 per contract.

There are also several publicly traded zinc producers, including Horsehead Holding Corporation. This company has been diversifying its platform by buying miners in areas like nickel.

LEAD

Lead has a blue-white color, is soft, and malleable. When exposed to air, the blue-white color changes to gray. When lead is melted, it turns to a silvery luster.

Of course, lead is toxic. Exposure can cause neurological and nervous disorders. Interestingly enough, the Romans used the metal for their water system.

Demand and Suppliers of Lead

The primary uses for lead include construction and batteries. The main producers of lead are China (37 percent), the United States (15 percent), and Germany (5 percent).

Lead Trading

You can trade lead on the London Metal Exchange (LME), under the product symbol PB. The minimum price fluctuation is $0.50 per ton, or $12.50 per contract.

TITANIUM

Titanium, which has a silvery color, is often referred to as the Space Age Metal because of its use in the NASA (National Aeronautics and Space Administration) program. The titanium commodity has a combination of corrosion resistance, a high strength-to-weight ratio, and high temperature performance.

Demand Sources for Titanium

The main use for titanium is in the aerospace industry. It will be a key to the next-generation of aircraft from Boeing and Airbus.

Some of the other uses for titanium include: medical implants, armor plating, desalination plants, and pollution control equipment. In emerging markets, there has been increases in demand for car production, geothermal facilities, and gas production installations.

Suppliers of Titanium

A large operator in the titanium market is Titanium Metals Corporation, which is traded on the New York Stock Exchange. The company produces titanium melted and mill products. Outside the United States, the top producers of titanium include Australia, Canada, China, South Africa, Norway and India.

Trading Titanium

There is currently no tradable futures contract on titanium. But there are a variety of publicly traded companies, including RTI International Metals, Inc. and Allegheny Technologies Incorporated.

MOLYBDENUM

Molybdenum is named after the ancient Greek word for lead. For many centuries, the commodity was actually confused for this element. It was not until 1778 that Carl Wilhelm Scheele discovered that molybdenum was an independent element. It is a silver-colored metal that has the sixth-highest melting point of any element.

Demand for Molybdenum

There was little use for molybdenum until World War I and II. During wartime, molybdenum became useful for things like steel armor plates. Because of its hard structure, it is used to strengthen steel and avoid corrosion. Interest in the metal was in a decline until the beginning of the twenty-first century.

Because of its effectiveness for green technologies, molybdenum has seen renewed interest over the past ten years. One of its uses is to minimize the environmental impact of nuclear power plants. In fact, molybdenum was one of the best-performing commodities over the past decade. It went from $3 per pound in 2000 to $45 per pound five years later. But when the 2008–2009 financial crisis hit, the price plunged to $10 per pound.

Suppliers of Molybdenum

A large amount of molybdenum is the by-product of copper. The largest producers include China (39 percent), the United States (25 percent), and Chile (16 percent).

Because of its large copper production, Freeport-McMoRan Copper & Gold Inc. is also a large player in the molybdenum market; 5 percent of the company's revenue comes from molybdenum. There are several pure plays in the industry including Thompson Creek Metals Company, which trades on the New York Stock Exchange. Much of its production is in North America.

Molybdenum Trading

You can trade futures contracts on molybdenum on the London Metal Exchange (LME), under the product symbol MO. The contracts were launched in early 2010.

LITHIUM

Lithium, which has a silvery-white color, is highly reactive, and flammable. When exposed to the open air, the color will change to gray and eventually to a black tarnish. Lithium is extracted from brine lakes, salt pans, clays, mineral springs, and igneous rocks. The largest amounts of lithium are found in South America, such as Chile, Argentina, and Bolivia. The U.S. Geological Survey (USGS) projects that the global reserves are about 11 million tons.

Demand Sources for Lithium

Until the tech revolution accelerated in the 1990s, the lithium market was fairly small. But the commodity has proved extremely useful for batteries. Lithium is light and can store large amounts of energy. In fact, it can be charged many times without much degradation. Consider that nowadays lithium batteries are in 90 percent of laptops and in over 60 percent of mobile devices.

Lithium is also cleaner than its alternatives, like lead and nickel. But perhaps the biggest growth opportunity for lithium is in batteries for electric and fuel-cell cars. There are already major government initiatives around the globe, such as from China, the United States, and Germany. Understanding the importance of this, Toyota purchased an interest in a lithium mine in Argentina.

Another possible source of demand is from the power-generation industry. It looks like lithium can be effective in enhancing alternative energy sources, such as wind and solar. From 2000 to 2010, the demand for lithium has roughly doubled. The growth is expected to continue, reaching 55,000 metric tons by 2020 (according to a research report from the TRU Group Inc.).

There are about 90 variations on lithium, which makes pricing complicated. Despite this, the overall prices have increased roughly three times from 2000 to 2010.

Suppliers of Lithium

One of the largest operators in the lithium market is FMC Corporation. Roughly 23 percent of its revenues come from the commodity. Sociedad Quimica y Minera de Chile S.A. (SQM), which is traded on the New York Stock Exchange, is another big lithium producer.

Lithium Trading

There is no futures trading in lithium. But investors have the option of purchasing exchange-traded funds (ETFs) for lithium. An example is the Global X Lithium ETF (LIT). It invests in the largest and highly liquid companies that explore or mine lithium, as well as produce the batteries.

ALUMINUM

Aluminum is the most abundant metal found on the earth's crust. It is actually a combination of over 270 minerals, with the main source being bauxite ore. Aluminum has a low density and is highly resistant to corrosion. It is also an effective conductor of electricity.

Demand Sources for Aluminum

Aluminum is used for construction, transportation, packaging, and aerospace. China is also the biggest consumer of aluminum.

Suppliers of Aluminum

The biggest producers of aluminum include China (35 percent), Russia (9 percent), Canada (8 percent), the United States (5 percent), and Australia (5 percent). The industry is also dominated by a few companies. One is Alcoa, which generates over $18 billion in annual revenues. Besides mining, Alcoa also refines, smelts, fabricates, and recycles aluminum. Alcoa has operations in 31 countries. Other aluminum suppliers include Rio Tinto and Norsk Hydro.

Even when aluminum prices increase, the impact may be delayed for companies like Alcoa. The main reason is that the aluminum industry relies mostly on long-term contracts. Another problem is energy, which accounts for large amounts of the company's costs. So a spike in the price of crude oil or coal can depress profits from aluminum.

Aluminum Trading

Aluminum futures used to be traded on the COMEX. But in late 2009, the exchange delisted the contract because of the lack of trading activity. Investors can still trade aluminum on the London Metal Exchange (LME), under the product symbol AA.

There are two exchange-traded funds (ETFs) for aluminum. One is the Global X Aluminum ETF (ALUM), which tracks companies involved in the industry. These include companies like Rio Tinto, Alcoa, Norsk Hydro, and Aluminum Corp. The other ETF is the iPath Dow Jones–UBS Aluminum Total Return Subindex ETN (JJU), which tracks futures.

STEEL

Steel is an alloy that consists primarily of iron and some level of carbon, which allows for hardening. Steel may also include manganese, chromium, vanadium, and tungsten.

Back in the late 1800s, industrialist Andrew Carnegie made his fortune from steel. He was responsible for several key innovations and made the necessary investments to scale production. By 1901, he sold the company to J. P. Morgan, who merged it with other companies. The result was U.S. Steel, which dominated its industry until the 1960s.

Types of Steel Companies

There are two main types of steel companies. They are listed below.

Integrated Producers

The large ones are known as integrated producers. They are large steel companies. They have mills that are involved in all aspects of steelmaking including conversion (turning iron to liquid steel), casting (solidifying the liquid steel), roughing/rolling (reducing the steel blocks), and product rolling (making the finished shapes).

Mini-mills

They get much of their iron from scrap (recycled from autos or equipment) and the facilities tend to be smaller. Their costs structures are usually lower than integrated producers because they have little or no pension obligations. However, profits can get squeezed if the cost of scrap increases significantly. Because of the strategic importance of steel, a variety of global operators have government subsidies. This often means lower cost structures.

Demand Sources for Steel

The main drivers for steel demand include the automotive and construction industries, which amount to over 50 percent of the global market. Of course, there is still considerable demand from appliances, electrical equipment, industrial machinery, and agriculture. In fact, steel has the highest amount of production for any industrial metal.

Suppliers of Steel

By far, the largest producer of steel is China, with 47 percent of the market. The other top producers include Japan (7 percent), Russia (5 percent), the United States (5 percent) and India (5 percent).

There are also a variety of steel companies that are publicly traded. This is the case with the world's largest steel producer, ArcelorMittal. The mastermind of the company is Lakshmi Narayan Mittal, who took over the family's steel business in India during the 1970s. He quickly grew the operation through many bold acquisitions, especially in foreign markets. Now the company generates revenues of $65 billion and Mittal has a net worth of $28 billion.

Another top company in the steel industry is Nucor, which focuses on mini-mills. The company has a long history of innovation and profitability.

Trading Steel

Investors need to be wary about investing in steel companies. Keep in mind that they tend to be regional. Despite a global rebound in steel, the major U.S. steel makers continued to struggle between 2009 and 2010. The reason was that the U.S. economy was fairly sluggish in its recovery. At the same time, the steel makers were experiencing higher labor, raw materials, and energy costs. Also, many steel makers must contend with legacy retirement and healthcare benefits. Often these are not issues for foreign steel makers.

The price of steel is also regional. So the local spot prices remained depressed in the United States, which meant added pressure on the steel makers.

COBALT

Cobalt has a silvery-gray color. Cobalt is produced through a process called reductive smelting, which makes the metal fairly hard. Much of the production comes as a by-product of copper and nickel mining.

Demand Sources for Cobalt

The traditional use of cobalt has been for glass, ceramics, and pottery. But over the years, the demand has increased significantly because cobalt is effective for use in rechargeable batteries for electric cars, cell phones, and other mobile devices.

Suppliers of Cobalt

The biggest deposits of cobalt are found in the Democratic Republic of Congo and Zambia. Since these areas are politically unstable, the supply of cobalt is periodically subject to disruption. While there are other promising sources of supply—such as in Canada, Australia, and Finland—it will take considerable time to realize any meaningful production.

Cobalt Trading

You can trade cobalt on the London Metal Exchange (LME), under the product symbol CO.

CHEMICALS

The chemicals industry is massive and global. A typical plant can easily cost a billion dollars and produce on a 24-hour basis. Chemicals are intermediate materials that become the core parts of many products.

A chemicals plant will use a process called cracking. This involves crushing hydrocarbons into two key materials: ethylene and propylene. Some of the world's largest chemical producers include Dow Chemical, BASF, and DuPont. Large oil companies like ExxonMobil and Chevron also have chemical operations.

Supply and Demand of Chemicals

The competitive environment in the chemicals industry is intense. To deal with this, there have been many acquisitions. Also, the industry has been focusing more on specialty chemicals, which usually have higher profit margins. Yet chemicals are also highly sensitive to changes in the economy. If there is a recession, demand can plunge.

Trading Chemicals

You can trade futures on propylene on the London Metal Exchange (LME), under the product symbol PP.

RARE EARTH METALS

Over the past few years, rare earth metals have gotten much attention from investors. It's even become a hot topic on CNBC. As the name implies, rare earth metals are definitely in short supply. Yet they are critical components for leading-edge technologies, such as the iPhone and electric cars.

Demand for Rare Earth Metals

The market for rare earths is still fairly small and is expected to reach only $3 billion by 2014. Japan is a big importer of rare earth metals.

In light of the heavy costs of mining, there may not be much motivation to make the necessary investments. Keep in mind that a new mine can easily cost several hundred million dollars.

More importantly, rare earth metals are also crucial for the Pentagon. Since much of the supply is in China, there has been much concern for military planners. Rare earth metals even have an impact on gasoline prices. The reason is that two of the metals—lanthanum and cerium—are a key part of the gasoline refining process. The result is likely to be lower profit margins.[2]

Suppliers of Rare Earth Metals

There are actually substantial amounts of rare earth metals across the world. But it takes many years to prepare a mine. Also, deposits are usually of low quality.

China has about 37 percent of the world's reserves of rare earth metals. As a result there will likely to be price squeezes for some time.

Interestingly enough, one of the top mines is based in Mountain Pass, California. But it had to be shut down because of water contamination from radioactive dust.

In light of the foreign policy implications, the federal government has been loosening things up. There is a fear that tensions

---

[2] http://online.wsj.com/article/SB10001424052748704055204576068270214808518
.html?mod=WSJ_hp_LEFTWhatsNewsCollection.

with China could make it more difficult to develop weapons. So the federal government has allowed the resumption of mining at Mountain Pass. The owner is a company called Molycorp. It plans to make substantial investments in the mine. As should be no surprise, Molycorp has had little trouble obtaining financing. It was able to secure $130 million from Sumitomo Corporation.

Even with the new sources of supply, the fact remains that China will still have a dominant share of the market. Estimates are that China will have about 67 percent of the world market by 2014.[3]

Other big deposits of rare earth metals are found in Chile, India, and Bolivia. However, these countries have stricter environmental laws, which has stunted mining. But as prices increase, this will probably change. Even so, it will easily take several years to see any meaningful production.

Trading Rare Earth Metals

There are no futures contracts on rare earth metals. But there are variety of publicly traded companies in the industry. Other than Molycorp, there is also Avalon Rare Metals and Rare Element Resources.

There is also an exchange-traded fund (ETF) for rare earth metals called the Market Vectors Rare Earth/Strategic Metals ETF. It consists of 26 companies in the industry, including Molycorp.

In this chapter, we have seen the many ways to invest in industrial metals. Besides futures, there are also a variety of exchange-traded funds as well as publicly traded companies. But investors need to understand the unique supply and demand factors for each of the metals, which can take lots of research. In the next chapter, we will look at the livestock and dairy industries.

---

[3] http://online.wsj.com/article/SB10001424052748704447604576007290928049906
.html?mod=WSJ_hp_LEFTWhatsNewsCollection.

CHAPTER 12

Livestock and Dairy

Key Concepts

- Understand the main drivers of livestock and dairy
- Learn how to invest in livestock and dairy
- Understand the various government reports

There are many definitions for livestock, which is also known as cattle. But in a broad sense, it refers to animals that are domesticated for some type of commercial purposes. When it comes to investing, the main categories of livestock include cows and hogs.

The livestock market provides supply throughout the year. Demand is usually fairly stable. An investor must account for the herd sizes, slaughter rates, and the cost of feed.

The dairy industry is unique and requires a specialized understanding of its supply and demand factors. Another major factor to be aware of is stringent government regulations.

THE HOG INDUSTRY

Listed below are the different aspects of the hog industry that influence the market.

The U.S. Hog Market

The hog market is fairly concentrated in the United States, with much of the operations in Iowa, Minnesota, Illinois, Ohio, and even North Carolina. The farms are mostly large so as to benefit from economies of scale, as well as leverage when negotiating with packers.

The Life Cycle of a Hog from Birth to Market

Let's take a look at the key elements of the hog market. A rancher will breed hogs twice a year, which results in more consistent production of baby piglets. The breeding is done with matching boars or by artificial insemination. A female hog will give birth to nine to ten piglets after a four-month gestation period. They will have a high-grain diet—including corn, barley, oats, and oilseed meal—that maximizes weight and growth.

Within six months, the hogs should be ready for slaughter. The weight of each hog will be about 250 pounds; the carcass will be about 200 pounds. Of this, about 20 percent will be ham, 20 percent loin, 15 percent belly, 10 percent picnic (a ham-like cut), 5 percent spareribs, and 5 percent butt.

Changes in the Hog Industry

Over the past 20 years, the hog industry has undergone some major innovations. Hog producers typically have hog factories, which are state-of-the-art facilities. They are made to minimize disease and to boost the size and grade of the hogs. The factories also protect the herd from adverse weather conditions.

The hog industry has also been sensitive to changes in the American diet. There has been a move to steadily reduce the fat component of hogs. At the same time, the National Pork Producers Council has been aggressive in promoting the benefits of this food.

The Effects of Feed Prices on the Price and Supply of Hogs

If the prices of the agricultural commodities used to feed the hogs increase, it will usually lead to higher hog prices. In fact, if feed prices are high, producers will usually increase the slaughter of hogs so as to lower costs. This is the same with the beef industry but the process tends to be quicker.

Supply and Demand for Hogs and Pork

The United States is the largest exporter of pork in the world. Interestingly enough, the largest amount goes to Japan. Other major importers include Canada, Mexico, Hong Kong, and China. To get a sense of the supply of hogs, an investor will analyze the inventory numbers. A big source of data comes from the United States Department of Agriculture (USDA), which is the federal agency that is responsible for the policies on farming, agriculture, and food. One of its divisions is the National Agricultural Statistics Service (NASS), which conducts hundreds of surveys every year and produces reports on many aspects of agriculture. A helpful survey is the Hogs and Pigs survey. It comes out on a quarterly basis and covers all 50 states. Another useful report from the NASS is the Livestock Slaughter report.

Hog Industry Trading

To predict futures prices, investors will try to estimate the number of expected hogs that will be slaughtered. One approach is to take the average of the slaughter to market numbers for the first and second quarters of the past five years. With this percentage, you will multiply it by the first quarter's inventory number. It's a rough calculation but tends to be accurate. But traders may want to adjust the number for exports and imports, as well as the death rate of the animals (usually 3 percent to 5 percent, depending on extreme weather conditions and so on). When it comes to investing in the hog industry, there are two main futures contracts: pork bellies and lean hogs.

Pork Bellies Futures Contract

A pork belly is the meat from the underside of a hog, with a weight of about 12 pounds. It is used for bacon. Pork bellies can be stored for up to a year before there is processing.

Trading was launched in 1961 on the CME and pork bellies were the first futures contract for frozen stored meats. The prices have seasonality, with the highest prices in the summer and the lowest prices in the spring, when inventories are large.

As for demand, it varies over a typical year. There is usually higher consumption during the summer months.

The problem of substitution affects demand. There are a variety of bacon-like products on the market that are made from turkey and other meats.

The product symbol for the pork bellies futures contract is PB. Each unit is for 40,000 pounds. The minimum price fluctuation is $0.0001, or $4 per contract. The trading months include February, March, May, July, and August.

However, over the past few years, trading in pork bellies has plunged and there are even indications that it will be shut down. Why? Keep in mind that frozen pork bellies were once important because of the changes in demand for bacon. During slow periods, such as during the winter, producers would store it. But over the years, bacon has become much more popular and less seasonal. As a result, the CME is now considering changing the futures contract to fresh pork bellies. This should ultimately lead to a revival in trading.[1]

Lean Hogs Futures Contract

A lean hog is actually a hog's carcass. About 50 percent of the production of lean hogs comes from China, 22 percent comes from the European Union, and 10 percent comes from the United States.

You can trade lean hogs on the CME, under the product symbol LH. The contract size is 40,000 pounds. The price fluctuation is $0.0001 per pound, or $4.00 per contract.

The contract is cash settled. Since it started to trade in 1997, the lean hogs contracts have been extremely volatile. A key reason is that the market is fairly illiquid and involves large commercial players. Another important driver is the outbreak of viruses. An example is the 2009 outbreak of swine flu. Because of the fears of consumers, the futures of lean hogs plunged.

---

[1] http://online.wsj.com/article/SB10001424052970204685004576046030368225052
.html?KEYWORDS=pork+bellies.

THE BEEF INDUSTRY

Listed below are the different aspects of the beef industry that influence the market.

The U.S. Beef Industry

Despite the health concerns, Americans still eat about 65 pounds of beef per year. Consider that this is the largest segment of the United States meat industry. But the market is saturated and the growth mirrors population increases. Of course, the big opportunity is in international markets, especially in Asia. As the wealth increases, so does the demand for protein.

The ranchers are in places like Texas, Kansas, Oklahoma, South Dakota, Montana, and Iowa. To grow a herd, a cattle rancher needs a certain amount of land for grazing, which is called the stocking rate. Often this varies based on weather. Where there is a large amount of rainfall, the stocking rate may be only five acres per cow-calf unit. But more arid climates may have a stocking rate of 150 acres.

The cattle ranch business is highly fragmented. Across the United States, there are 690,000 ranches, but about three-quarters of sales come from just 35,000 ranches.

Life Cycle of a Calf from Birth to Market

Let's take a look at the key elements of the beef market. A cattle rancher will breed cows to produce calves naturally or by artificial insemination. The latter approach has become more popular because it allows for improved genetics, which should mean better yields. In some cases, there will be a failure to conceive. If this happens, the cow will likely be taken to slaughter. The cull rate is anywhere from 15 percent to 25 percent of the herd.

Breeding typically occurs in August, which means the calves will be born in the spring. This is to avoid weather problems and ensure that there will be enough forage for the calves.

A cow will give birth to only one calf. After a calf is born, the cow will nurse it. But over the next couple of months, the calf will start eating grass and then grain.

In six to eight months, the calf is weaned and then placed into a stocker operation. This will last from six to ten months until the calf gets to 600 to 800 pounds.

Then it is time to put the calf into a feedlot, which is essentially an animal feeding operation. These may have thousands of livestock and are highly regulated, such as for environmental concerns.

When a calf reaches the feedlot, the calf is referred to as feeder cattle. The diet is now focused on the maximum weight gain. This involves a combination of grain, protein supplements, and roughage.

The feedlot stage can last from 90 days to 300 days. Why the wide range? The primary reason is weather. If it is unusually hot, then the animal will have a lower appetite. Cold weather, on the other hand, will mean that the animal will use food energy for heat. Yet in the feedlot stage, the animal will gain about three pounds per day. Once the animal is about 1,200 to 1,300 pounds, it is sent to be slaughtered and then transported to a packing plant or sold at an auction.

Supply and Demand for Cattle and Beef

For investors, predicting the supply of slaughtered cattle is some-what more difficult than for hogs. The reason is that there is more variation in the length of time from birth to slaughter. An inves-tor will first look at the Cattle on Feed report from the National Agricultural Statistics Service (NASS). It will have estimates for the number of cattle that has been placed in feedlots. From this, an investor can predict supply for the next four to five months, because this is the amount of time it will take until the cattle go to slaughter. But the report only accounts for 85 percent of the total. So an investor needs to use the following formula:

Feeder Placement Number / 85% = Market Supply

This should give an estimate of the number of cattle that will go to slaughter and reach the market. But it can vary. One main reason is the weather. Unusually cold or wet weather can extend the feedlot process.

At the same time, there should be adjustments for exports and imports. This is found in the Livestock, Dairy, and Poultry Situation and Outlook report from the Economic Research Service (ERS). Interestingly enough, there can be wide swings in exports. This could be from new tariffs or disease. For example, in 2003, there was a breakout of the mad cow disease. The result was a plunge in beef exports.

Herd Size and Beef Prices

Over the next decade, there may actually be a general increase in the price of beef. This is based on the analysis of Derrell Peel, who is a cattle expert at the Oklahoma State University Cooperative Extension. His main contention is that the total cow herd has been shrinking. True, part of the reason is that the industry has developed new techniques to increase the size of the animals. But this is not enough to make much of a difference over the long haul.

From 1990 to 2010, the size of the cow herd has gone from 32.5 million to 26.1 million head. Part of this was the result of the increase in slaughter rates because of feed prices. There have also been various droughts and breakouts of diseases.

Cattle and Beef Trading

For investors, there are ways to invest in beef and other livestock. One way is through an exchange-traded fund (ETF) such as the iPath Dow Jones–UBS Livestock (COW) ETF. It is a subset of the Dow Jones–UBS Commodity Index, where the live cattle futures contract represents 63 percent of the fund and the remaining is in the lean hogs futures contract.

But beware. The trading volume is light, with average daily volume of only 42,000 shares. Also, the performance has been lackluster. From 2005 to 2010, the average annual return came to −10.92 percent.

Instead, traders focus mostly on buying and selling futures when investing in livestock. The contracts include live cattle, feeder cattle, lean hogs, and pork bellies.

Live Cattle

When the CME introduced the futures contract on live cattle in 1964, it was a historic event. Until this time, an exchange would focus on only those commodities that are *stored*. But with live cattle, the commodity is still alive! It makes sense there was much interest in this type of contract. After all, a cow is a versatile animal. It does not move much and mostly eats grass. Of course, a cow is a big source of beef and even milk.

A rancher will usually breed a cow in the summer so that the calf is born in the spring, when the weather is moderate. There is then a regimented process, where the rancher will expedite the diet to produce the most weight. This is generally 1,200 pounds. At this point, the cow is ready for slaughter.

You can trade a live cattle futures contract on the CME, under the product symbol LC. The contract size is 40,000 pounds. The price fluctuation is $0.00025 per pound, or $10.00 per contract.

Feeder Cattle

Feeder cattle generally includes steers, which are castrated cows, as well as heifers, which are females that have not given birth. But there are usually many more steers. According to an old saying: "Feeders are the leaders." In other words, if prices of feeder cattle increase or decrease, there will eventually be the same impact on live cattle.

In 1971, the CME launched futures on feeder cattle. The underlying price is based on the seven-day average of an index, called the CME Feeder Cattle Index.

You can trade a feeder cattle contract on the CME, under the product symbol FC. The contract size for one unit is for 50,000 pounds (or about 60 animals). The minimum fluctuation is $0.0001, or $5.00 per pound. The trading months include January, March, April, May, August, September, October, and November.

CYCLES IN THE HOG AND BEEF INDUSTRIES

In terms of prices, the hog and beef industries tend to track each other in consistent cycles—which covers the peak and trough for inventory levels. For the hog market, the cycle is four years. The cycle is 10 to 12 years for the beef industry. The reason for the longer length of the beef industry is that it takes lots of time to raise female cattle.

When prices begin to increase, ranchers will want to hold onto females longer. This is the case for both cattle and hogs. This means fewer animals available for slaughter, which increases the price even more.

But eventually, a larger supply will come onto the market and prices will stabilize. When this happens, it gets expensive to hold onto females. So the rancher will cull the herd, which adds even more to the supply for slaughter.

INVESTING IN MEAT PRODUCERS

Investors can invest in a variety of meat producers. The main ones include Tyson Foods (TSN), Smithfield Foods (SFD), and ConAgra Foods (CAG). Their stock is traded on the New York Stock Exchange (NYSE).

There are factors that influence the value of the stock. If there is a general increase in livestock prices, these meat producers should benefit. However, these companies also need to buy large amounts of feed grains. If these agricultural commodities increase in price, there will be a squeeze on margins. Because of the volatility, profits can quickly plunge, which means that stock valuations are usually fairly muted for the sector.

One factor that impacts on grain prices is the use of corn for ethanol production instead of grain. In past years, the U.S. government encouraged this use for corn, but over the past couple of years, it looks like this policy has been waning.

There is usually a lag when it comes to higher input costs, such as grains. The reason is that by the time prices for grains have increased or decreased, a large amount of cattle are already prepared for slaughter. So it may take another year until there is an impact, when the breeding starts again.

A weaker U.S. dollar is a boost for meat producers. Because of their focus on exporting to the overseas markets, the meat products are likely to be more price competitive. But this could stir up some problems overseas. After all, countries like China could resort to quotas and tariffs to protect its own domestic producers.

Keep in mind that meat producers often have little pricing power. The reason is that they sell their products to major chains, like Walmart. But over the past decade, meat producers have been trying to improve things by introducing more premium brand offerings.

THE DAIRY INDUSTRY

Listed below are the different aspects of the dairy industry that influence the market.

The U.S. Dairy Industry

In the United States, the dairy business amounts to about $48 billion. The primary source is the milk from cows. However, some milk comes from goats and sheep. Unlike the United States, half of the milk consumption in India comes from water buffaloes. For the typical cow in the United States, a farmer will milk it two to three times a day throughout the year. Even though the agriculture industry has many regulations, the U.S. dairy industry is one of the most intensively regulated.

Dairy Cooperatives and Federal Price Supports

In terms of the industry, a typical dairy farmer will belong to a cooperative. This helps with pricing power, distribution, as well as managing shortages or oversupplies. The federal government has price support programs for cheese, butter, and milk. However, the federal government has also been gradually lowering the price supports over the years, which adds to the volatility. Because of this, there is certainly much interest in dairy futures.

Supply and Demand and Dairy Prices

Dairy prices are highly sensitive to changes in supply and demand. Just a 1 percent or 2 percent change can result in a swing in prices of over 50 percent. At the same time, there are usually pressures on high prices. The result is that there will be an influx of imports, which is the case even with tariffs and quotas.

A big problem for the dairy industry is that major retailers will deeply discount milk as a way to drive customer traffic. It appears to be a long-term trend, which will pressure margins for milk producers.

For investors, they will tend to focus on milk production. The rate of growth in the United States has averaged about 1 percent or so. But this can easily change based on weather, government programs, and the number of cows. Another factor is the use of genetics to improve the production of cows. In fact, some cows can generate over 20,000 pounds of milk per year.

Demand fluctuates throughout the year. For example, about 5 percent of milk is consumed at schools. So when classes are in session, the demand will tend to be higher.

Tracking the Dairy Industry

Investors can track the dairy industry by looking at several key reports. The one that gets the most attention is the Milk Production report, which is released by the federal government. It has the production levels for 20 states that account for 85 percent of the United States' milk. If there is a falloff from the prior year's numbers, then investors see this as a bullish sign. But if the production is 1 percent or higher, then prices may be poised for a drop.

The Agriculture Price report is also helpful because it has the milk-feed price ratio. This shows the relationship between the price of milk and the cost of cow feed. If the ratio is increasing, then it is becoming more profitable to produce milk and farmers are likely to increase production.

The Livestock Slaughter report is also useful. When there is an increase over the prior year, it should mean lower production—since there are fewer cows.

The Dairy Futures Contracts

The main contracts for dairy commodities include milk, butter, and dry whey. There are various contracts on milk, which are traded on the CME.

Cheese Milk Futures Contract

One is cheese milk (Milk Class III), which is mostly for cheddar cheese. It also has the largest amount of volume for the milk contracts.

Butter and Nonfat Dry Milk Futures Contract

Then there is butter and nonfat dry milk (Milk Class IV). Nonfat dry milk comes from the manufacturing of butter, which can be stored and reconstituted into milk. Butter is also placed into storage, which is done before the Christmas holidays. Butter requires roughly ten quarts of milk to produce one pound. The result is that butter tends to track the price of milk. Yet because of health concerns about cholesterol, butter consumption has been falling. Instead, there has been a shift to alternatives like margarine, which is based on vegetable oil.

Dry Whey Futures Contract

Dry whey is used in crackers, breads, and protein bars. It is even a good source of animal feed.

Dairy Company Stocks

While investors can invest in dairy companies, the options are fairly limited. Many of the operators are privately owned or traded on foreign exchanges.

But in the United States, the largest dairy processor and distributor is Dean Foods (DF), which is publicly traded on the New York Stock Exchange (NYSE). It has more than 50 brands that include WhiteWave-Morningstar, Silk, and Horizon Organic. The growth strategy of the company has been mostly through acquisitions. From 1994 to 2010, the company struck 40 transactions as sales went from $150 million to $11 billion.

THE EGG INDUSTRY

Below are the aspects of the egg industry that influence the market.

Supply and Demand for Eggs

In a modern-day farm, a chicken will lay 265 to 285 eggs per year. While the main purpose is for food, eggs also have some applications in medicine, such as vaccines.

In the United States, demand for eggs is about 1 percent per year. The average per capita consumption ranges between 248 to 258 eggs per year.

Feed Cost and Egg Prices

The major cost for the production of eggs is feed for the chickens. So the prices for corn and soybean meal will have a major influence on egg prices.

Investing in Egg Producers

There are no futures on eggs. Rather, investors will look at egg producers. While the market is fragmented, there are not many publicly traded companies. One of the few is Cal-Maine Foods.

When it comes to commodities investing, livestock and dairy often get little coverage. Yet it is a massive industry and is likely to see growth for the long haul. A big driver will be the increase in wealth in countries like India and China. The result will be changes in diets, which will affect food demand. In the next chapter, we will take a look at investing in miners and learn how to evaluate reserves.

CHAPTER 13

Investing in Miners

Key Concepts

- Understand the differences between juniors and major producers
- Evaluate reserves
- Learn how to research miners

TYPES OF MINING

There are two main types of mining, which depend on the type of resource being extracted. There is surface mining, which is also known as strip mining, and there is underground mining. Surface mining tends to be cheaper and uses fewer miners.

Surface Mining

With surface mining, there will be the use of massive earthmoving equipment to extract resources from soil and rocks. The next step usually involves the use of explosives, which unlocks the resources.

Underground Mining

The second type is underground mining. This requires drills to penetrate deep into the earth's crust. It will mean digging various tunnels and implementing systems to carry out the resources.

MINERS

Some of the biggest companies in the world are miners. The largest operator in the industry is BHP Billiton, which has a market capitalization of $258 billion. It has 40,990 employees across 25 countries and mines aluminum, energy coal, metallurgical coal, copper, manganese, iron ore, uranium, nickel, silver, and titanium minerals. BHP Billiton generates about $50 billion in revenues and $18.9 billion in operating cash flows.

Miners have also been good investments for commodities traders. In fact, investing in miners can also provide investors exposure to commodities that are not traded on futures exchanges. Examples include iron ore, potash, and metallurgical coal. However, when evaluating an investment, there are some specialized techniques and strategies.

EXPLORATION COMPANIES

The global mining industry is quite diverse. There are companies that mine for commodities like gold, silver, uranium, coal, potash, industrial metals, and diamonds. But mining usually does not involve non-renewable resources, like crude oil and natural gas. Despite this, the investment approaches explained in these chapters are also applicable to oil and natural gas company investments.

The mining process involves a variety of key steps. The first is for exploration of the resource. This often involves small companies, which have staffs of geologists. They will search around the world for potential rich deposits and use sophisticated equipment and drills to test them. It can easily take several years to find a location that shows positive results.

When deposits are found, the exploration company will issue a press release. Often there will be a spike in the stock price. But this can be misleading for investors. Drill results can often be off the mark.

It is not until the company issues a feasibility study that there is better confirmation that a deposit is economically viable. When this is the case, there will be another big move in the stock price.

Investing in Shares of Exploration Companies

Because of the huge profit potential, investors certainly like to specu-late in the shares of exploration companies. A large number of them trade on the Canadian TSX Venture Exchange and the Australian Stock Exchange. These markets are geared to the specialized needs of exploration companies and allow for quicker access to capital.

To be successful, an investor really needs to have a deep back-ground in the mining industry. Usually, this means being a geolo-gist and even visiting the mine. Unfortunately, most exploration companies fail and shareholders get wiped out. In a way, it's like investing in an Internet start-up. For every Facebook, there are thousands of others that go nowhere.

Despite this, there are a variety of newsletter writers and bloggers who claim they know the next big exploration company. Unfortunately, they often have little knowledge of the situation. Even worse, some are paid by the exploration companies they cover. This is certainly unethical and perhaps even illegal. But it is commonplace, especially for penny-stock exploration companies. The executives may actually be stock promoters, using hyped press releases and media appearances to give the impression of success. Yet the companies have little hope of generating any profits or even revenues.

Bre-X Minerals Ltd.

Perhaps some of the most notorious examples come from the gold industry. As Mark Twain once said, "A gold mine is a hole in the ground with a liar on top."

Consider a company called Bre-X Minerals Ltd., based in Calgary, Canada. Bre-X was focused on exploration in Kaliman-tan, Indonesia. The problem was that their land holdings had no gold. So management decided to manipulate the samples. Viola! The management claimed that Bre-X was sitting on one of the big-gest gold finds ever—with estimated reserves of about 200 mil-lion ounces. Wall Street went wild and so did the stock price. At the height, Bre-X reached a market value of $6 billion. Still, there were no revenues. Eventually, analysts found out that Bre-X was a massive fraud. Fairly quickly, the value of the company's shares became worthless.

PROSPECT GENERATORS

To deal with the risks of exploration companies, a new model has emerged for exploration. It is called the prospect generator. The company will bring in a financial partner, for which it will get a substantial percentage of the ownership in the property. The prospect generator will work on a variety of properties. Each property will have its own financial partner. In other words, this is a way to leverage capital and increase the odds of finding a rich deposit. If the property succeeds, the prospect generator will only get a fraction of the upside. Then again, it will not have to worry about going bust because several of its other properties failed.

Keep in mind that there are some drawbacks with the prospect generator. Often the first property will be a dud. Also, the financial partner may be slow in providing new capital. This could stunt the growth of the prospect generator. Another problem is that it is not easy to find financial partners. But, if a commodity market is showing strength, the process should be easier.

THE JUNIORS

A junior is a company that has gone beyond the exploration phase and has one or more producing properties. There is still a lot of risk. For example, the company's management may overspend or not adequately raise enough capital. Or, there may be political problems in the country or even injuries to the miners to deal with. Despite all this, a junior is still in an enviable position. This is especially the case if it is based in a relatively safe jurisdiction and has a deposit with substantial reserves. Because of the lower-risk profile, a junior is attractive to a large producer.

THE LARGE PRODUCERS

A large producer is a global mining company. Such a company has the tremendous resources necessary to construct a mine. This involves making large purchases for equipment like trucks, cranes, and drills. A large producer will need to hire miners, as well as get the necessary governmental permits. Most likely there will be a need to build infrastructure, such as housing and transportation facilities. Once everything is in place, the mining company will begin production. This could take several years to a decade, depending on the recoverable amounts.

When it comes to large producers, investors are seeking leverage. This means that a small increase in a commodity will have a much higher increase in profits.

To understand this, let's take a look at an example. XYZ Mining Corp. produces silver at a cost of $20 per ounce. With the current price of silver at $30, the profit is $10. Suppose that silver increases by $6 or 20 percent. This will mean that XYZ Mining Corp's profit margin will be 80 percent.

But leverage can also magnify losses. So if the commodity falls, the profits will suffer more—and so should the stock price.

In a way, leverage for miners is similar to the concept of beta. Beta is the relationship between the stock price of a company and the market. For miners, beta is the relationship between the stock price and the underlying commodity. With gold mining stocks, the beta is roughly 3. That is, a 1 percent increase in the gold price will result in a 3 percent increase in the stock price.

Something else to consider is that the profits of the large producers are cyclical or highly sensitive to the business cycle. For example, during the 2008–2009 global recession, many large producers saw plunges in their stock prices as commodities prices fell. So when investing in large producers, investors will buy aggressively when the economy is in the early stages of an economic expansion and may even short stocks when the economy starts to weaken.

Large producers also need to raise large amounts of capital. While part of this is from debt offerings, there is usually a sizeable amount raised from the issuance of new stock. In rising markets, investors tend to ignore this. But it is a real cost because of dilution of the existing amount of stock.

Evaluating a Large Producer

When considering an investment in a large producer, an investor will often look at several key areas. An important one is the cash cost. It is the cost of production—such as transportation, administrative, smelting, salaries, royalties, and environmental protections—at a mine per unit of output.

Cash costs can vary significantly from one company to the next. Part of the difference comes down to strong management capability. But other factors are beyond the management's capabilities. They include the political environment of a country, the infrastructure of the country and the mine, and the quality of the deposits. If a company has a cost structure that is volatile—compared to its peers—or is higher than the norm, then the valuation is likely to be muted.

Another issue is if a mine has by-products, which generate revenues. An example would be a copper mine that produces gold as a by-product. In this case, the value of the gold would be subtracted from the cash cost.

Because of the complexities, a company's cash costs can be far from perfect. In fact, there are a variety of quirks. For example, if the value of a by-product is fairly high, the cash cost may actually be negative! No doubt, this makes the metric somewhat suspect. So for investors, they still need to focus on the overall profitability of the operation.

Operating Profit Margin

One approach is to look at the operating profit margin, which is calculated as:

$$Operating\ Income\ /\ Sales = Operating\ Profit\ Margin$$

The operating income is a company's earnings *before* subtracting interest and taxes. By excluding these two numbers, it is easier to compare the metric to industry rivals. The reason is that each company is likely to have a different tax basis and debt structure.

If a large producer has an operating margin that is higher than the industry average, then this is an indication of the strength of management and the quality of the mines. But investors should look at the operating margins over several years. The industry can be quite volatile. With a healthy operating margin, a company will have more resources to invest back into its business. The result is that its lead is likely to increase even more.

Reserves

Another important consideration for investors is reserves. This is the amount of a resource that is still in a company's deposits. There are different types of reserves to consider.

- **Proven & Probable (P&P)**: These reserves are the most accurate and are based on third-party feasibility studies.
- **Measured & Indicated (M&I)**: These reserves have involved extensive analysis, but their accuracy is still somewhat uncertain.
- **Inferred**: These reserves have involved some analysis, but the reserve amounts are fairly speculative.

If the total reserve amount is known, then an investor can actually determine the viability of a company.

To understand this, let's take a look at an example. Suppose XYZ Mining Corp. has 100 million ounces of proven reserves of gold. If the company extracts 2 million ounces per year, then the company will be able to produce for 50 years.

What happens after this? In theory, the company will disappear. In fact, there are a variety of mining companies that have depleted a large amount of their reserves.

To increase reserves, a company has a variety of approaches. One is to invest in exploration. But for large producers, this is far from easy. These operators tend to have expertise in scaling operations, not engaging in speculative activities.

Another way to increase reserves is to search for new sources around an existing mine. This is known as brownfields exploration. All in all, this is quite effective. An advantage is that there is already an existing infrastructure to extract the resource.

But perhaps the most common way for large producers to get more reserves is to buy companies. Over the years, there has been a surge in mergers and acquisitions across the mining industry. The trend is likely to continue for some time.

Yet there are risks. Integrating two companies can be time-consuming and lead to culture clashes. But perhaps the biggest problem is the valuation of the purchase. A major producer will likely need to pay a large premium for an acquisition. If commodities prices continue to be healthy, this may not be a problem. But even a small drop in prices can make an acquisition unprofitable.

Interestingly enough, the rise in a commodity price can lead to increased reserves. How? Keep in mind that reserves are those deposits that are economical to extract. So with a higher price, this should make more reserves recoverable. At the same time, the higher price will likely incentivize more exploration.

VALUATION METRICS

The different approaches when valuing a stock are price-earnings ratio, market capitalization per ounce, net present value, and effect of supply and demand.

Price-earnings Ratio

Many investors will use earnings-based approaches when valuing a stock. One of the most common is the price-earnings ratio (P/E ratio), which is calculated as:

$$Stock\ Price\ /\ Net\ Income\ for\ the\ Past\ 12\ Months = Price\text{-}Earnings\ Ratio$$

The P/E ratio does have some drawbacks, though. The P/E ratio is backward-looking but investors are focused on the future. One tweak to the P/E ratio is the forward price-earnings ratio (P/E ratio). This is based on the forecast for net income for the next 12 months. An investor will then look at the P/E ratio and compare it to others in the industry. There will also be comparisons to different periods of time. For example, a P/E ratio is likely to be quite low during recessions and much higher during expansions. These metrics are certainly useful for miners.

Market Capitalization per Ounce

Investors will also rely heavily on valuing the assets of the company. After all, this is the prime source of profits. One approach is to calculate the market capitalization per ounce of the resource.

To understand this, let's take a look at an example. Suppose XYZ Mining Corp. has 100 million ounces in reserves of silver, which trades at $30 an ounce. This puts the value of the reserves at $3 billion. But XYZ Mining Corp. has a market cap of $1 billion.

In other words, if you bought the whole company, you would get $2 billion in reserves for free.

As with any valuation metric, the market capitalization per ounce metric has flaws. One of the biggest is that the calculation does not account for the time value of money. This means that a dollar is worth more now than getting one a year from now. In the case of XYZ Mining Corp., it will likely take many years to get revenues from the reserves.

Net Present Value

To account for the time value of money, an investor will use a sophisticated calculation called the net present value (NPV) method. The net present value is the current value of future cash flows from an asset, such as a mine. This is based on what an investment can get a return on for an alternative investment with similar risks. In the mining industry, this is usually 10 percent.

In theory, a mining company should trade at roughly the same value as the P/NPV, or the price divided by the net present value. But this is often not the case. Instead, the market value of the stock is usually at a premium. Why? Part of this could be from speculative activity. Although, this is probably only a factor for the short term. Rather, investors are expecting that a miner will eventually find more reserves. This could be from additional discoveries or acquisitions. Plus, there may be higher metal prices in the future.

Effect of Supply and Demand on Valuation

When computing a valuation, investors will try to gauge the overall supply and demand levels. Each commodity industry has its own information sources, as explained in Chapter 6. Investors want to be aware of difficulties in supply, while demand continues to grow.

Besides looking at industry statistics, investors will analyze the futures markets. If commercial operators are aggressively purchasing futures contracts, then the supply/demand profile is probably promising.

However, a large producer may still have problems. This is when a company's production starts to fall off. This could be due to difficulties with labor or governmental regulations, weather, or even the quality of the deposits. While a decline can be temporary, it is still a big red flag. If it persists, investors will probably sell shares.

ANALYZING THE FINANCIAL STATEMENTS

Throughout the year, public companies are required to make disclosures of their financials. These documents are typically long and complicated. But for investors, there are only a few that warrant much attention. These include the 10-Q, the 10-K, and insider transactions. Even if a company is based in another country, it will still need to make these disclosures if it is traded on the Nasdaq or the New York Stock Exchange (NYSE).

There are many places to get a company's financial disclosures. One of the easiest is from the company's website, which is usually in the Investor Relations area. Other helpful sources include Yahoo! Finance (finance.yahoo.com) and the website of the Securities and Exchange Commission (SEC)(www.sec.gov).

The 10-Q Filing

The "10-Q" filing reviews a company's results for the first, second, and third quarter. What about the fourth quarter? This is actually covered in the 10-K. A company must release the 10-Q within 35 days of the end of the quarter.

A key area to focus on is the Management's Discussion and Analysis (MD&A) section. This is management's description of recent trends and forecasts. Easy to understand, the MD&A provides a good overview of a company.

Of course, an investor will then look at the income statement, the balance sheet, and the statement of cash flows. Are revenues and profits increasing? Is the company generating more cash? Or are expenses starting to get bloated?

Other important sections to review include Legal Proceedings and Labor Negotiations. Are there are any new lawsuits or regulatory actions?

The 10-K Filing

The 10-K filing is a comprehensive disclosure for the full year. Like the 10-Q filing, you want to read the Management's Discussion and Analysis (MD&A), as well as look for trends in the balance sheet, the income statement, and the statement of cash flows. A company must file a 10-K within 60 days of the end of the year.

The 10-K is also audited. This involves a third-party accounting firm that examines a company's financials, procedures and even computer systems. The firm will conduct interviews with vendors and suppliers, as well as count inventory. An audit can be expensive and time-consuming, costing several million dollars. While an audit is far from foolproof, it is usually effective and is a protection for investors. If there are issues with the audit, then this is certainly a red flag.

Auditor's Report
An auditor's report will have several versions.

- **Unqualified or clean opinion:** This is the best opinion. This means that there are no known problems with the financials and that everything is in accordance with Generally Accepted Accounting Principles (GAAP). GAAP is the main standard for financial statement reporting.
- **Qualified opinion:** This opinion means that there are disagreements with management on material areas of the financials, and you should be wary.
- **Adverse opinion:** This opinion means that the auditor thinks the financials are misleading and has elected to disclaim the opinion and end its engagement.
- **Going concern opinion:** This opinion means that the auditor believes that the company will not have enough cash to operate. Unless there is a quick improvement in the business or a new round of financing, the outcome may be bankruptcy.

Often investors will confuse the 10-K filing with the annual report. But they are different. An annual report is much smaller and usually has glossy pictures. Despite this, it is still a useful document to get a better understanding of how the business works. There may be helpful charts and diagrams. Investors will also read the Chairman's Letter. It is a recap of the year and looks to the company's future prospects. Investors will look for words like challenging, difficulties, and restructuring. It is also a good idea to look at prior Chairman's Letters to determine if the company has followed through on its initiatives and projects.

INSIDER TRANSACTIONS

Savvy investors will analyze purchase and sale transactions of executives in their company's stock. After all, the executives have access to proprietary information. But isn't insider trading illegal? This is correct. Because of this, the federal government requires extensive disclosures of the transactions. Also, executives must hold on to their positions for at least six months to keep any profits.

In addition, executives must report these transactions. The law covers other insiders of a company. These include large shareholders, board members, and some key employees.

Insider transactions are disclosed on a variety of forms, which include Form 3, Form 4, Form 5, and Form 144. Websites like Yahoo! Finance consolidate these transactions and make them much easier to follow.

Insider Purchasing

Investors will look to see if insiders are making large purchases. Positive signs would be if there are several insiders that are making these transactions and that it has come after a period of little activity. Also, investors will look for transaction amounts that are two to three times an insider's existing position. These are definitely bullish signs indicating that there may be an eventual increase in the stock price.

Insider Selling

Insider selling may indicate just the reverse—there may be an eventual decrease in the stock price. Yet investors do not put as much weight on this. The reason is that there are many legitimate reasons for selling. Examples include gifts to children and relatives, diversification into other investments so as to lower the overall risk of the portfolio, contributions to charities, dividing assets for a divorce, and even paying for a large tax bill. In fact, some insiders will develop a plan where they sell a fixed amount every quarter.

But if three or four insiders suddenly sell large amounts, then this would be a red flag. Be wary if the sales represent 10 percent or more of an insider's current position.

DEBT AND LIQUIDITY RATIOS

Because large producers rely heavily on debt, investors will scrutinize the amounts. If the debt is too high or expensive, then a company may have a lower credit rating. The result is that it will be difficult for the company to raise more capital, which will likely crimp growth.

Debt-to-Equity Ratio

One common method to measure the levels of debt is the debt-to-equity ratio. Here's the formula:

$$Total\ Debt\ /\ Total\ Equity = Debt\text{-}to\text{-}Equity\ Ratio$$

Times Interest Earned Ratio

To get a better reflection of the leverage, an investor will include short-term and long-term debt. If the ratio is more than 70 percent, there should be some caution. The main reason is that it could be difficult to pay off the debt. To this end, an investor will look at a company's liquidity. An indicator to measure this is the times interest earned ratio. Here's the formula:

$$Earnings\ Before\ Interest\ and\ Taxes\ (EBIT)\ /\ Interest\ Expense = Liquidity$$

While it has some flaws, EBIT is a quick way to measure a company's cash flow. In fact, lenders will typically use this metric when extending loans. For example, a bank may require that a company maintain a ratio of 7. If this is not maintained, the company will be in default of the loan, which could cause a major drop in the stock price.

If a company is posting negative cash flows, an investor can measure the burn rate. This involves finding the average quarterly reduction in the cash balance and assuming it will continue at the current rate. In light of this, how long will it take for the company to run out of cash? If it is within two years, investors need to be wary.

Current Ratio

Investors may also use the Current Ratio to measure a company's liquidity. Here's the formula:

$$Current\ Assets\ /\ Current\ Liabilities = Liquidity$$

If the ratio is 2:1, then it is generally in a safe area.

TOXIC FINANCING

Because of the frequent capital raises, investors need to be wary of dilution when investing in mining companies. This is the reduction in the value of the ownership positions for existing investors. For smaller operators, they may have no choice but to use a toxic financing. This is when the cost of capital is extremely high, which typically results in a reduction in the stock price.

Private Investment in Public Equity

The most common structure of a toxic financing is private investment in public equity, known as a PIPE. Like any type of investment, it is not necessarily bad. However, it is often used for companies that are in desperation. A PIPE is the issuance of securities through a process called a private placement. Because of regulatory requirements, there are only a select number of institutional investors that can participate in the financing. They do not require as much disclosure, which makes the deals quicker to close.

However, an investor can get some of the main details in a filing known as an 8-K. Some of the red flags are listed below.

- **Warrants:** This gives the PIPE investor the right to buy
  more shares. The result is that there is more dilution.
- **Convertible Security:** This gives the PIPE investor the
  right to convert its security into common stock. If there is a
  reset feature, then the dilution can be substantial. In some
  cases, it is called a death spiral.
- **Liquidation Preference:** This gives the PIPE investor
  priority in the event of a liquidation. In some cases, it can
  actually wipe out common shareholders.

THE RISKS FACING MINERS

Miners certainly face several major risks. Some of the risks they
face are political instability, the worldwide commodity boom,
government regulation, global climate change, and environmental risks.

Political Instability

One of the most important risks is from the country where the mine
is located. While investors would like to have a company that has
operations in safe locations, this is unrealistic. The fact is that many
large deposits are in politically unstable areas. Because of this,
investors like to see that a large producer has a long history of dealing with these types of countries.

A prime example is Freeport–McMoRan Copper & Gold
(FCX). Through deft managerial skills, the company was able to
build a highly successful mine in Indonesia. After this was done,
Freeport-McMoRan then invested billions in a copper operation in
the Democratic Republic of the Congo. It could be one of the largest
producers of the commodity in over twenty years.

Even safe countries can pose many risks for large producers.
As profits start to rise, more countries are imposing special taxes
and fees. For example, in 2010, the Australian government declared
a 40 percent supertax on the miners. The goal was to help fund
public pensions.

This supertax was bad news for a variety of companies like BHP Billiton and Rio Tinto, which have large operations in the country. Their stock prices plummeted on the news.

Investors can find information on the stability of a country in the Survey of Mining Companies from the Fraser Institute (www .fraserinstitute.org). In the 2010 report, there was a focus on countries, like Quebec and Australia, which have increased taxes. There were also big drops in the rankings for countries like Russia and Kazakhstan.

The Worldwide Commodity Boom

Interestingly enough, even the worldwide commodity boom is a risk to miners. As demand increases—and prices surge—the industry needs highly qualified employees. However, mining skills have lagged over the years and it has become tough to find qualified employees. The result is that compensation levels have increased significantly. As of 2010, the highest rates were in Australia.

To deal with this, companies have been increasing their training programs. But another approach is to invest in new technologies. This will certainly be a boon for equipment providers like John Deere and Caterpillar Inc.[1]

Government Regulation

Another key risk for mining companies is government regulation. However, there can certainly be major differences from county to country. The laws in China and Africa tend to be relatively lax. But in the United States, this is not the case. The laws are extensive and span federal, state, and local jurisdictions.

The regulation coverage areas include discharge, employee health and safety, permits, storage requirements, air standards, reclamation, and materials management. Violations of these rules can result in fines, cease-and-desist orders, and even criminal sanctions.

---

[1] http://online.wsj.com/article/SB10001424052748704543004576052202890106490 .html?mod=WSJ_hp_LEFTTopStories.

Global Climate Change

Perhaps one of the biggest liability concerns for mining companies is global climate change. Because of fossil fuel combustion, it appears that the average temperature is increasing. No doubt, this could lead to significant environmental damage. President Obama and members of the U.S. Congress have pushed initiatives to regulate carbon emissions. But so far, nothing has passed.

Yet it appears that many other countries will eventually implement their own rules. The result will be higher costs for mining companies. One of the biggest to be impacted would be coal. The industry accounts for 30 percent of carbon emissions.

Environmental Risks

The coal industry pose some of the largest risks to the environment. You can usually find the lawsuits and other problems in a company's financial statements in the section called Contingencies.

One company that has faced lawsuits is Massey Energy, one of the largest coal companies in the United States. One lawsuit was for claims that the company contaminated water wells because of improper slurry injection and impoundment practices from 1978 to 1987. Some of the alleged problems resulting from the alleged contamination include neurological injury, cancers, gallstones, and kidney problems.

On April 5, 2010, the infamous explosion at the Upper Big Branch mine, another Massey Energy mine, resulted in 29 deaths of miners. In fact, it was the worst mining disaster in the United States since the late 1960s. It is too soon to evaluate the damages. But they are likely to be large. As a result, Massey Energy has been seeking a buyer.

ROYALTY COMPANIES

The volatility of miners can be too stomach-churning for many investors. But there is an alternative: royalty companies. These companies provide upfront financing for miners to engage in the exploration and extraction of the deposits. For this, the royalty company will get an ongoing percentage of the revenues. If the reserves are substantial, the fees can continue for decades. Notable examples include Royal Gold (RGLD) and Silver Wheaton (SLW).

Benefits and Risks of Royalty Companies

Buying the shares of a royalty company can be a cost-effective way to hold a commodity. There are no storage or insurance costs. A royalty company also does not engage in any complex derivatives or leverage. Another benefit is that the costs are mostly fixed.

Consider that Silver Wheaton has long-term fixed contracts to purchase silver at only $3.90 per ounce. So if there is a price spurt in the commodity, the profits will soar.

But there are certainly risks. Because of the requirements to provide large amounts of capital, a royalty company may have a significant amount of debt. In the early years, this could reduce cash flows. If a mining property fails to generate enough royalties, it could pose the risk of a debt default.

As seen in this chapter, there are different types of miners for investors. For those looking for higher returns, there are many exploration companies. But if an investor wants to reduce the risk levels, there are strong larger producers. In the next chapter, we will look at the benefits and risks in investing global commodities, and learn about foreign futures exchanges.

CHAPTER 14

Global Commodities Investing

Key Concepts

- Look at the benefits and risks of investing in foreign markets
- Analyze the foreign futures exchanges
- Learn how to invest in foreign markets

A legend in global investing is Mark Mobius. Now an executive chairman of Templeton Asset Management, he researches investments in 15 emerging economies. But he does not sit in an office. Instead, he spends much of his time visiting countries. While it can be stressful, it has resulted in strong long-term profits for investors.

Mobius even has a blog (mobius.blog.franklintempleton.com), where he writes about his travels. On one post, he described what it was like to go down a mine shaft in the middle of the Kazakhstan steppes. He had to get a safety briefing and wear a mining outfit, with an oxygen container. Of course, to be a successful commodities investor, you do not have to visit far-off countries. But it is still important to have an understanding of foreign markets, such as their stock and futures exchanges.

THE REWARDS AND RISKS OF FOREIGN INVESTMENTS

The rewards and risks of foreign investments, which are listed below, are access to international miners and commodities, diversification, political instability, and changes in currency.

Access to International Miners and Commodities

As we've seen in this book, the commodities market is international. So if investors want to benefit from the growth, it is a good idea to look at foreign markets. Some of the best miners are in countries like Canada, Russia, Australia, and China. In some cases, there are certain commodities that are traded only on foreign futures exchanges.

Diversification

Diversification is another important benefit to investing in foreign companies. Keep in mind that the U.S. markets and the foreign ones do not necessarily move in the same direction. After all, each economy has its own dynamics.

If anything, emerging market economies have shown tremendous growth over the past 20 years. A big part of the growth has been from commodity demand.

But the diversification is not foolproof. If the United States has major problems—such as in 2008 to 2009—the impact is likely to spread around the world. So on a temporary basis, diversification may not happen.

Political Instability

One of the major risks to investing in foreign countries is political instability. Emerging economies are vulnerable to coups, wars, and social unrest. The result can be devastation for investors.

Just consider the revolutionary protests in Egypt in early 2011. Because of the protests, the country's stock exchange plunged 20 percent and had to be shutdown for a period of time.

So before investing in another country, it is a good idea to get a sense of the political environment. One helpful resource is the CIA World Factbook. Information can be found at https://www .cia.gov/library/publications/the-world-factbook/docs/refmaps .html. It provides in-depth analysis on over 100 countries.

Change in the Currency

Another key risk for foreign investments is a change in the currency. When investing in a foreign company, there will need to be the purchase of the country's currency to buy the shares. So after the purchase, there is likely to be fluctuations in the currency relative to the U.S. dollar.

Exchange Rates

To avoid mistakes, an investor will need to understand exchange rates. Keep in mind that the market for currencies is the world's largest, transacting on a seven-day, 24-hour basis. Trading volume is about $4 trillion daily.

There is no central exchange. Instead, currencies are traded directly among buyers and sellers in the Over-the-Counter market. The current price of a currency is known as the spot rate. It is the value relative to another currency.

To understand this, let's take a look at an example. Suppose that the exchange rate for the dollar is 1.50 euros. This means that for each dollar you will get 1.50 euros. If you divided this by one— or 1 divided by 1.50—then each euro is converted into .666 dollars.

Currency Appreciation and Depreciation

Investors need to understand currency appreciation and depreciation. This is the increase or decrease between two currencies. Suppose the dollar exchange rate goes from 1.50 euros to 1.60 euros. In this case, the dollar has appreciated because it will get *more* euros. The reverse would be a depreciation in the dollar.

If you invest in foreign markets, you actually want the foreign currency to appreciate. The reason is that when you sell your investment, you will get more dollars back.

To understand this, let's take a look at an example. Suppose you purchase ABC Mining Corp., which is based in Brazil. The share price is 10 real. It takes one dollar to buy 1.50 reals. So to purchase 1,000 shares, it takes 10,000 reals, or $6,666.66.

A few months go by and the stock price remains at 10 real. However, the currency has increased in value. One dollar now buys 1.40 reals. This means that your investment is now worth $7,142.85.

As you can see, your investment can stay in place—or even fall—in value on the stock exchange, but you could still have a gain because of a favorable currency move. Of course, a depreciation in the foreign currency has the opposite impact. Does it make sense to try to hedge this volatility? Some investors try this but it can be complicated and even expensive. Besides, one of the benefits of foreign investments is to diversify your home currency into other country's currencies.

Currency Pegging

Investors also need to realize that some foreign currencies are not freely traded on markets. Rather they are pegged to another currency, and trade within a certain band. This is the case with the Chinese yuan, which is pegged to the U.S. dollar.

Currency Controls

Investors also need to be aware of currency controls. Basically, this is when a government prevents investors from taking their money out of the country. No doubt, this can be a big problem for foreign investors, who may want to get ready access to their cash.

In late 2006, the government of Thailand was worried about the increase in its currency, the Thai baht. So it imposed various currency controls. However, the move rattled investors and the Thailand stock exchange crashed 15 percent. Realizing that it was a wrongheaded policy, the government quickly reversed its policy.

HOW TO INVEST IN FOREIGN MARKETS

Interestingly enough, an easy way to participate in foreign markets is to buy shares in U.S. multinational companies. Firms like Freeport-McMoRan, Alcoa Inc., and others have extensive global footprints. While there is nothing wrong about investing in these companies—it is a good strategy—it is still not like investing in foreign companies. Buying a multinational will give you broad exposure in many markets. Plus, the stock values are likely to mirror the U.S. averages and economy.

But if you buy a miner in Canada, Australia, or even China, your investment will certainly be different. You will have a different management team and even benefit from the advantages these companies have in their home market. The good news is that investors have many ways to invest in foreign markets.

Mutual Funds and Exchange-Traded Funds

One of the easiest ways to invest in foreign markets is through mutual funds and exchange-traded funds (ETFs). These provide diversification because they invest in *many* companies. They also have professional managers who can monitor the portfolio on a day-to-day basis. The fees are reasonable and it is not difficult to buy and sell shares.

American Depositary Receipts

Another approach is to invest in American depositary receipts, or ADRs. These are foreign companies that are publicly traded on the New York Stock Exchange (NYSE) or the Nasdaq. Purchasing ADRs is no different than buying or selling any other stock. In fact, there are over 2,000 ADRs available. ADRs have been around since the 1920s and were created in response to the difficulties individual investors had in participating in foreign markets.

With this structure, a bank will buy a bulk of a company's securities on a foreign exchange and then list them in the United States. The bank will handle all of the fees, the dividend payments, and the currency conversions.

ADRs must abide by the stringent U.S. federal securities laws. This means that investors can get detailed access to a foreign company's financial statements and other disclosures.

There is a special type of ADR, the Level 1 ADR, which means that the foreign company does not want it to be listed on an exchange. In other words, there will be little disclosure and the trading will be on the Over-the-Counter (OTC) Bulletin Board or the Pink Sheets, which is a market that has few requirements for listing a company's shares. These markets can be quite volatile and have low amounts of liquidity.

HOW TO MAKE DIRECT INVESTMENTS IN FOREIGN STOCK MARKETS

Two ways to make direct investments in foreign stock markets are setting up an American brokerage account and setting up a foreign brokerage account.

Set Up an American Brokerage Account

When investing in foreign stock markets, one method is to set up a brokerage account at a U.S. firm. Over the years, a variety of online brokers—like E*TRADE, Charles Schwab, and Interactive Brokers—have provided trading in foreign markets. They make it fairly easy and handle the complicated details, such as converting currency.

But there are drawbacks to using a U.S. broker. Consider that the U.S. brokers cater only to the larger markets. This can certainly limit your investment opportunities. Another issue is that the fees can be high. It's not uncommon for a brokerage to add 1 percent to 2 percent to the bid-ask spread. There may also be monthly account fees, say for $20. In fact, sometimes a broker will not purchase the stock on a foreign exchange, but instead make the purchase in the Over-the-Counter (OTC) Bulletin Board. As seen earlier in this chapter, this market can be highly illiquid.

Set Up a Foreign Country Brokerage Account

Another approach is to set up a brokerage account in the country where the stock exchange that you want to trade on is based. While this seems forbidding—and risky—it has become much easier.

The prevalence of the Internet has been a big help. Often there are foreign brokerage exchanges that have online platforms that allow overseas investors to place their trades and monitor their positions. There will also likely be access to helpful research reports (this is usually not the case for the U.S. brokers).

Find Names of Brokers

The first step in finding a good broker is to check the Internet. For example, if you want to locate a firm in Australia, you can enter into Google the following query: "brokerage firms Australia." In many cases, the first page should provide the highest quality firms. Then you can do a further Google search on several of the firms. Are there complaints? Or good reviews?

Research the Brokers

You should also get a sense of the financial stability of the broker. This is possible if the firm is publicly traded on the exchange.

Check out the financials. Has the firm been growing? Has the firm been paying dividends? Has the cash balance been increasing?

Another way to gauge the stability of the firm is to check out the country's stock exchange and see if the broker is a member. If so, the foreign broker has likely met some stringent requirements.

Contact the Foreign Brokerage Firms

After you have narrowed your list, contact the brokerage firms. Is the website in English? Do several of the brokers speak English? What are the fees? How comprehensive is the market data? Are there trading tools?

Check to see if you can engage in short selling. This essentially allows you to make money when the value of a stock falls. It's done by borrowing shares and immediately selling them on the market. Then you will later buy the shares, hopefully at a lower price. If so, you will make a profit. Short selling can be an effective tool for any investor.

Foreign Brokerage Account Application and Set-up Fees

When you have decided on a firm, you will then fill out an account application. It will probably look similar to the ones you've seen in the United States. That is, you will need to provide your personal information, investment background, and goals.

It can take a couple of days to process the form because of the time differences. But once your account is approved, you will need to wire money into the account. There will likely be a minimum amount. You will also need to pay a wire fee to your bank, which can be about $40. Interestingly enough, a foreign broker will give you an option to denominate your account in various currencies. Of course, this will be dependent on the firm's location.

Set Up Foreign Bank Account

You may need to get a bank account in the foreign country that you will be trading. This is especially the case with the dividend payments. If not, the company will send the check to you. The problem is that your local bank will probably not cash it in.

Setting up a local bank account is not time-consuming. But just like with your brokerage account, you should do an online search before selecting a bank. Actually, a foreign bank account can be a way to generate higher returns. After all, the interest rates may be higher.

Even though investing through foreign brokers and banks is fairly straightforward, there may still be problems. Just as with any financial institution, there could be clerical errors or other mishaps. So long as you are persistent, it should be resolved. But it could still take awhile, at least compared to the United States.

Foreign Income and Taxes

Dealing with tax payments on foreign income can be difficult, though. The Internal Revenue Service (IRS) does not care what country the profits come from. The IRS taxes worldwide income.

If you have foreign accounts over $10,000, you will need to file Form TD90-22. It is actually an easy form to fill out.

However, when computing your taxes, this can be extremely difficult. Some countries will tax your earnings and some will not. Some countries will even pay an additional dividend to makeup for the taxes taken out. Or, there may be a tax credit. So it is important to get a tax professional to sort out these matters.

Financial Disclosures

It is common for financial disclosures from foreign brokers to be released every six months, not on a quarterly basis as in the United States. The fact is that U.S. investors tend to be short-term oriented.

A foreign-company financial disclosure may also be much shorter than what you will see with a 10-Q filing or a 10-K filing. The accounting principles may not conform to GAAP, or Generally Accepted Accounting Principles. Instead, they are likely to conform to the International Financial Reporting Standards (IFRS). This is not a problem since this set of rules is highly regarded.

Corporate Structure and Holding Companies

The corporate structure of a foreign company can be complicated. The reason is that the foreign brokerage firms may have diverse interests in different types of companies. To facilitate this, the firms will often have holding companies, which own these divisions.

Differences in Spelling, Language, and Social Conventions

One area of confusion is with the expression of common conventions. For example, some countries may express decimals with a comma and thousands with decimals. This would look like $1.000,00 instead of $1,000.00.

Some key terms are used instead of American terms. Various countries use the word *turnover* instead of the word *revenues*.

Due to cultural differences or inexperience with public companies, communicating with foreign brokers and managers could lead to confusion or misinformation. In terms of finding information, the Web is definitely a tremendous resource. You might also want to read local foreign newspapers and publications, which can be excellent sources to get new foreign investment prospects.

THE FOREIGN STOCK MARKETS AND EXCHANGES

When investing in a foreign stock market, it is important to focus on those exchanges that provide substantial liquidity. This is the ability to sell a security without suffering a loss in the trade because it is difficult to find a buyer. There are some exchanges that have a small number of shares and the trading volume is fairly light. While there may be some good opportunities in these markets, the valuations can be expensive, because of the high markups. Keep in mind that these markets can also be vulnerable to crashes and even suspensions of trading.

The Structure of a Foreign Stock Market

No doubt, the structure of a foreign stock market may be different. Consider that some countries prefer small-priced stocks. This gives the impression that they are more affordable. Even a high-quality company may be trading at penny-stock levels.

Some exchanges may require board lots. Essentially, this is a minimum amount of shares that must be bought or sold per transaction.

Even the stock symbols may different. In some countries, they are in the form of numbers! For example, HSBC is traded under the symbol of 0005 on the Hong Kong exchange.

Something else to consider is the Initial Public Offering, or IPO. This is when a company issues stock to the public for the first time. In the United States, it can be difficult to get allocations of the IPOs. But this is not necessarily the case in foreign markets.

By getting an IPO in a foreign market, you will probably get the shares at a lower valuation. Besides, this is a company that is in the early stages of development and offers much growth potential. In the commodities markets, many of the IPOs would be for exploration and junior miners.

Let's now take a look at some of the major stock and futures exchanges across the world.

Australian Stock Exchange

The Australian Stock Exchange (ASX) is fairly young, with its founding in 1987. It was actually the result of a merger of six stock exchanges, which had their roots back in the nineteenth century. In 2006, the ASX merged with the Sydney Futures Exchange.

The ASX is the eighth largest stock exchange in the world. The total market value is about $1.3 trillion and there are 2,216 listed companies. About 23 percent of the value is from resources stocks. The website is www.asx.com.au.

Australia has experienced strong growth over the years. It is ranked as the fourteenth largest economy in the world. It is the fourth largest economy in the Asia-Pacific region. Australia has a thriving resources sector, such as in iron ore and copper. It helps that the country is relatively close to China and Japan.

Toronto Stock Exchange

Founded in the 1850s, the Toronto Stock Exchange (TSX) is one of the top exchanges for miners. In 2001, the exchange purchased the Canadian Venture Exchange, which was renamed the TSX Venture Exchange. Its website is www.tmx.com.

The market allows for the issuance of early-stage companies. Because of this, there are over 1,000 commodity exploration companies on the exchange. In fact, the TSX has 55 percent of the world's mining company listings and 35 percent of the world's energy company listings. The TSX also owns the Natural Gas Exchange (NGX). It's a leading market for trading and clearing in natural gas and electricity contracts.

Canada's economy, which has a rich resources base, has generated strong growth over the past decade. The economy also has a low amount of government debt and the corporate taxes rates are fairly low.

Santiago Stock Exchange

The Santiago Stock Exchange (SSE) is the main stock exchange in Chile. Founded in 1893, the SEE trades equities, options, futures, and even gold and silver coins. The total market value of the listed companies is about $128 billion. The website for the SSE is www.bolsadesantiago.com/web/bcs/home.

Chile has a population of 16.6 million people and the government is one of the most stable in South America. The economy has also been fairly steady over the past 30 years, with a conservative fiscal policy and an open policy on trade. Then again, Chile benefits tremendously from its copper mines. CODELCO, or Corporación Nacionel del Cobre, is the largest mining company in the world.

Russian Trading System

The Russian Trading System (RTS) was the first stock market in Russia and was created in 1995. Modeled on the Nasdaq, the marketplace is fully electric. The RTS has been quite volatile over the years. Also, the Russian government has intervened from time to time. The website for RTS is www.rts.ru/en/.

Russia has a population of 141.9 million and a gross domestic product (GDP) of about $1.23 trillion. Some of its major natural resources include petroleum, natural gas, precious metals, and timber. Russia is also rich in grain and dairy products.

Bombay Stock Exchange

Founded in the 1850s, the Bombay Stock Exchange (BSE) is the oldest in Asia. It has seen much evolution over the years, with the market going electronic in the mid-1990s. Actually, it was the first to provide for Internet trading. Then in 2000, the BSE introduced futures trading. Options were launched a few years later. The total market value of the BSE is about $1.6 trillion. It is the fourth largest exchange in Asia. The website is www.bseindia.com. India has a population of 1.2 billion and a GDP of $4 trillion. In 2010, the economy grew about 8.4 percent.

Bolsa de Valores, Mercadorias & Futures de São Paulo

The Bolsa de Valores Mercadorias & Futures de São Paulo (BM&FBOVESPA) came about through the merger of the Brazilian Mercantile & Futures Exchange (BM&F) and Sao Paulo Stock Exchange (Bovespa). The exchange trades stocks, foreign currencies, and various agriculture commodities like corn, live cattle, and soybeans. The exchange is electronic and has a value of $1.3 trillion. Once owned by the Brazilian government, it is now a for-profit organization. The website for BM&FBOVESPA is www.bmf.com.br.

Brazil's GDP is $2.2 trillion, which was up 7.5 percent in 2010. The country is also rich in resources, such as with oil, lumber, coffee, sugarcane, and iron ore.

London Metal Exchange

The origins of the London Metal Exchange (LME) go back to 1571, when Elizabeth I was queen. Traders in metals came together frequently to conduct business. As the British empire expanded across the globe, there was a tremendous increase in trade, which required sophisticated exchanges. Over the years, the LME has continued to grow and add new product offerings. Although the main focus is on metals, with a long history of trading in copper and tin.

The LME generates a tremendous amount of volume, with an annual market value of $7 trillion. This amounts to about $29 billion per day. The exchange is also global, with about 95 percent of business coming from foreign investors. The futures contracts on the LME include:

- Non-ferrous metals, including aluminum, aluminum alloy, copper, lead, zinc, nickel, and tin
- Minor metals, including cobalt and molybdenum
- Steel
- Gold
- Plastics, including linear low-density polyethylene and polypropylene

The exchange's website is www.lme.com.

Shanghai Futures Exchange

Founded in 1998, the Shanghai Futures Exchange (SHFE) was the result of a merger between the Shanghai Metal Exchange, the Shanghai Cereals and Oil Exchange, and the Shanghai Commodity Exchange. In fact, it was not until 1990 that China reopened its various commodities exchanges, so as to allow for economic development. The SHFE has been growing at a rapid rate, tripling its volume from 2008 to 2009. The exchange is now ranked the sixth largest stock exchange in the world.

The most popular contract on the SHFE is the Fuel Oil Futures. But the exchange also has a thriving business in copper, aluminum, and natural rubber. In fact, the SHFE is now the top metals exchange in Asia.

Keep in mind that much of the trading comes from domestic investors. So as China loosens its restrictions on foreign investment, there is likely to be a tremendous flood of capital into the exchange. This is likely to be the case with other futures exchanges in China, such as the Dalian Commodity Exchange (which trades oils like soy and palm) and Zhengzhou exchange (which focuses on plastics).[1]

---

[1] http://www.theaustralian.com.au/business/news/china-ranked-no1-in-world-commodity-exchanges/story-e6frg90o–1225850743531.

The main contracts for the SHFE include copper cathode, aluminum, zinc, gold, steel rebar, steel wire rod, fuel oil, and natural rubber. The website for SHFE is www.shfe.com.cn/Ehome/index.jsp.

Shanghai is the most populous city in the world, with roughly 23 million people. It is located on the eastern coast of China and has become a power in commerce and finance.

Tokyo Commodity Exchange

Futures trading got its start in Osaka, Japan, during the seventeenth century. The original contracts were on rice. At the time, rice was actually used as payment to the samurai. Although, the futures exchange had many problems. When there were food shortages, there was usually blame for the traders.

Japan continues to be a global leader in futures, with the Tokyo Commodity Exchange (TOCOM). However, over the years, the market influence has been diminishing. Of course, the exchanges in China are starting to get traction.

To help to improve things, TOCOM has actually liberalized its rules on participation of foreign brokers. This should improve trading volume and liquidity. The main contracts on the TOCOM include gold, silver, palladium, gasoline, kerosene, gas oil, crude oil, Chukyo gasoline, Chukyo kerosene, and rubber. The website for TOCOM is www.tocom.or.jp/index.html.

TAX HAVENS

When looking to invest in overseas markets, some investors want to find tax havens. These are jurisdictions—like the Bahamas or Switzerland—that have banking secrecy laws. The belief is that this will allow for tax-free investments.

However, the IRS and the Justice Department have been cracking down on these offshore tax havens. A prime example is the agreement to compel UBS to disclose the names of over 4,000 U.S. citizens who were in violation of U.S. tax laws. They were subject to a full-blown audit unless they provided voluntary disclosure. Interestingly enough, over 18,000 U.S. citizens did this, which has resulted in a windfall of tax revenue.[2]

---

[2] http://www.irs.gov/newsroom/article/0,,id=231520,00.html.

As seen in this chapter, it is important to understand global economics and trends when investing in commodities. The fact is that many of the opportunities are from companies in places like China, Brazil, Canada, and Russia. In the next chapter, we will take a look at buying physical commodities, including bars and coins.

CHAPTER 15

Buying Physical Commodities

Key Concepts

- Look at the different ways for physical ownership of commodities
- Analyze the market dynamics for owning bullion bars and coins
- Understand the rare coins market

For some investors, the best approach is to own the physical commodity. True, this is not practical for some metals, like copper and uranium. Yet there are certain commodities that have been perennial holdings for investors. These are usually the precious metals, which include gold, silver, platinum, and diamonds.

WHY PHYSICAL OWNERSHIP OF COMMODITIES?

While often dismissed as being paranoid, the gold bugs are people who believe that you should physically own precious metals. One reason is that gold and silver have intrinsic value and can be used as a currency, especially in the event of the breakdown of the world economic system. But other investors own precious metals by purchasing rare coins. Over the long term, this has proven to be a lucrative investment.

When buying a precious metal, you need to find a place to store it. One approach is to get a vault. Because precious metals are fairly small, you do not need a large one. Some believe it is important that a vault be earthquake-proof and even have a security system. You should have the vault in a place that is hard to detect, such as beneath the floor. Remember that it's important that the precious metals retain their qualities and not get tarnished. To this end, there are specialized canisters for this. You should also purchase insurance.

Another approach is to store your gold at a bank, such as in a safety deposit box. There are also security holding companies, like GoldSilver.com, which provide storage options as well as bullion dealers.

However, some gold bugs think this is a bad idea since a bank may go under, making it difficult to get to your gold or silver. Keep in mind that during the 1930s, President Roosevelt made gold ownership illegal. So if this happens again, then having gold at a bank could make it vulnerable to seizure.

As should be no surprise, there are many interesting stories about how people have stored precious metals. One is Ted Binion, who was the heir to Binion's Horseshoe casino in Las Vegas. After his death in 1998, law enforcement authorities found a 12-foot deep vault in a desert area in Nevada. It had six tons of silver bullion, 100,000 rare coins, and Horseshoe chips. No doubt, there were suspicions about his death. His wife and her lover were charged with murder, but they were later acquitted.

JEWELRY

As an investment in precious metals, jewelry is typically the wrong approach. When bought at a retail store, there are usually high markups, which can be 200 percent to 300 percent or more.

Yet some people will convert their existing jewelry for cash, which has been popular over the years. The problem is that the jewelry's gold content is likely fairly small. In fact, there may be little value, especially in light of the low valuation from the store. The discounts are especially deep for karat weights of 20 or lower.

A karat shows the fineness of gold, with each karat representing 1/24 part of pure gold. So 24 karat gold would be 100 percent gold.

Interestingly enough, some stores provide you with packets in which you can send your gold jewelry through the mail. Obviously, this can be risky. What if the store is really a scam?

Instead, it may be worth more selling the jewelry as is. Consider that there is a market for well-crafted designs, such as through online marketplaces, like eBay, or local jewelry stores. These are usually better options than pawn shops.

To this end, you can get the jewelry appraised. Reputable places include the National Association of Jewelry Appraisers and the American Society of Appraisers. Fees can be several hundred dollars or more.

BULLION

Bullion is a common method for investors to benefit from the rise in value of precious metals. This is a pure form of a metal, with a minimum of 99.5 percent. Bullion is in the form of coins or bars, which have serial numbers. As for the coins, they have no numismatic value. This means they do not have any qualities like being rare. As a result, bullion coins tend to have little markup to the underlying precious metal value, say 1 percent to 3 percent or so. This makes bullion attractive to investors.

An investor can also buy bullion bars for gold, silver, and platinum. But the two most common ones are for gold and silver. In fact, with gold, there are roughly 20 or so sizes for bullion bars, which range from one ounce to 100 ounces. Thus, it is possible for investors to buy smaller amounts.

Investors will invest in those bullion bars that are fairly standardized, such as the 100-ounce versions. These have high amounts of trading volume, which translates into lower markups.

There are also ingots, which are bars with some type of design. Because of this, they often sell at a premium to bars.

Bullion Coinage

Types of bullion coins include gold coins, silver coins, and platinum and palladium coins.

The Background of U.S. Coinage

Before looking at the bullion coinage market, let's first take a look at the background of coinage. It was President George Washington who signed the first coinage Act in 1792. Before this, trade was conducted by barter or various foreign currencies. But to allow for the growth in commerce, there was a need for a national currency. To do this, the federal government established the United States Mint. Some of the first coins included the $10 Gold Eagle, $1 dollar silver coins, silver dimes, copper pennies, and even half cents. The coinage was based largely on the Spanish system of reales.

As the price of gold increased, Congress passed new coinage acts to adjust the value of the currency. The goal was to keep a consistent ratio between the value of silver and gold. Interestingly enough, the coinage acts caused some controversy with silver miners. They believed the ratio undervalued their silver reserves.

The U.S. government eventually moved to the gold standard, which further devalued silver. Another important development was in 1965. This is when Congress passed the Coin Act, which phased out silver for various coins because of the depletion of the stockpiles. In place of silver, future coins would have zinc, nickel, and copper.

Government mints create bullion coins. Because of this, bullion coins might be guaranteed to be authentic—so there is no need to get an assay, which is a way to determine the quality—and even considered legal tender. This means you can use it as a currency. There are many bullion coins available for investors. However, it is important to focus on the common ones because there is more liquidity.

Gold Coins

The most popular coin in the United States is the American Eagle, which came out in 1986. It is 22 karat gold and the design is based on the $20 gold eagle by the artist Augustus Saint-Gaudens (who was a favorite of President Teddy Roosevelt). An American Eagle is available in the following sizes: one ounce (the most common), half-ounce, one-quarter ounce, and even one-tenth ounce.

Another sought-after coin is the Krugerrand, which first hit the market in 1970. Also 22 karat gold, this is from the South African government. Krugerrands are the most plentiful bullion coins in the world. Because of this, they generally have the lowest premiums.

Then there is the Canadian Maple Leaf, which is from the Royal Canadian Mint. It is 24 karat gold.

The American Buffalo is also 24 karat gold. It has been in lower demand than the American Eagle. However, the popularity of the American Buffalo has increased over the past couple years as more investors buy gold bullion coins. It comes from the U.S. Mint at West Point, NY.

Silver Coins

Silver certainly has a variety of bullion coins. The highest-selling one is the American Eagle coin, which came out in 1986. It comes in a one ounce size and has a silver content of 0.999. You can purchase silver American Eagles in a tube that consists of 20 coins.

Another popular silver coin is the Silver Kookaburra, which comes from the Perth Mint in Australia. A new design comes out every year.

Investors also like to purchase the junk silver bags. While the name is dubious, it is actually a solid investment. This is a bag of $1,000 in face value of silver coins. A common type is a 90% bag, which means the silver content is 90 percent. The coins are those that have been minted up until the mid-1960s. Each bag will have either dimes, quarters, or half dollars (there are no mixed bags), although half dollars tend to sell at a slightly higher premium.

So why are they called junk? Well, the coins are of low quality. But for investors, this is fine since they are more interested in the silver content. While the $1,000 version is common, it is also possible to get one for $500. But if you do purchase one that has a 90-percent level, you will be required to report the transaction to the Internal Revenue Service. A bullion dealer will provide you with the necessary paperwork.

Platinum and Palladium Coins

Bullion coins are even available for platinum and palladium. Some of the popular versions for both include the American Eagle and the Canadian Maple Leaf. While the trading is much lower than gold and silver coins, there has been increasing demand over the years. More investors consider platinum and palladium coins to be good alternatives.

Value of Bullion Coins over Time
While bullion has little premium at the time of purchase, there may be an increase over time. Some vintages have seen strong demand. At the same time, the supply is finite, which adds to the pricing pressure. For example, some American Eagles from the 1980s are selling for several times the metal content.

Buying Bullion

To purchase bullion bars or coins, you will need to find a reputable dealer. Just as with many professions nowadays, a Google search can be an effective way to do research. Has the bullion dealer been the subject of investigations or criticisms? You should also check the Better Business Bureau.

There are also websites that have listings of top dealers, like the Numismatic Guaranty Corporation (www.ngccoin.com) and Coin-Info.com. Some of the top bullion dealers include Kitco and Monex.

Another popular one is the Perth Mint Certificate Program (PMCP). A key attraction is that the organization is guaranteed by the Australian government. What's more, the minimum investment amount is $25,000.

Even with a reputable dealer, there still may be differences in fees. So make sure you understand what the total costs include, such as storage, shipping, and commissions. Keep in mind that there is a spread, which is the difference between the bid and the ask price. This can add up.

Allocated and Unallocated Bullion
While you can take possession of the precious metal, many investors actually retain it with the bullion dealer. This can be either allocated or unallocated. Allocated means that that the metal will be identified in the vault and segregated from the other customers' holdings. For some investors, this provides more comfort and security. However,

it can be expensive and some dealers may require high minimum amounts, say $100,000.

Unallocated, on the other hand, means that you own a portion of the existing metal in the vault. If you want to get physical possession, you can still request it.

Leverage

Some bullion dealers will allow investors to make purchases using leverage. This means the dealer will lend you a percentage of the value of the bars—as much as 80 percent.

To understand this, let's take a look at an example. Suppose you want to buy $10,000 worth of gold bullion. A dealer will lend you $8,000 against this purchase. If the value increases 10 percent to $11,000, then your profit is actually 50 percent. This is $1,000 divided by your $2,000 cash investment.

Of course, if the value decreases, you can quickly lose money. That is, if the value of bullion falls by 20 percent, your $2,000 investment will be wiped out.

A bullion dealer will require that you provide more cash if the value of the investment falls. If the money is not forthcoming, the bullion dealer will liquidate your account. As such, when buying bullion with leverage, it is important to use a non-recourse loan. This means that if the value of the investment falls, your personal assets will not be subject to seizure.

REDEEMABLE EXCHANGE-TRADED FUNDS

Exchange-traded funds (ETFs) that are backed by a physical commodity have been popular over the years. It is an easy and cost-effective way to own gold, without the storage and insurance costs.

Despite these advantages, there are some investors who are skeptical. Does the ETF really have the gold in the vault? What if the financial institution has financial troubles and takes the gold for itself? This sounds kind of paranoid but it is a common sentiment. Besides, some investors like the idea that they can get ready access to their gold.

As should be no surprise, several financial institutions have launched redeemable ETFs. There are also closed-end funds that are redeemable in gold. But there are limitations:

- The redemption is usually allowed once a month.
- There is a minimum amount requirement, such as 400 troy ounces.
- There are also shipping and security fees. Keep in mind that delivery is often done using an armored car.

Interestingly enough, there is a tax advantage with owning a commodity-backed closed-end fund. If you hold onto the stock for over a year, you should be able to get taxed at the lower capital gains tax rate of 15 percent. ETFs, on the other hand, are taxed as collectables, at a tax rate of 28 percent.

INDIVIDUAL RETIREMENT ACCOUNTS

While the rules are restrictive, it is possible to put precious metals in an individual retirement account (IRA). First of all, you need to establish a self-directed IRA, which allows for more flexibility. It also has higher fees.

There are only a handful of precious metals that can be transferred to an IRA. For gold bars and coins, the purity must be 24 karats. The exception is the U.S. Gold Eagle, which is 22 karats. The bars also must be NYMEX or COMEX approved. The allowable sizes for bars are one ounce, ten ounces, 32.15 ounces (one kilo), 100 ounces, and 400 ounces.

Silver coins must have a minimum fineness of 0.999. The allowable silver coins include the U.S. Silver Eagle, the Canadian Maple Leaf, and the Mexican Silver Libertad.

Gold bars must be either 100 ounces or 1,000 ounces. Investors can also transfer platinum and palladium into an IRA, so long as the fineness is a minimum of 0.9995.

Finally, regardless of the metal, the storage must be an approved vault. You cannot store the bullion in your own vault.

RARE COINS

On television and the Web, you will find many advertisements about commemorative coins. They may have the likeness of a President or celebrity. Of course, they are well done and give the impression that they are great investments. Unfortunately, they usually are not. The fact is that commemorative coins are usually mass produced and are not independently recognized as rare. As a result, they may have little value above the metal content, known as the melt value. This means you may be paying 100 percent to 200 percent or more for the underlying value.

Instead, investors will look for coins that have numismatic value. These are coins that typically have values at multiples of the metal content. In some cases, a coin may fetch more than $10 million.

Over the years, rare coins have generally been strong investments. But they tend to have bursts of price increases. Besides, the market is highly fragmented and the liquidity is often light.

Another attraction to rare coins is their perceived safety. When gold was outlawed in the 1930s, rare coins were made an exception. With rare coins, an investor needs to do a great deal of research. Actually, this can be quite fun, especially for those who enjoy being collectors and studying the history of various coins.

Factors that Drive Coin Values

There are several key factors that drive the value of a coin.

Rarity of a Coin

One of the most important factors is how rare it is. There are cases where a mint produced a small amount of a coin—because of a war or some other event. One type is gold proof coins, which are extremely rare. Perhaps only as many as 20 to 30 coins have been minted.

Often, rare coins are fairly old, say over 100 years. Table 15-1 details some of the years that have seen strong rare coin values.

TABLE 15-1

Rare Coins

Time Period	Description
1860–1915	Gold coins generally
1795–1838	Gold coins generally
1795–1916	Silver coins generally
1878–1935	Morgan dollars
1916–1947	Walking Liberty half dollars

Grade of a Coin

Another important factor is the grade. This is essentially the condition of the coin. There is an independent standard called the Sheldon Scale. It has been around since the 1950s and provides dealers and investors the ability to gauge the quality of a coin. The system goes from 1 to 70, with MS-70 being flawless. For investors, they will try to focus on coins between MS-50 to MS-70. The definitive guide that ranks the grade of coins is the *Official ANA Grading Standards for the United States*.

What if your coin does not have a grade? You can have it inspected by a third party. There are also a myriad of helpful publications for research. Two of the top ones are *World Coin News* and *Coins* magazine published by Krause Publications. *The Official Redbook* is also a widely read book.

Coin Dealers

Just as with bullion, you will typically use a dealer when buying and selling rare coins. There are many firms in the marketplace, with varying quality. So it is important to do some investigation.

Some investors will try to find buyers directly. This can be through online sites like eBay or other forums. For the most part, investors focus on gold and silver coins. They tend to have the highest value and the most liquid markets. But there are some other types of coins that have robust demand. These include certain nickels and pennies, like the Liberty nickels and the Flying Eagle pennies.

Collecting Rare Coins

Some investors have made substantial amounts of money from rare coins. One of the most well-known is John Jay Pittman. He came from a middle class family and started his career as a chemical engineer at Eastman Kodak. But his passion was collecting rare coins, which he did over a period of 60 years.

Since he did not have much money, he focused on lower-priced coins. To find good values, he would travel around the world and conduct in-depth research. Pittman's collection eventually reached roughly 12,000 coins. And what is the total value? Estimates are about $40 million.

DIAMONDS

A diamond is formed with carbon, which is part of a lattice that creates a beautiful look. It is the hardest natural element on earth. But diamonds are not just for jewelry. Because of their hardness and conductivity, diamonds are used in a variety of industrial applications, such as cutting tools (about 80 percent of demand). For example, during the 2010 BP spill in the Gulf of Mexico, the company tried to use a diamond cutter to stop the flow of oil.

Investing in Diamonds

Like the rare coins industry, the diamond industry has many collectors. It can be a difficult market to understand, but people have made fortunes from it. While there are many varieties of diamonds, investors tend to focus on white ones. They are considered the standard in the industry.

Over the years, there has been the emergence of a variety of funds that invest in high-end diamonds. A big driver is the increase of new wealth in countries like China and India. As should be no surprise, they want to live a luxurious life. What better way than with diamonds?

There is no central marketplace for trading diamonds. However, there are major auctions at places like Sotheby's. The prices can be substantial, with a diamond going for $5 million to $10 million.

There is no futures exchange that trades diamonds. Then again, it is hard to come up with a standardized contract. Value is often based on complex factors and nuances, such as the cut of the diamond.

There is an online auction exchange called RapNet. Daily it lists over 500,000 diamonds. There are also a variety of diamond producer stocks. However, they all trade on foreign exchanges.

Global Supply of Diamonds

The global supply of diamonds is in tight control. About 35 percent of the world's production of diamonds comes from Botswana. The major producer is the De Beers Group, which has a virtual monopoly on the world price. Other major countries where diamonds are mined include Russia, Canada, and Australia.

Diamonds are often mined in war-torn areas where there are human rights violations. This has caused a perception problem for the industry. Concern over purchasing blood diamonds from these areas has actually resulted in lower demand for diamonds. This came out in a 2006 movie, which starred Leonardo DiCaprio.

As seen in this chapter, there are logical reasons to hold physical commodities, especially gold and silver. Yet there are more efficient approaches than buying a vault, such as with ETFs and certificate programs. But if you are interested in rare coins, then you will likely have a vault or rent a facility. In the next chapter, we will take a look at mutual funds, exchange-traded funds, and hedge funds.

CHAPTER 16

Funds

Key Concepts

- Learn about easier ways to invest in commodities
- Look at the advantages and disadvantages of mutual funds, ETFs, and hedge funds

When it comes to investing in commodities, investors have a variety of options. These include options, futures, and even purchasing the physical commodity. Despite this, the analysis and process can get complicated. After all, even top traders will only focus on a handful of markets. But investors can rely on top-notch portfolio managers to get exposure to commodities. There are many choices available, including mutual funds, hedge funds, and exchange-traded funds (ETFs).

MUTUAL FUNDS

A mutual fund is a pool of investor money, which focuses on a certain investment strategy like blue chips, foreign companies, and even commodities companies. This investment offers investors a cost-effective approach to building a portfolio.

All mutual funds have a net asset value (NAV). The NAV is equal to the sum of all the fund's assets minus the liabilities and expenses. The result is then divided by the number of shares out-standing. A mutual fund is required to disclose the NAV at the close of each trading day. There are two main types of mutual funds: open-end funds and closed-end funds.

Open-end Mutual Funds

The open-end mutual fund will issue new shares when investors buy more and reduce the number of shares when there are redemptions, which is when investors sell back their shares. Because of this, the net asset value will always *equal* the value of the shares (although there will be adjustments for fees).

Being able to redeem shares—on any trading day—is a nice feature for investors. This is especially the case when there is a need for ready cash. However, if many investors redeem their shares at the same time, the portfolio manager of the mutual fund will be in a bind. He or she will be forced to dump shares, which will likely put undue pressure on the prices.

Unfortunately, the investment options for commodities is fairly limited for mutual funds. They mostly involve funds that invest in companies that mine for precious metals or natural resources, like coal, natural gas, or energy.

Closed-end Mutual Funds

With a closed-end mutual fund, the investment fund will sell shares in a public offering. These are often found on the American Stock Exchange. For those closed-end mutual funds related to commodities, there is a thriving market on the Toronto Stock Exchange.

Just like any stock, you will need to pay a commission on any purchase and sale. But this will not have any impact on the number of shares outstanding. The result is that there is often a difference between the net asset value and the stock price, which is usually at a discount.

To understand this, let's take a look at an example. Suppose XYZ Corp.'s net asset value (NAV) is $10 per share but the stock is trading at $9.00. The discount is 10 percent from the NAV.

This can be strange for investors. Why is there such large under-valuation of assets? A key reason is that the management fees can be substantial and take a toll on the asset values. Keep in mind that the sizes of closed-end funds tend to be smaller than open-end funds.

For commodities, there are two types of closed-end funds. One will focus on purchasing companies in a sector, like energy or gold miners. The other will invest in the physical commodity. But all will focus on precious metals.

Master Limited Partnership

A variation on the closed-end mutual fund is the master limited partnership (MLP), or publicly traded partnership (PTP). While a Master Limited Partnership (MLP) trades on a stock exchange—usually the New York Stock Exchange—there are no "common shares." Rather, an MLP is made up of "units." This is because the legal structure is a partnership, not a corporation.

A general partner (GP) operates an MLP. The GP is usually a management company and will get an incentive structure for these services, which will include a 2 percent fixed fee and an additional percentage of the profits. This is disclosed in the MLP partnership agreement, which must be disclosed. In the document, you will also notice that the GP has a tremendous amount of control over the MLP. For example, there is no requirement for an annual meeting and voting is limited. This is why it is important to research the team of the GP. Do they have a good track record in managing profitable MLPs?

What is the attraction of a master limited partnership? The partnership structure actually provides tax benefits. So long as at least 90 percent of its income comes from commodities investments, the partnership does not pay taxes.

But the owner of the units will owe taxes for any distributions and capital gains. An investor will also receive a form, called a K-1, which will report any gains or losses. For the most part, MLPs focus on areas like energy storage and pipelines. Because of the high cash-flow generation of these activities, MLPs often pay relatively high distributions.

Advantages of Mutual Funds

Since the early 1980s, the mutual fund industry has seen tremendous growth. There are now over 7,500 funds, with about $11.5

trillion in assets. The federal government has in place stringent regulations on the mutual fund industry. The result is that fraud is virtually nonexistent.

There are many reasons to explain the popularity. One is the low minimum investments, which can be as little as $100 (although the typical amount is $1,000). It is also easy to have money deducted from your salary into a mutual fund, which makes 401(k) investments easy.

But, for relatively small fees, an investor will get the advantage of top-notch money managers. They will spend their full time on putting together the best portfolios. These will span virtually any type of market or investment style.

Disadvantages of Mutual Funds

Of course, mutual funds are far from perfect. A key problem is performance. Keep in mind that most funds are actively managed. This means a portfolio manager is trying to get higher returns than the market, with lower risks. Unfortunately, the fact remains that many funds fail to do this. As a result, more investors are turning to index funds, which have much lower costs.

The management fees are often the reason that actively managed funds underperform the market averages. For commodities funds, these can easily range from 1 percent to 1.5 percent of the net asset value. Another problem with performance is attracting strong money managers. It is not uncommon for them to prefer running hedge funds, which offer more compensation and flexibility.

Mutual funds can be tax-inefficient for investors. Consider that they must distribute all gains and dividends to investors. The result could be that a new investor will get hit with a higher-than-expected tax bill. This situation is more likely for a fund that has a high turnover, which is the percentage of the portfolio that is traded for the year. A high level is 200 percent or more. To help deal with the tax inefficiency, an investor may want to put a mutual fund in a tax-advantaged vehicle, like an IRA or 401(k).

Investors need to evaluate other costs, such as commissions. These are often referred to as loads. A front-end load is the commission you pay when you purchase shares. A back-end load is the commission you pay when you redeem your shares. These fees can add up over time, reducing your returns. The good news is that there are many funds that are no-load.

Index Mutual Funds

Back in 1997, Oppenheimer Funds launched the first mutual fund that tracked a commodities index. Given the lack of interest in the industry at that time, it was a prescient move. The fund was the only one of its kind until 2002, when PIMCO launched its own offering. Since then, more index funds have hit the market.

Index Mutual Funds all use sophisticated derivatives—such as options, futures, and swaps—to track, and even beat, the indexes. Because this type of trading requires low margin amounts, the index funds will usually have large amounts of funds left in their coffers. As a result, they will try to find low-risk ways to generate higher returns on these balances. This can often be a key differentiator among index funds.

There are funds for all the major indexes, like the Goldman Sachs Commodity Index, Deutsche Bank Liquid Commodity Index and Dow Jones–UBS Commodity Index. There are also ones focused on market segments like oil and gas, basic materials, and precious metals.

To enhance returns, some indexes employ leverage. An example is a Bull 2X Return Fund. This means that if the index is up 1 percent, then the fund will increase by 2 percent. However in practice, this is not always a 1-to-1 relationship. What's more, the risk can be substantial for investors.

Country Mutual Funds

Some economies are heavily dependent on natural resources. For example, Russia generates huge profits from oil. Brazil generates large gains from sugar and coffee. These countries could certainly benefit from rising commodity prices. The result could be stronger growth in gross domestic product (GDP), which could lead to stronger stock prices. Or, the currency value could increase in value. Even the real estate markets could see strength as well.

Interestingly enough, some people move to these countries because of the potential for growth or to buy additional properties. An alternative possibility for an investor is to buy stocks in the country or the currency, such as with mutual funds. There are offerings for over 100 hundred countries.

But there are risks with purchasing country mutual funds. One of the biggest is political instability. In some cases, a country might wind up nationalizing the key commodity-producing companies. There may be a tightening of capital flows into the country. Such moves could definitely be a big problem for investments.

EXCHANGE-TRADED FUNDS

An exchange-traded fund (ETF) pools investors' assets into market indexes. Over the past decade, these types of investments have become quite popular. There are now roughly 920 ETFs on the market, with assets over $900 billion. An ETF is traded on a stock exchange. This provides investors with much flexibility.

Margin and Leverage

It is possible to use margin to leverage a portfolio. To understand this, let's take a look at an example. Suppose you have $5,000 and want to invest in the ABC ETF, which is trading at $100 per share. With a margin account, you can borrow up to 100 percent of your liquid assets. In this case, it would be an additional $5,000 of ABC ETF.

Now suppose the value of the stock increases by 10 percent, which would be a gain of $1,000. Since your initial out-of-pocket investment was only $5,000, your return actually would be 20 percent ($1,000 divided by $5,000). But leverage can be risky. Let's say that ABC ETF falls by 50 percent, or $5,000. In this case, you would have lost your $5,000 investment.

Short Selling

Another key advantage with an exchange-traded fund (ETF) is short selling. This involves the process of borrowing shares and buying them back later, with the hope of the price being lower.

In other words, this is a way of making money when the stock price falls.

To understand this, let's take a look at an example. Suppose you think the ABC ETF will fall from $100 to $80. You short 100 shares, which comes to $10,000, which is set aside in an escrow account. Then in a few months, the stock prices indeed falls to $80 and you buy back the shares for $8,000. The $2,000 difference is your profit.

Types of Exchange-Traded Funds

When it comes to commodities, there are various types of exchange-traded funds (ETFs).

Stock-Based ETF

One category is the stock-based ETF. With this, there will be investments in certain companies in a sector or index.

Futures-Backed ETF

A futures-backed ETF will use sophisticated systems to purchase futures on a particular commodity or an index. These contracts are usually short-term, say a couple of months. This creates the potential problem of a roll penalty. When the fund needs to sell an expiring futures contract, there needs to be the purchase of a new one. Of course, the reason is that the ETF does not want to take delivery of the commodity.

However, the repurchase of the futures contract is often at a higher price because of the contango. This means that the futures price is *higher than* the spot price. Over time, this can result in higher costs and lower returns.

In fact, it is possible for the commodity ETF to show a negative return even though the underlying commodity has increased! This happened to the United States Oil (USO) ETF during 2010. Because of this, there were redemptions from investors, which put even more pressure on the ETF.

To deal with this, a new breed of exchange-traded funds (ETFs) has found strategies to minimize the roll penalty. These include funds like the Greenhaven Continuous Commodity Index Fund, the Deutsche Bank's PowerShares DB Oil Fund, and the

United States Commodity Index Fund. Essentially, these funds take an active role in terms of *timing* the repurchases and finding the best prices. Despite all this, there are still problems. In volatile markets, there may be bad decisions in terms of the repurchase of the futures.[1]

The futures-backed ETF must comply with exchange regulations, such as limit rules. This means that if a commodity increases to a certain level, trading must stop. This can make it nearly impossible for a futures-backed ETF to operate. The result is that it may actually stop issuing new shares. To avoid the U.S. limit requirements, some futures-backed ETFs have chosen to focus on foreign futures exchanges.

A futures-backed ETF does pose tax complications. The investor must treat the investment as if he or she were buying and selling futures. This means that the tax rate is half the ordinary tax rate and the long-term capital gains rate, or 15 percent. An investor must also mark-to-market at the end of the calendar year. This means that he or she will need to report gains or losses at the end of each year—even if he or she has not sold any of the ETF shares.

Physically Backed ETFs

Until the early 2000s, it was not easy for individual investors to participate in commodities. Instead, the main approach was to invest in commodity producers and related firms. While this can be an effective strategy, there are still drawbacks. But what if an investor wants to own the actual commodity, such as a bar of gold? To do this, there are a variety of expenses, such as transportation, insurance, and a vault.

Perhaps there could be a better way? Interestingly enough, the World Gold Council (WGC) felt there was. A trade association for the mining industry, it was actually struggling. So in 2002, the WGC hired a high-level financier, James Burton, who set forth a way to allow individual investors to easily trade gold. He did this by creating a new type of exchange-traded fund (ETF). While ETFs traditionally focused on owning a basket of stocks—like the S&P 500—a gold ETF would own physical gold bars.

---

[1] http://online.wsj.com/article/SB10001424052748704008704575638842042951392
.html?KEYWORDS=commodities.

This involved some complicated structures to allow for regulatory approval of the new product. First, Burton retained HSBC PLC as the holder of the gold, through its massive vaults. Next, he partnered with State Street Global Advisors to sell the gold ETF to investors. There was also the need for a third party to calculate the value of the gold ETF. This was the role for Bank of New York Mellon.

In 2004, Burton launched the new ETF, called the SPDR Gold Shares. It was traded on the New York Stock Exchange (NYSE) under the product symbol GLD. It was an immediate hit. In two years, assets under management reached $10 billion. As of now, they are over $55 billion. Interestingly, many top investors are holders of GLD shares, including hedge fund legends George Soros and John Paulson.

In light of the success of the gold ETF, other physically backed ETFs have been created. They offer ETFs for commodities like silver, platinum, palladium, copper, and uranium.

Of course, there is still skepticism about physically backed ETFs, which is inevitable for any newfangled Wall Street innovation. First of all, there are concerns that if there is a major drop in a commodity, a physically backed ETF will see a large amount of redemptions. SPDR Gold Shares has about one million investors. This could be exaggerated because many of the investors are individual investors and may not necessarily have long-term perspectives. As a result, a physically backed ETF may undergo much stress and could even have problems meeting its obligations.

Another concern is that demand for physically backed ETFs may result in temporary shortages of the actual commodity. After all, the ETF will need to buy up more and more of it. If this means less of the commodity for industrial purposes, then perhaps there may ultimately be regulatory actions?[2]

Physically backed ETFs are structured as trusts, so they do not pay taxes. But there is an interesting wrinkle. An exchange-traded fund has to sell its assets in order to pay for its expenses. These will change the tax basis in the fund, which can certainly get complicated when determining capital gains or losses.

---

[2] http://online.wsj.com/article/SB10001424052748703628204575618602535514506 .html.

Another tax problem is the tax rate. The general rule with stock sales is that long-term gains are taxed at favorable rates, which range from 0 percent to 15 percent. These rates apply only if the investor holds onto the investment for over one year. But with an ETF, the Internal Revenue Service considers the investment to be a collectible. This means the maximum tax rate on long-term gains is 28 percent. The short-term gains are taxed at ordinary rates. Because of this, some investors prefer to put their physically backed ETFs in an Individual Retirement Account (IRA).

EXCHANGE-TRADED NOTES

While often confused by investors, exchange-traded notes (ETNs) are not the same as exchange-traded funds (ETFs). There are some similarities, though. For example, both trade on stock exchanges. So what makes them different?

Started in 2006 by Barclays Bank PLC, an exchange-traded note (ETN) is a debt and is focused on several commodities indexes. The debt is in the form of a senior note, which is backed by an investment bank. This means that in the event of a bankruptcy, these holders will get first dibs on the money. The senior note will have a term of five to 30 years. After this time, the investment bank will pay all the returns in the index, which is netted by an ongoing annual fee. An investor can sell an ETN on the open market or redeem it with the investment bank. But this is usually for large amounts and is done on a weekly basis. An investor can also choose to wait until the note matures. At this point, the investor will receive the cash. Generally, these financial institutions are global giants, but it is still important to assess the backing. If the investment bank has problems, the note may be in jeopardy of default.

Advantages of Exchange-Traded Notes

A key advantage to an exchange-traded note (ETN) is taxes. Unlike the case with futures-backed ETFs, an ETN investor will only pay taxes when he or she sells the security. The reason is that the ETN is not considered to be a futures investment. Instead, it is a prepaid contract.

Another benefit of ETNs is the avoidance of tracking risk. That is, based on the structure, there should be no deviation between the value of the ETN and its underlying index. This is in contrast to futures-backed ETFs, which can have large amounts of tracking risk.

HEDGE FUNDS

Back in the 1950s, sociologist Alfred Winslow Jones created the first hedge fund. It was focused on investing in stocks, but had an interesting twist. To protect his portfolio in down markets, part of Winslow's portfolio had short-sale positions. The belief was that this would provide for returns that would beat the averages. This additional amount of gain is known as alpha, which is not easy to generate. Winslow also wanted to generate absolute returns. This means getting a return even if the overall market is down. No doubt, short selling is critical for this strategy.

All in all, Winslow's approach turned out to be a winning strategy as the hedge fund posted 27 percent per year returns from 1949 to 1966, which compared to 11 percent annual returns for the Dow Jones Industrial Average. It was a track record that was similar to Warren Buffett's performance.

Winslow also created an innovative compensation structure to encourage above-market returns. A money manager would get 1 percent to 2 percent of the money in the fund, as well as 20 percent of the profits, which is known as the carried interest.

Because of the success, Wall Street took note and now the hedge fund is a multitrillion-dollar global industry. While the main focus is still on stocks, this is beginning to change quickly. Since the bull market got its start in 2000, there has been a surge of assets into commodities hedge funds. A variety of hedge funds have over $1 billion in assets, even though they have been in existence for only a few years. However, hedge funds are geared mostly for institutions, like pension and endowments, and wealthy investors. The main reason is that the risk levels are high. What's more, the minimum investment amounts can be high, such as $1 million or more.

Advantages of Hedge Funds

With its compensation structure, hedge funds attract some of the world's top money managers. Consider Chris Levett. After a stellar career as a trader at Moore Capital, he left the firm in 2007 to start Clive Capital. It now has over $4 billion in assets. Another example is Merchant Commodity Fund, whose managers include Michael Coleman and Doug King. They were both top traders at Cargill.

But compensation is definitely not the only attraction. Hedge funds also allow for a tremendous amount of flexibility, which can be essential for a commodities trader. In light of the volatility, it is important to be able to quickly go long on a position, which means purchasing securities, or short, which allows for making money when the price of a security drops. The flexibility also extends to the types of investments. For example, a top commodities hedge fund will often have trades in dozens of markets, spanning from agriculture, precious metals, energy, and so on. Thus, for investors looking for top management expertise and sophisticated strategies, commodities funds are certainly attractive.

Because of their scale and resources, hedge funds also have the ability to physically own commodities. They will handle the necessary requirements for storage, insurance, and transportation. This can be particularly important for dangerous commodities, like uranium.

In fact, some hedge funds will even own storage facilities and crude oil tankers. An example is the hedge fund Platinum Partners LP, which has about $750 million in assets. While the fund invests in stocks, it also buys oil properties. These are usually fields that have been abandoned because of low production levels. Yet with new technologies—as well as some investments in equipment—Platinum Partners has been able to get higher yields.[3]

Another attraction of hedge funds is that many of the portfolio managers have a substantial amount of their own wealth in them. This is to allow a better alignment of interests.

Most hedge funds will have a high-water mark. This means that if a fund has a loss, there will be no carried interest earned

---

[3] http://online.wsj.com/article/SB10001424052748704055204576067852780435770
.html?mod=WSJ_Commodities_LEFTTopNews.

until the value reaches the prior level. However, if the current value of the portfolio is at a steep discount to the high-water mark, the fund manager may decide to close down the operation and create a new fund.

Disadvantages of Hedge Funds

In light of the financial panic of 2007 to 2008, the U.S. government has enacted more regulations for the hedge fund industry. Despite this, the requirements are still not up to the levels for investments on regulated stock exchanges. As a result, investors still need to take precautions before investing in hedge funds. One of the most notorious examples is the $64 billion Ponzi scheme of Bernie Madoff.

Another big issue for hedge funds is the size, which is especially the case for commodities. These markets may not have as much liquidity and thus a large fund may not be able to invest in some of them for fear of pushing up prices. Thus, a hedge fund manager may sit on a large amount of capital and take its 2 percent management fee. For multibillion-dollar funds, this can turn into substantial amounts. But for the investors, it is really an expensive way to park money.

Many hedge funds also have lock-ups. These are contractual arrangements that prevent investors from redeeming their shares for a fixed period of time, such as a year. The reason is to prevent undue dumping of shares, which would harm the portfolio. But during volatile times, this could also mean that investors will not get access to their funds, even though they may need it.

Another big issue is that a hedge fund may engage in highly risky activities. A classic example is Amaranth Advisors. In 2004, the firm hired Brian Hunter, who was in his early thirties. His expertise was in trading natural gas futures. Based on his trading, he realized there were some repeatable patterns in prices, especially when there was a colder winter or even hurricanes. His strategy was to go short on the summer contracts and to go long on the winter contracts. It was a traditional spread trade.

Year after year, the trading resulted in substantial returns. In 2005, Amaranth Advisors had the biggest win, with a $1.26 billion profit. Of course, this was because of Hurricane Rita and Hurricane Katrina.

Eventually this type of trade became popular with other firms, so it was getting tougher for Hunter to have an edge. By 2007, his positions accounted for roughly 60 percent of the natural gas contracts. So when prices began to fall, Hunter was unable to unload his positions. It was not long until Amaranth Advisors suffered losses. By the end of the year, the fund had to be closed and the losses came to about $6 billion.

MANAGED FUTURES FUND

A managed futures fund is a pool of investors' money for investments in futures contracts and options. This segment has roughly $250 billion in assets and some of these funds are focused on commodities, known as commodities pools. Others will invest in areas like currencies, interest rates, and stock indexes. Interestingly enough, the managed futures industry got its start more than 60 years ago. Back then, the focus was mostly on retail investors. However, in the past decade, institutional investors have become big players in the market.

A commodity pool operator (CPO) will create a managed futures fund and be responsible for managing its operations. He or she will then retain commodity trading advisors (CTAs), who will carry out the trading strategies. A CTA must meet licensing and regulatory requirements from both the Commodity Futures Trading Commission (CFTC) and the National Futures Association (NFA).

All investors in a managed futures fund are called limited partners. This means they only invest money in the fund and do not have any discretion on the management of the investments or the operations. This is important since it means that the investors get limited liability protection. This means that they can only lose up to their investment amount, and are not liable for anything more.

Another big attraction of a managed futures fund is that the commodity trading advisors have the discretion to go long as well as short. This flexibility can be critical in generating strong returns. After all, this is important in times like 2008, when many commodities plunged.

Keep in mind that a typical managed futures fund may not have the same high returns as a long-only commodities hedge fund, which does not engage in short selling. The reason is that there is more emphasis on reducing overall volatility. There are even some commodity pool operators (CPOs) that have investment guarantees, in which investors will get back their initial allocation. This is done by the fund purchasing a zero-coupon bond or using a bank letter of credit. A zero coupon bond is a debt that is priced at a discount to the face value, which will be paid in the future. The difference is the return on the investment.

Typically a managed futures fund has a fee structure similar to a hedge fund, with a 1 percent to 2 percent fee for assets under management and 20 percent of the profits. However, some funds charge a per-trade fee.

It can be difficult to get access to a managed futures fund. This is because it may actually require payment of a substantial fee of 3 percent to 5 percent to an introducing broker. In terms of investment approach, a typical commodities trading advisor will use technical analysis. This is because he or she is looking for short-term investment opportunities.

To look at the overall performance of CTAs, there is the Barclay CTA Index. It tracks the returns for a large group of CTAs.

There is also an exchange-traded fund (ETF) for managed futures, called the WisdomTree Managed Futures Strategy Fund (WDTI), which is based on the Diversified Trends Indicator (DTI). Besides exposure to commodities, there are also investments in currency and fixed-income futures. The commodities part is spread across energy, grains, precious metals, industrial metals, and livestock.

STOCKPILING COMPANIES

With the commodities bull market, there has been the emergence of stockpiling companies. These are firms that raise money through an initial public offering (IPO) and then stockpile a commodity. Often, these are rare earth metals or other specialized commodities, which can be difficult to obtain and invest in.

There are no risks of mining or exploration. Instead, the value should generally track the spot price of the underlying commodity. The company will then take care of the costs for storage and insurance.

However, the Securities and Exchange Commission (SEC) has concerns about these offerings. The main one is that the metals have low amounts of liquidity. This could ultimately hurt investor returns. So the SEC has instituted a variety of rules, such as the requirement that at least 85 percent of the proceeds go to the metal and to have an independent committee measure the value of the stockpile.[4]

COMMODITY TRADERS

While investment banks are household names—such as Goldman Sachs and Morgan Stanley—this is not the case with commodities trading firms. Yet these operations are massive and have been growing quickly. Consider Glencore International AG. Marc Rich founded the firm in 1974 and created the crude oil spot market. However, because of legal troubles, he left the firm in 1993.

As of now, Glencore is one of the world's largest commodities traders. Besides crude oil, the firm trades in coal and various agriculture products like grains and sugar. There are over 2,000 employees across 40 countries. Glencore also operates various plants, mines, and freight operations. In 2009, revenues were about $106.4 billion.

So why do these commodities traders not have much visibility? There are several reasons. One is that these firms are usually structured as closely held partnerships, which means they are not mandated to make disclosures. This is to help protect a firm's trading strategies, as well as provide more flexibility. Another reason is that many commodities firms are based in foreign countries. They will often set up in key points of global commerce, such as Amsterdam.

Yet, over the next few years, it looks like commodities traders will go public. Interestingly enough, clients want more transparency of the financials. Commodities firms will need more capital to capitalize their growth. These public offerings will likely be on foreign exchanges, such as in London and Hong Kong.

---

[4] http://online.wsj.com/article/SB10001424052748704376104576122582519496442 .html?mod=WSJ_Commodities_LEFTTopNews.

As seen in this chapter, there are a variety of easy, low-cost ways to invest in commodities. Mutual funds and ETFs are certainly a common way for individual investors to participate in these markets. But managed-futures funds and hedge funds are also good options.

In this book, we have looked at the main parts of the commodities world. We have analyzed the main investment vehicles, like futures, options, and funds. But we have also focused on the importance of understanding each market. While speculation may be a driver in the short run, the commodities markets will ultimately track the overall supply and demand trends.

In light of the importance of growth in emerging markets as well as the threats from inflation, commodities are an important component to any portfolio. But most important, it is critical to take time to research the markets and investments.

FUTURES CONTRACTS REFERENCE

ENERGY

Commodity	Crude Oil
Exchange	CME
Symbol	CL
Size	1,000 US barrels or 42,000 gallons
Trading Hours	*Open Outcry*: Monday–Friday 9:00 a.m.–2:30 p.m. *Electronic*: Sunday–Friday 6:00 p.m.–5:15 p.m. with a 45-minute break each day beginning at 5:15 p.m.
Minimum Price Change	$10.00

Commodity	Unleaded Gasoline
Exchange	CME
Symbol	RB
Size	1,000 barrels or 42,000 US gallons
Trading Hours	*Open Outcry*: Monday–Friday 9:00 a.m.–2:30 p.m. *Electronic*: Sunday–Friday 6:00 p.m.–5:15 p.m. with a 45-minute break each day beginning at 5:15 p.m.
Minimum Price Change	$10.00

Commodity	Coal
Exchange	CME
Symbol	QL
Size	1,550 tons
Trading Hours	*Open Outcry*: Monday–Friday 9:00 a.m.–2:30 p.m. *Electronic*: Sunday–Friday 6:00 p.m.–5:15 p.m. with a 45-minute break each day beginning at 5:15 p.m.
Minimum Price Change	$15.50

Commodity	Heating Oil
Exchange	CME
Symbol	HO
Size	1,000 barrels or 42,000 gallons
Trading Hours	*Open Outcry*: Monday–Friday 9:00 a.m.–2:30 p.m. *Electronic*: Sunday–Friday 6:00 p.m.–5:15 p.m. with a 45-minute break each day beginning at 5:15 p.m.
Minimum Price Change	$4.20

Commodity	Natural Gas
Exchange	CME
Symbol	NG
Size	10,000 million British thermal unit (mmBtu)
Trading Hours	*Open Outcry*: Monday–Friday 9:00 a.m.–2:30 p.m. *Electronic*: Sunday–Friday 6:00 p.m.–5:15 p.m. with a 45-minute break each day beginning at 5:15 p.m.
Minimum Price Change	$10.00

Commodity	Electric Power
Exchange	CME
Symbol	JM
Size	40 megawatt hours per peak day
Trading Hours	*Open Outcry*: Monday–Friday 9:00 a.m.–2:30 p.m. *Electronic*: Sunday–Friday 6:00 p.m.–5:15 p.m. with a 45-minute break each day beginning at 5:15 p.m.
Minimum Price Change	$10.00

Commodity	Uranium
Exchange	CME
Symbol	UX
Size	250 pounds of U308
Trading Hours	*Open Outcry*: Monday–Friday 9:00 a.m.–2:30 p.m. *Electronic*: Sunday–Friday 6:00 p.m.–5:15 p.m. with a 45-minute break each day beginning at 5:15 p.m.
Minimum Price Change	$10.00

Commodity	Ethanol
Exchange	CME
Symbol	EH
Size	29,000 gallons
Trading Hours	*Open Outcry*: Monday–Friday 9:00 a.m.–2:30 p.m. *Electronic*: Sunday–Friday 6:00 p.m.–5:15 p.m. with a 45-minute break each day beginning at 5:15 p.m.
Minimum Price Change	$10.00

INDUSTRIAL METALS

Commodity	Copper
Exchange	CME
Symbol	HG
Size	25,000 pounds
Trading Hours	*Open Outcry*: Monday–Friday 8:10 a.m.–1:00 p.m. *Electronic*: Sunday–Friday 6:00 p.m.–5:15 p.m. with a 45-minute break each day beginning at 5:15 p.m.
Minimum Price Change	$12.50

Commodity	Palladium
Exchange	CME
Symbol	PA
Size	100 troy ounces
Trading Hours	*Open Outcry*: Monday–Friday 8:30 a.m.–1:00 p.m. *Electronic*: Sunday–Friday 6:00 p.m.–5:15 p.m. with a 45-minute break each day beginning at 5:15 p.m.
Minimum Price Change	$5.00

Commodity	Aluminum
Exchange	CME
Symbol	AL
Size	44,000 pounds
Trading Hours	*Open Outcry*: Monday–Friday 7:50 a.m.–1:15 p.m. *Electronic*: Sunday–Friday 6:00 p.m.–5:15 p.m. with a 45-minute break each day beginning at 5:15 p.m.
Minimum Price Change	$5.00

Commodity	Tin
Exchange	London Metal Exchange
Symbol	SN
Size	5 tonnes
Trading Hours	*Open Outcry*: Monday–Friday 11:45 a.m.–5:00 p.m. *Electronic*: Monday–Friday 24-hours
Minimum Price Change	N/A

Commodity	Nickel
Exchange	London Metal Exchange
Symbol	NI
Size	6 tonnes
Trading Hours	*Open Outcry*: Monday–Friday 11:45 a.m.–5:00 p.m. *Electronic*: Monday–Friday 24-hours
Minimum Price Change	N/A

Commodity	Zinc
Exchange	London Metal Exchange
Symbol	ZS
Size	25 tonnes
Trading Hours	*Open Outcry*: Monday–Friday 11:45 a.m.–5:00 p.m. *Electronic*: Monday–Friday 24-hours
Minimum Price Change	N/A

Commodity	Lead
Exchange	London Metal Exchange
Symbol	PB
Size	25 tonnes
Trading Hours	*Open Outcry*: Monday–Friday 11:45 a.m.–5:00 p.m. *Electronic*: Monday–Friday 24-hours
Minimum Price Change	N/A

Commodity	Molybdenum
Exchange	London Metal Exchange
Symbol	MO
Size	6 tonnes
Trading Hours	*Open Outcry*: Monday–Friday 11:45 a.m.–5:00 p.m. *Electronic*: Monday–Friday 24-hours
Minimum Price Change	N/A

Commodity	Cobalt
Exchange	London Metal Exchange
Symbol	CO
Size	1 tonne
Trading Hours	*Open Outcry*: Monday–Friday 11:45 a.m.–5:00 p.m. *Electronic*: Monday–Friday 24-hours
Minimum Price Change	N/A

PRECIOUS METALS

Commodity	Gold
Exchange	CME
Symbol	GC
Size	100 troy ounces
Trading Hours	*Open Outcry*: Monday–Friday 8:20 a.m.–1:30 p.m. *Electronic*: Sunday–Friday 6:00 p.m.–5:15 p.m. with a 45-minute break each day beginning at 5:15 p.m.
Minimum Price Change	$10.00 per contract

Commodity	Silver
Exchange	CME
Symbol	SI
Size	5,000 troy ounces
Trading Hours	*Open Outcry*: Monday–Friday 8:25 a.m.–1:25 p.m. *Electronic*: Sunday–Friday 6:00 p.m.–5:15 p.m. with a 45-minute break each day beginning at 5:15 p.m.
Minimum Price Change	$25.00 per contract

Commodity	Platinum
Exchange	CME
Symbol	PL
Size	50 troy ounces
Trading Hours	*Open Outcry*: Monday–Friday 8:20 a.m.–1:30 p.m. *Electronic*: Sunday–Friday 6:00 p.m.–5:15 p.m. with a 45-minute break each day beginning at 5:15 p.m.
Minimum Price Change	$5.00 per contract

AGRICULTURE

Commodity	Cocoa
Exchange	CME
Symbol	CO
Size	10 metric tons
Trading Hours	*Open Outcry*: Monday–Friday 8:00 a.m.–11:50 p.m.
Minimum Price Change	$10.00 per contract

Commodity	Cotton
Exchange	CME
Symbol	CT
Size	50,000 pounds
Trading Hours	*Open Outcry*: Monday–Friday 10:30 a.m.–2:15 p.m.
Minimum Price Change	$5.00 per contract

Commodity	Coffee
Exchange	CME
Symbol	KC
Size	37,500 pounds
Trading Hours	*Open Outcry*: Monday–Friday 8:30 a.m.–12:30 p.m.
Minimum Price Change	$18.75 per contract

Commodity	Sugar
Exchange	ICE
Symbol	SB (Sugar #11)
Size	112,000 pounds
Trading Hours	*Open Outcry*: Monday–Friday 8:10 a.m.–12:30 p.m.
Minimum Price Change	$11.20 per contract

Commodity	Soybeans
Exchange	CME
Symbol	ZM
Size	100 tons
Trading Hours	*Open Outcry*: Monday–Friday 9:30 a.m.–1:15 p.m.
Minimum Price Change	$10.00 per contract

Commodity	Orange Juice
Exchange	ICE
Symbol	OJ
Size	15,000 pounds
Trading Hours	*Open Outcry*: Monday–Friday 6:00 a.m.–12:30 p.m.
Minimum Price Change	$7.50 per contract

Commodity	Corn
Exchange	CME
Symbol	ZC
Size	5,000 bushels
Trading Hours	*Open Outcry*: Monday–Friday 9:30 a.m.–1:15 p.m.
Minimum Price Change	$12.50 per contract

Commodity	Wheat
Exchange	CME
Symbol	ZW
Size	5,000 bushels
Trading Hours	*Open Outcry*: Monday–Friday 9:30 a.m.–1:15 p.m.
Minimum Price Change	$12.50 per contract

Commodity	Rough Rice
Exchange	CME
Symbol	ZR
Size	91 metric tons
Trading Hours	*Open Outcry*: Monday–Friday 10:30 a.m.–2:15 p.m.
Minimum Price Change	$10.00 per contract

Commodity	Oats
Exchange	CME
Symbol	ZO
Size	86 metric tons
Trading Hours	*Open Outcry*: Monday–Friday 10:30 a.m.–2:15 p.m.
Minimum Price Change	$12.50 per contract

Commodity	Lumber
Exchange	CME
Symbol	LB
Size	110,000 board feet
Trading Hours	*Open Outcry*: Monday–Friday 10:30 a.m.–2:15 p.m.
Minimum Price Change	$5.00 per contract

Commodity	Rubber
Exchange	Tokyo Commodity Exchange
Symbol	JN
Size	50,000 kilograms
Trading Hours	*Open Outcry*: Monday–Friday 10:30 a.m.–2:15 p.m.
Minimum Price Change	$5.00 per contract

LIVESTOCK

Commodity	Lean Hogs
Exchange	CME
Symbol	LH
Size	40,000 pounds
Trading Hours	*Open Outcry*: Monday–Friday 10:05 a.m.–2:00 p.m.
Minimum Price Change	$4.00 per contract

Commodity	Pork Belly
Exchange	CME
Symbol	PB
Size	40,000 pounds
Trading Hours	*Open Outcry*: Monday–Friday 9:10 a.m.–1:00 p.m.
Minimum Price Change	$4.00 per contract

Commodity	Live Cattle
Exchange	CME
Symbol	LC
Size	40,000 pounds
Trading Hours	*Open Outcry*: Monday–Friday 10:05 a.m.–2:00 p.m.
Minimum Price Change	$10.00 per contract

Commodity	Feeder Cattle
Exchange	CME
Symbol	FC
Size	50,000 pounds
Trading Hours	*Open Outcry*: Monday–Friday 9:05 a.m.–1:00 p.m.
Minimum Price Change	$5.00 per contract

GLOSSARY

Absolute Return: The focus of a fund to get positive returns in any market environment.

Allocated: This is an account with a vault where the owner of the metal wants it to be segregated.

Alloy: A compound of two or more metals. An example is a combination of zinc and copper, which creates a brass alloy.

Alpha: The additional return a fund generates because of superior investment management.

Alternative Investment: A class of investments that do not include stocks or bonds. Examples are hedge funds, venture capital, and commodities.

American Depositary Receipts (ADRs): These are foreign companies that list on the New York Stock Exchange (NYSE) or the Nasdaq.

American Eagle: A bullion gold coin that came out in 1986. It contains 22 karat gold.

Annual Crop: A crop that is planted and harvested within a year. Examples include corn and wheat.

Arbitrage: This is when an investor makes a profit because there are gaps in valuation in two markets. It often means shorting the overvalued commodity and buying the undervalued one.

Ask: The price at which a trader will buy a futures contract.

Assay: A scientific analysis to determine the quality and weight of a precious metal.

Avoirdupois Ounce: This is an ounce used in the measurement of gold jewelry.

Backwardation: This is when the spot price of a commodity is higher than the prices on the futures contracts.

Base Metal: A non-precious metal. Examples include nickel and copper.

Bear Market: A market that is generally falling in value. The rule of thumb is a 20 percent decrease.

Bid: The price at which a trader will sell a futures contract.

Black-Scholes Model: A pricing model for call and put options.

Breakout: A key principle in technical analysis. This is when the price moves out of a certain trading range, which may be a trigger to make a trade.

British Thermal Unit (BTU): A unit of measure of energy, which is roughly 1,055.05585 joules.

Brownfields: Reserves that are found close to an existing mine.

Bullion: A precious metal that is in the form of bars or ingots, not coins. The bars must be at least 99.5% pure.

Bull Market: A market that is generally rising in value. The rule of thumb is a 20 percent increase.

Calendar Spread: This involves buying a futures contract in one month and selling one in another month.

Call Option: The right to buy a fixed number of a commodity at a certain price for a period of time. The call option will generally have value if the underlying futures contract increases.

Candlestick Charts: Developed in Japan, this is a form of technical analysis, with a focus on the open and close for the commodity. These types of charts have unique symbols.

Cash Cost: The cost of production—such as extraction, transportation, smelting, salaries, and royalties—at a mine per unit of output.

Channel: This is the band of the support and resistance levels for an uptrend or downtrend in the prices of a commodity.

Clearinghouse: This is when a commodities exchange will take the other side of a transaction and guarantee the obligations.

Closed-End Mutual Fund: An investment fund that raises money through a public offering. Because of this, the stock price may be above or below the Net Asset Value.

CME Group: A large commodities futures exchange.

Cocoa: A bean that is planted mostly in West Africa. It is used primarily for chocolate.

Commodity: A good for which there is demand, but there is little or no differentiation between one good and another one. Examples of commodities include wheat, live cattle, copper, and gold. Often, commodities are raw materials to make finished products.

Commodity Futures Trading Commission (CFTC): The federal agency that regulates futures trading.

Commodity Trading Advisor (CTA): A person who manages futures accounts for clients.

Complement: This is when the demand for one good increases the demand for another.

Complex: A group of similar commodities.

Consolidation: This is when a stock trades within a range of its support and resistance levels.

Contango: This is when futures prices are higher the longer the contract terms.

Continuation Pattern: This is a formation in technical analysis that indicates that a trend is likely to continue.

Convertible Bond: A bond that the investor can turn into shares of the company.

Corner: A manipulation of the markets where a trader will buy up a large amount of a commodity to boost profits.

Correction: A temporary fall in the market, which is usually about 10 percent.

Counterparty Risk: This is the possibility that the other party to a transaction will not uphold his or her obligations.

Crack Spread: This is purchasing the crude oil contract and then selling contracts for gasoline and heating oil.

Crossover: This is using two moving averages, with different time periods. If the lines cross, there may be a bullish or bearish signal.

Cyclical: This refers to a commodity or company that is highly sensitive to the changes in the economy.

Daily Limit: The maximum a price of a futures contract can increase or decrease for a trading session. This is to allow for more orderly markets.

Day Order: A market order that is open for the trading day.

Deflation: A general fall in the prices in an economy. This is usually when there is a recession or even a depression.

Delivery Date: In a futures contract, this is when the seller of a contract is required to deliver the underlying commodity to the futures buyer.

Delta: The ratio of the option price change to the futures price change.

Derivative: An investment that is based on the price movement of an underlying asset. Examples include options and futures.

Double Bottom: A chart formation in technical analysis that looks like a W.

Double Top: A chart formation in technical analysis that looks like an M.

Downstream companies: Companies that are focused on the selling of a commodity, such as gas stations.

Downtrend: This is when the trading of a commodity is trending lower, which usually involves lower highs and lower lows.

Drawdown: Any loss that happens between two peaks in equity.

Efficient Market Hypothesis (EMH): The academic theory that says that it is nearly impossible for an investor to get stronger returns than the market averages over the long run. The main reason is that all public information is quickly incorporated into commodities prices.

Elastic Price: This is a price where a small change in the price of a commodity will have a major impact on the demand for it.

Elliott Wave: Based on the research of Ralph Elliott, this involves using complex waves to predict commodities prices.

Exchange Rate: The rate that one currency trades against another one.

Exchange-Traded Fund (ETF): An investment fund that usually invests in an index. An ETF can be traded like a stock and can even be shorted.

Exchange-Traded Note (ETN): An investment fund that is traded on an exchange. However, it is a debt instrument that is backed by an investment bank.

Expiration: The time that a call option will be terminated, which is a fixed period of time. It usually lasts three months. When an option expires, the buyer has the right to take delivery of the underlying asset.

Exponential Moving Average (EMA): This is a moving average with the most recent prices getting more weight.

Feasibility Study: Analysis of a deposit to see if it is economical to extract the minerals.

Federal Reserve (The Fed): The central bank of the United States. The Fed has the power to increase or decrease the money supply in the economy, which can have a major impact on interest rates.

Feeder Cattle: Usually steers that are fed forage and grain until they are slaughtered. They are traded on the CME.

Feedlot: An animal feeding operation, which may contain thousands of livestock.

Fiat Currency: The official currency of a country.

Fibonacci Retracement: This is when traders use a sequence of unique numbers to predict the fall in a commodity's price.

Forward Contract: A variation of a futures contract. This allows for the purchase of a fixed quantity of a commodity for delivery in the future. However, the transaction is not on an exchange but between a buyer and seller.

Fundamental Analysis: The analysis of supply and demand factors when trying to predict the prices of commodities.

Futures Commission Merchant (FCM): A futures broker that handles the full cycle of services, such as taking possession of funds, confirming trades, and making sure the account is in compliance with the exchanges.

Futures Contract: An investment vehicle that allows for the purchase of a fixed quantity of a commodity for delivery in the future.

Galvanization: A process that helps to prevent rust and corrosion for metals like steel and iron.

Gamma: Shows the changes in delta for an option.

Gap: A major move in the price of a commodity that shows up as empty space on the chart.

Generally Accepted Accounting Principles (GAAP): These are the core standards for corporate financial statements.

Globex: An electronic exchange for futures and options.

Gold Proof Coins: Extremely rare coins.

Gold-Silver Ratio: Ratio that shows the value of gold versus silver. If there is a wide divergence, it may represent an investment opportunity for traders.

Gold Standard: This is when a paper currency is backed by a certain amount of gold. This is to help avoid inflation.

Good-'Til-Canceled (GTC) order: A market order that will remain open until the trader cancels it.

Grade: The quality of a commodity.

Gross Domestic Product (GDP): The total value of goods and services produced in an economy for the year.

Head and Shoulders: A chart formation in technical analysis with three peaks. The head is the highest price in the move; the shoulders are the lower prices.

Hedge Fund: An investment fund that typically is focused on sophisticated strategies and is meant for institutions and wealthy investors.

Hedging: Using an investment vehicle, such as a futures contract or an option, to provide downside protection.

Hog Factories: State-of-the-art facilities for hogs. They are built to minimize disease and increase output.

Hyperinflation: When inflation is running at an extreme rate. This is at least 50 percent per month.

Index: A group of investments that track an asset class. The commodities industry has many indexes, which are usually based on futures contracts.

Individual Retirement Account (IRA): A vehicle that allows investors to deduct contributions and earn returns tax-free. Some IRAs allow for bullion coin investments.

Inelastic Price: This is a price where a change in the price of a commodity has little impact on the demand for it.

Inferred Reserves: Shows the amount of reserves of a deposit. But the analysis is fairly speculative.

Inflation: A general increase in the prices of an economy.

Ingot: A gold bar that has some type of design on it.

Institution: A large investor. Examples include endowments, insurance companies, and pensions.

Inter-Exchange Spread: This involves trading the same type of contract on different exchanges.

In-the-Money: For a call option, the futures price is higher than the strike price. For a put option, the futures price is lower than the strike price. This means that the option has intrinsic value.

Intrinsic Value: This is when it is profitable to exercise an option.

Introducing Broker (IB): A commodities broker who actually facilitates trades through another firm, known as a futures commission merchant (FCM).

Junior: A mining company that has gone beyond the exploration phase and has one or more producing properties.

Junk Silver Bags: A bag of silver coins that have a face value of $1,000.

Karat: Indicates the fineness of gold, with each karat representing 1/24 part of pure gold.

Krugerrand: Launched in 1970, it is the gold bullion coin from South Africa. It contains 22 karat gold.

Lean Hogs: A hog's carcass. It is traded on the CME.

Legal Tender: This means you can use a coin as a currency.

Leg Off a Spread: This is when a trader takes off one of the positions on a spread.

Light-Sweet Crude: A high-quality crude that is preferred by refineries.

Limit Order: When buying or selling a futures contract, a limit order will set a price to make the transaction at.

Live Cattle: A cow that is ready for slaughter and has reached a weight of about 1,200 pounds. It is traded on the CME.

Livestock: An animal that is domesticated for a commercial purpose. Also known as cattle.

Load: A commission for a mutual fund.

Lock-Up: A provision that prevents investors from redeeming their shares in a fund. This often applies to hedge funds.

Log-Scale Chart: This is a mathematical technique to smooth out a chart for volatility.

Long Position: The purchase of a futures contract that will make money if the value increases.

Long-Term Equity Anticipation Security (LEAP): A call or put option that has a long expiration period, such as over one year.

Managed Account: An account that helps to create and manage strategies for investors. This is from a futures trading firm.

Managed Futures: A fund that has one or more professional managers to invest in futures.

Margin: A good faith deposit against a commodity futures contract.

Margin Call: If a margin account goes below the minimum level, a broker will require more cash in the account or liquidation of the holdings.

Market Order: A order that is for the next best available price.

Mark-to-Market: This is the daily adjustment that a futures exchange makes to the margin accounts for all traders. This is to allow for lower risks and a more orderly market.

Master Limited Partnership (MLP): A publicly traded partnership that allows for special tax breaks. This is common for pipeline operators.

Measured and Indicated Reserves: The amount of reserves of a deposit. But it is based on less accurate analysis.

Melt: The value of a coin when the precious metal is extracted.

Metallurgical Coal: Coal that is used primarily for the creation of steel.

Mini Contract: A futures contract that has a lower underlying commodity amount. This is to make it easier for individual investors to trade them.

Mini Mills: Companies that produce steel primary with scrap.

Minimum Price Fluctuation: *See* **Tick.**

Moving Average: This shows the average price of a commodity on a chart. This is often a 50-day or 200-day moving average. Investors will track these to get a sense of when a stock or commodity is ready for a move on the upside or downside.

Moving Average Convergence-Divergence (MACD): A common indicator for technical analysis. It is based on a 12-day and 26-day moving average.

Multiplier: This is used to calculate a futures price.

National Agriculture Statistics Service (NASS): Part of the United States Department of Agriculture, this division conducts hundreds of surveys every year and produces reports on many aspects of agriculture.

National Futures Association (NFA): An industry association that enforces standards and compliance for futures trading.

Net Asset Value (NAV): The total value of a mutual fund's assets minus the liabilities and expenses. This is published at the end of each trading day.

Numismatic Value: The value of a coin that goes beyond its metal content.

Offsetting Trade: This is when a futures trader closes out a current position. If it is a long futures contract, then it will be offset with a short position, and vice versa.

Oil Services Company: A company that helps to find and extract oil, such as setting up rigs and using sophisticated software analysis.

On Balance Volume: An indicator in technical analysis that looks at the overall changes in volume. This often indicates bullishness or bearishness.

Open-End Mutual Fund: A fund that will issue new shares when investors buy more and reduce the number of shares when there are redemptions. This means that the Net Asset Value is always equal to the share price.

Open Interest: The number of futures contracts that have not been closed out with offsetting trades.

Open Outcry: This is a physical trading floor where traders buy and sell commodities.

Ore: A rock that contains metals valuable enough to be mined.

Organization of Petroleum Exporting Countries (OPEC): A global organization of some of the largest oil producers. They will coordinate actions to help provide for higher oil prices.

Oscillator: An indicator in technical analysis, which has a value that ranges from 0 to 100. Often, an oscillator provides the general level of sentiment.

Out-of-the-Money: For a call option, the futures price is lower than the strike price. For a put option, the futures price is higher than the strike price. This means that there is no intrinsic value.

Outright Positions: Buying or selling a futures contract.

Over-the-Counter Market: Where trading is done directly between buyers and sellers. There is no central exchange.

Peak Oil: The belief that worldwide production is in decline and that there will be higher prices for the long term.

Perennial Crop: A crop that is planted and harvested over a period of at least two years.

Pit: A place on an exchange where traders buy and sell commodities. A pit usually has an octagonal shape and several steps that go downward.

Point-and-Figure Charts: A charting approach that looks only at prices, not time. A rise is indicated by an X and a fall by an O.

Pork Belly: The meat from the underside of a hog, which is used for bacon. It is traded on the CME.

Potash: A mixture of salts that have potassium. It is used mostly for fertilizers.

Premium: The cost of purchasing a call option or a put option.

Private Investment in Public Equity (PIPE): This is a type of financing known as a private placement. The investors tend to be institutions and the regulations are less strenuous than a public offering of securities.

Prospect Generator: An exploration company that will have a portfolio of deposits but find partners to help finance the mining operations.

Proven and Probable Reserves: These are the most accurate amount of reserves and are based on third-party feasibility studies.

Pure Silver: Bullion that has the highest content of silver.

Put Option: The right to sell a fixed number of a commodity at a certain price for a period of time. The put option will generally have value if the underlying futures contract decreases.

Quantity: In a futures contract, this is the total amount. It is usually what can fit in a railcar.

Real Interest Rate: The difference between the current interest rate and inflation.

Rebalancing: When an index changes the weightings of its positions.

Redeemable Exchange-Traded Funds: These are funds that own physical precious metals. However, the investor can request the delivery of his share.

Relative Strength Indicator: An indicator in technical analysis that measures overall sentiment in a commodity.

Reserves: The amount of a resource that has yet to be extracted from a deposit.

Resistance: The price where a commodity's price reaches a top and sellers come into the market.

Rolling over a Position: When a futures contract is close to expiring, a trader will need to close it out and buy a new contract if he or she wants to maintain the position.

Round Turn: A commission charged on the purchase and sale of a futures contract.

Royalty Company: A company that provides upfront financing for a mine. For this, it will get ongoing royalties from the production.

Scrap: This is a commodity that comes from recycling products, like jewelry and electronics equipment.

Seat: This is a membership on a commodities exchange.

Serial Option: This is when the option and futures expire in different months.

Short Position: Selling a futures contract that makes money if it falls in value.

Short Selling: Borrowing and then simultaneously selling the security. The investor will then buy it back at a lower price to make a profit.

Side-by-Side Trading: This is when there is electronic and floor trading in the same commodity.

Simple Moving Average (SMA): *See* **Moving Average**.

Smelting: The process of extracting a metal from its ore.

Softs: Commodities that include various foods and fibers. These include coffee, cotton, sugar, cocoa, and orange juice.

Sovereign Wealth Fund (SWF): An investment fund that is funded and managed by a government.

Speculators: These are traders in commodities futures. These include individuals and hedge funds. Speculators are key for providing liquidity in the markets.

Spot Price: This is the price of a commodity for current delivery.

Spread: Buying or selling different types of futures contracts to take advantage of price discrepancies.

Squeeze: When traders will aggressively buy up a futures contract— close to expiration—to cause a spike in the price.

Standard Option: When the option and futures contracts expire during the same month.

Sterling Silver: An alloy of 7.5% copper and 92.5% silver. This helps to increase the durability.

Stocking Rate: The amount of land for grazing for cattle and other livestock.

Stop-Loss Order: An order that will get out of a position if a futures price hits a certain level.

Straddle: An option strategy where it is possible to make money if the underlying futures contracts increases or decreases in value.

Strategic Stockpiling: When a country buys up large amounts of a commodity.

Strike Price: The price that the buyer of a put option or a call option has the right to exercise.

Strip Mining: Mining that is above ground, which means removing large rocks and soil. This typically involves heavy equipment and even explosives.

Support: This is the price where a commodity's price reaches a bottom and buyers come into the market.

Tariff: A tax on exports.

Technical Analysis: Using price and volume to predict the prices of a commodity.

10-K filing: A financial disclosure that reviews a company's results for the year as well as for the fourth quarter.

10-Q filing: A financial disclosure that reviews a company's results for the first, second, and third quarters of the year.

Thermal Coal: Coal that is used primarily for electricity generation.

Theta: Shows the rate of change of the decay in an option's time value.

Tick: The smallest amount the price can go up or down.

Ticker: Usually one to two characters. They represent a certain commodities futures contract.

Time Value: This is an option that has value that is above the intrinsic value. The time value decreases as the option gets closer to expiration.

Tonne: This refers to metric tonne, which is equivalent to 1,000 kilograms or 32,150.7465 troy ounces.

Trailing Stop: This is when a trader sets a new stop price as the futures price increases.

Unallocated: This is an account with a vault where the owner of the metal will not have it segregated.

Upstream Companies: These are commodity companies that focus on the exploration, extraction, and refining process.

Uptrend: This is when the trading of a commodity is trending higher, which usually involves higher highs and higher lows.

United States Department of Agriculture (USDA): A federal agency that is responsible for the policies on farming, agriculture, and food.

Volume: The total number of contracts traded for the day.

Warrant: A security that allows an investor to purchase more shares in a company, at a fixed price.

Writer: The party that creates a call or put option. For this, he or she will receive the premium.

PHYSICAL COMMODITIES

Listed below are the Web resources for physical commodities.

Bullion Dealers

- Kitco: www.kitco.com
- Monex: www.monex.com
- National Association of Jewelry Appraisers: www.najaappraisers.com
- American Society of Appraisers: www.appraisers.org/ASAHome.aspx

Rare Coins

- Coin World: www.coinworldonline.com
- Daily Numismatic & Gold Investment News: www.cointoday.com
- PCGS: www.pcgs.com
- ANACS: www.anacs.com

Industrial Metals

The industrial metals are copper, aluminum, coal, and nickel.

Copper

- International Copper Study Group: www.icsg.org
- Copper Development Association: www.copper.org

Aluminum

- Aluminum Association: www.aluminum.org

Coal

- World Coal Institute: www.worldcoal.org

Nickel

- International Nickel Study Group: www.insg.org
- Nickel Institute: www.nickelinstitute.org

Energy

The main energy commodity is crude oil.

Crude Oil

- International Energy Agency (IEA): www.iea.org

Precious Metals

The precious metals are gold, silver, and platinum.

Gold

- World Gold Council: www.gold.org
- GFMS: www.gfms.co.uk
- CPM Group: www.cpmgroup.com/main.php
- Gold Sheet Mining Directory: www.goldsheetlinks.com

Silver

- The Silver Institute: www.silverinstitute.org
- SilverStrategies.com: www.silverstrategies.com/defaultNS.aspx

Platinum

- Platinum Metals Review: www.platinummetalsreview.com/dynamic/

- Platinum Today: www.platinum.matthey.com
- The International Platinum Association: www.ipa-news.com/en/

Agriculture

The physical commodities for agriculture are cocoa, sugar, corn, lumber, livestock, and dairy.

Cocoa

- International Cocoa Organization: www.icco.org

Sugar

- International Sugar Organization: www.isosugar.org

Corn

- Prospective Plantings Report: www.usda.mannlib.cornell.edu/ MannUsda/viewDocumentInfo.do?documentID=1136

Lumber

- Residential Construction Report: www.census.gov/const/ www/newresconstindex.html
- American Forest & Paper Association: www.afandpa.org/

Livestock

- Hogs and Pigs Report: www.usda.mannlib.cornell.edu/ MannUsda/viewDocumentInfo.do?documentID=1086
- Livestock Slaughter Report: www.usda.mannlib.cornell.edu/ MannUsda/viewDocumentInfo.do?documentID=1096
- Cattle on Feed Report: www.usda.mannlib.cornell.edu/ MannUsda/viewDocumentInfo.do?documentID=1020
- Livestock, Dairy, and Poultry Outlook: www.ers.usda.gov/ Publications/LDP/

Dairy

- Milk Production Report: www.usda.mannlib.cornell.edu/ MannUsda/viewDocumentInfo.do?documentID=1103

FUTURES EXCHANGES

- Buenos Aires Futures Exchange (Argentina): www.matba.com.ar
- Sydney Futures Exchange (Australia): www.sfe.com.au
- Bolsa de Marcadorias & Futures Exchange (Brazil): www.bmf .com.br
- Toronto Futures Exchange (Canada): www.tse.com
- Santiago Stock Exchange (Chile): www.bolsadesantiago.com
- Shanghai Futures Exchange (China): www.shfe.com.cn
- Hong Kong Futures Exchanges and Clearing (China): www .hkex.com.hk
- Dalian Commodity Exchange (China): www.dce.com.cn
- Frankfurt Stock Exchange (German): www.deutsche-boerse.com
- National Stock Exchange of India: www.nseindia.com
- Tokyo Commodity Exchange (Japan): www.tocom.or.jp
- Osaka Securities Exchange (Japan): www.kanex.or.jp
- Malaysia Derivatives Exchange: www.mdex.com.my
- Singapore Commodity Exchange: www.sicom.com.sg
- London Metal Exchange (U.K.): www.lme.co.uk
- CME group (U.S.): www.cme.com
- Kansas City Board of Trade: www.kcbt.com
- Minneapolis Grain Exchange: www.mgex.com
- ICE (U.S.): www.theice.com

FOREIGN INVESTMENTS

- CIA World Factbook: www.cia.gov/library/publications/ the-world-factbook/docs/refmaps.html

TECHNICAL ANALYSIS

- Barchart.com: www.barchart.com
- FuturesPros.com: www.futurespros.com

INDEX

ABOUT THE AUTHOR

Tom Tauli founded the companies BizEquity, ExamWeb, and Hypermart.net and is the author of several investing books, including *Investing in IPOs and Stock Options* and *All About Short Selling*. He lives in San Jose, CA.